Why Do You Need this New Edition?

If you're wondering why you should buy this new edition of *Workplace Communications: The Basics*, here are ten good reasons!

1 An increased focus on ethics throughout. This helps you understand and successfully navigate ethical dilemmas in workplace communications, thereby satisfying the demands of both conscience and the law.

2 Greatly expanded treatment of electronic communication, particularly e-mail. By devoting a separate chapter to the memo and e-mail (rather than discussing them along with the business letter, as in past editions), the new edition places appropriately greater emphasis on e-mail and better enables you to see how it has evolved from the traditional paper memo.

3 New examples of visual elements in reports. Updated illustrations assist you in grasping the principles governing effective tables, graphs, charts, and illustrations.

4 An updated chapter on the employment application process. Expanded discussion of on-line job search strategies offers practical advice about designing a scannable résumé and using key words to craft the personal summary.

5 Many new sample documents. Updated examples throughout reinforce the book's "real world" flavor, helping you relate to the situations portrayed, and providing models to guide your own writing.

6 An entire new chapter on preparing proposals. Analysis of the strategies that characterize persuasive writing enables you to create convincing proposals, a highly valued workplace skill.

7 Helpful checklists. As in past editions, step-by-step guidelines allow you to assess your work with respect to format, content, and execution as you complete each kind of assignment.

8 Revised "Tech Tip" pointers. Updated discussion of various aspects of the computerized workplace brings you up-to-date on the latest technological developments.

9 Increased coverage of documenting on-line sources. In recognition of our ever-expanding use of the Internet when conducting research, this new edition features many new Web-based examples and explains in far greater detail how to document such material.

10 A new appendix on avoiding plagiarism. This supplemental section provides concrete suggestions for quoting, summarizing, and paraphrasing to give you the information you need to avoid accusations of—and penalties for—plagiarism.

PEARSON
Longman

Workplace Communications

The Basics

FOURTH EDITION

George J. Searles

Mohawk Valley Community College

PEARSON
Longman

New York San Francisco Boston
London Toronto Sydney Tokyo Singapore Madrid
Mexico City Munich Paris Cape Town Hong Kong Montreal

To Ellis

Senior Acquisitions Editor: Katherine Meisenheimer
Senior Supplements Editor: Donna Campion
Senior Marketing Manager: Sandra McGuire
Production Manager: Eric Jorgensen
Project Coordination: Pre-Press PMG
Cover Design Manager: John Callahan
Cover Designer: Base Art Co.
Cover Image: Courtesy of Artville
Senior Manufacturing Buyer: Roy L. Pickering, Jr.
Printer and Binder: RR Donnelley & Sons Company / Harrisonburg
Cover Printer: RR Donnelley & Sons Company / Harrisonburg

Library of Congress Cataloging-in-Publication Data

Searles, George J. (George John), 1944-
      Workplace communications : the basics / George J. Searles. – 4th ed.
         p. cm.
      Includes bibliographical references and index.
      ISBN 0-205-60336-X (alk. paper)
      1. English language–Business English. 2. English language–Technical English.
      3. Business writing–Problems, exercises, etc. 4. Technical writing–Problems,
      exercises, etc. 5. Business communication–Problems, exercises, etc. 6. Commercial
      correspondence–Problems, exercises, etc. I. Title.

   PE1479.B87S43 2008
   808'.06665--dc22   2007036034

Please visit us at www.pearsonhighered.com

ISBN-13: 978-0-205-60336-7
ISBN-10: 0-205-60336-X

   3 4 5 6 7 8 9 10—DOH—11 10 09

Contents

3

Business Letters   51

4

Effective Visuals: Tables, Graphs, Charts, and Illustrations   77

5

Short Reports: Page Design, Formats, and Types   99

6

Summaries   141

7

Mechanism and Process/Procedure Descriptions   157

11

Proposals   257

12

Long Reports: Format, Collaboration, and Documentation   289

Preface

Workplace Communications: The Basics originated as the solution to a problem. Semester after semester, I had searched unsuccessfully for a suitable text to use in my English 110 course, Oral and Written Communication, at Mohawk Valley Community College. Designed as an alternative to traditional first-year composition, the course satisfies curricular English requirements for students anticipating careers in such fields as welding, air conditioning, and electrical maintenance. As might be expected, English 110 is a highly practical, hands-on course that meets the specialized needs of its target audience by focusing exclusively on job-related communications.

Although some excellent texts had been written in the fields of business and technical communication, nearly all were aimed at the university level and were therefore quite beyond the scope of a course like English 110. Finally, I decided to fill the gap and meet my students' needs by creating a textbook of my own. More than five years in the making, the first edition of *Workplace Communications: The Basics* was published in 1999. My students at Mohawk Valley responded enthusiastically, citing the book's accessibility, clarity, and pragmatic, down-to-earth emphasis as particularly appealing features. To my great satisfaction, it met with similar success at many other colleges, and new editions appeared in 2003 and 2006.

Now, however, rapid changes in the workplace environment—particularly with respect to technology—necessitate further revision. I'm delighted, therefore, that Longman has given me the opportunity to once again update the book. The fourth edition retains all the essential features of the earlier versions while incorporating much new material. Short on theory, long on practical applications, and written in a simple, conversational style, it's exceptionally user-friendly. The book is appropriate not only for recent high school graduates but also for returning adult students and other nontraditional learners. It's comprehensive and challenging enough for trade school and community college courses such as English 110 and for similar introductory-level classes at most four-year institutions.

Like the earlier editions, it includes many helpful features such as the following:

- Learning objectives and outlines for each chapter
- Numerous examples, illustrations, and exercises based on actual workplace situations
- Useful checklists at the ends of major sections
- Realistic exercises that reflect each chapter's focus

I'm looking forward to using this fourth edition in my classes, and I'm hopeful that other instructors will find it valuable as well. The updated Instructor's Manual offers teaching guidelines for each chapter, sample course outlines, keys to the exercises, and additional material. All the visuals are reproduced at high-quality resolution in order to facilitate photocopying or scanning for the creation of overhead transparencies or PowerPoint slides. Please send me your comments and suggestions by e-mail to gsearles@mvcc.edu or by conventional mail to the Humanities Department, Mohawk Valley Community College, 1101 Sherman Drive, Utica, NY 13501.

Permit me some acknowledgments. First, I wish to thank my reviewers: Daniel D. Ding, Ferris State University; Suzanne Griffith, Olympic College; Rima S. Gulshan, George Mason University; Arthur Khaw, Kirkwood Community College; Thomas Mantey, Ohio University; David D. Pitcher, Broome Community College; Cheli Turner, Greenville Technical College, and Rebecca Gilpin and Katherine Meisenheimer at Pearson/Longman and Lindsay Mateiro at Pre-Press PMG. And thanks to Teresa Ward, for her work on the Instructor's Manual.

On a more personal note, I wish also to thank my students, who have taught me so much over the years. And I would be remiss indeed if I neglected to acknowledge the editorial advice of Cynthia Eaton Tvelia, of Suffolk Community College, along with the technical assistance of my Mohawk Valley Community College colleagues Louise Charbonneau, Norma Chrisman, Barbara Evans, Jim Fiore, Colleen Kehoe-Robinson, and Ron Miller. I must also mention the longtime support of my valued friend and colleague Marie Czarnecki. In addition, I salute my lifelong friend Frank Tedeschi and my "basketball buddies," Mike Cosgrove and John Lapinski, who continue to provide much-appreciated diversion, encouragement, and companionship.

Most importantly, of course, I thank my wife, Ellis, and my sons, Jonathan and Colin.

GEORGE J. SEARLES

Introduction

As even its title suggests, *Workplace Communications: The Basics* is in no sense a typical English textbook.

Appropriate as such topics may be in a traditional composition text, you'll find nothing here about how to write 500-word essays, and nothing about how to critique English literature. Instead, it focuses on the purpose, audience, and tone of communications. Throughout, there is great emphasis on the essential features of effective workplace writing: concision, clarity, and proper formatting. In keeping with the book's highly practical nature, you'll work exclusively with nonacademic forms of writing, the kind done on the job. Among these are memos, e-mail, business letters—including the application letter and résumé—and both short and long reports.

In addition, chapters detail how to handle specific tasks: writing summaries, descriptions, instructions, and proposals; delivering oral reports; and enhancing oral and written presentations by using visual aids such as tables and graphs. Every chapter includes numerous examples and illustrations, advice on using computers, and exercises that enable you to practice applying specific principles. Through the use of commonsense strategies, you'll learn to express yourself quickly and directly, with no wasted words. Once you begin to communicate more confidently and efficiently, you'll be better motivated to eliminate any basic mechanical errors that have weakened your writing in the past.

The communication skills you'll develop are important not simply for the sake of completing a course and satisfying an English requirement. Combined with specialized training in your major field of study, these skills will also help equip you for success in the highly competitive environment of today's workplace. In survey after survey employers repeatedly mention good communication skills along with character, technical knowledge, and computer literacy when asked what they consider to be the most desirable attributes a job candidate can possess. Fortunately, you need not major in English to learn to communicate better. Anyone can. It requires only three components: desire, effort, and guidance. The first two are your responsibility. Coupled with your instructor's efforts, this text will provide the third.

The content of *Workplace Communications* is based on the author's experience of more than 30 years not only as a writing teacher but also as a professional social worker, widely published freelance journalist, and communications consultant to numerous businesses, organizations, and social service agencies. This new edition also benefits from valuable suggestions provided by my students and by other college-level instructors who have used earlier editions in their classes. The emphasis, therefore, is not on the abstract theory but on practical application. This text is designed specifically for *you*, the student. After completing the book you'll know a great deal more than you did before about written and oral communication in the workplace. You'll be better prepared to confront any communication challenges your chosen career presents. And if you decide to continue your education, what you've learned will provide a solid foundation for further study.

GEORGE J. SEARLES

1

The Keys to Successful Communication: Purpose, Audience, and Tone

Learning Objective When you complete this chapter, you'll be able to identify your communication purpose and your audience, thereby achieving the appropriate tone in every workplace writing situation.

☐ **Purpose**
☐ **Audience**
☐ **Tone**
Exercises

Every instance of workplace writing occurs for a specific reason and is intended for a particular individual or group. Much the same is true of spoken messages, whether delivered in person or by phone. Therefore, both the purpose and the audience must be carefully considered to ensure that the tone of the exchange will be appropriate to the situation. Although this may seem obvious, awareness of purpose, audience, and tone is the single most crucial factor in determining whether your communication will succeed. This opening chapter concentrates on these fundamental concerns, presents a brief overview of the basic principles involved, and provides exercises in their application.

Purpose

Nearly all workplace writing is done for at least one of three purposes: to create a record, to request or provide information, or to persuade. A caseworker in a social services agency, for example, might interview an applicant for public assistance to gather information that will then be reviewed in determining the applicant's eligibility. Clearly, such writing is intended both to provide information and to create a record. The purchasing director of a manufacturing company, on the other hand, might write a letter or e-mail inquiring whether a particular supplier can provide materials more cheaply than the current vendor. The supplier will likely reply promptly. Obviously, the primary purpose here is to exchange information. In yet another setting, a probation officer composes a presentencing report intended to influence the court to grant probation to the offender or impose a jail sentence. The officer may recommend either, and the report will become part of the offender's record, but the primary purpose of this example of workplace writing is to persuade.

The first step in the writing process is to consciously identify which of the three categories of purpose applies. You must ask yourself, "Am I writing primarily to create a record, to request or provide information, or to persuade?" Once you make this determination, the question becomes, "Summarized in one sentence, what am I trying to say?" To answer, you must zoom in on your subject matter, focusing on the most important elements. A helpful strategy is to employ the "Five W's" that journalists use to structure the opening sentences of newspaper stories: Who, What, Where, When, Why. Just as they do for reporters, the Five W's will enable you to get off to a running start. Consider, for example, how the Five W's technique applies in each of the following situations:

- *Caseworker writing to provide information and create a record*

WHO   WHAT   WHERE

Carolyn Matthews visited the downtown office of the County

    WHEN WHY

Social Services Department on May 15 to apply for public assistance.

- *Purchasing director writing to request information*

    WHO   WHAT

I'd like to know whether you can provide gaskets for less than

    WHERE   WHEN

$100/dozen, shipped to my company on a monthly basis,

 WHY

because I am seeking a new supplier.

- *Probation officer writing to persuade*

WHO   WHAT

Jerome Farley should be denied probation and sentenced to

WHERE   WHEN   WHY

state prison, effective immediately, because he is a repeat offender.

▟ Audience

Next ask yourself, "Who will read what I have written?" This is a crucial aspect of the communication process. To illustrate, consider these two examples. The first is from a *USA Today* newspaper story about an article published in the *Journal of the National Cancer Institute,* and the second is an excerpt from the abstract accompanying that article.

Prostate Cancer Study Focuses on Vitamins

Doctors are investigating a possible link between heavy multivitamin use and the most serious types of prostate cancer, according to an article in today's Journal of the National Cancer Institute.

Researchers followed 295,344 men. Men who reported taking multivitamins more than seven times a week had a slightly greater risk of advanced or fatal prostate tumors. If doctors followed 10,000 men for 10 years, there would be about 30 extra cases of advanced prostate cancer and seven or eight extra cases of fatal prostate cancer associated with heavy supplement use, says lead author Michael Leitzmann of the NCI.

Authors found no increase in the risk of early prostate tumors among heavy vitamin users. They also found no heightened risk among men who took only one vitamin a day, Leitzmann says. He stressed the study was not designed to prove that vitamins affect cancer risk.

To prove that, scientists would have to randomly assign half of patients to take supplements and half of men to follow some other regimen.

Vitamin users should be cautious about taking more than the recommended daily allowance, he says.

(From *USA Today,* 16 May 2007: 7D)

Abstract

Background: Multivitamin supplements are used by millions of Americans because of their potential health benefits, but the relationship between multivitamin use and prostate cancer is unclear. Methods: We prospectively investigated the association between multivitamin use and risk of prostate cancer (localized, advanced, and fatal) in 295344 men enrolled in the National Institutes of Health (NIH)-AARP Diet and Health Study who were cancer free at enrollment in 1995 and 1996. During 5 years of follow-up, 10241 participants were diagnosed with incident prostate cancer, including 8765 localized and 1476 advanced cancers. In a separate mortality analysis with 6 years of follow-up, 179 cases of fatal prostate cancer were ascertained. Multivitamin use was assessed at baseline as part of a self-administered, mailed food-frequency questionnaire. Relative risks (RRs) and 95% confidence intervals (CIs) were calculated by use of Cox proportional hazards regression, adjusted for established or suspected prostate cancer risk factors. Results: No association was observed between multivitamin use and risk of localized prostate cancer. However, we found an increased risk of advanced and fatal prostate cancers (RR = 1.32, 95% CI = 1.04 to 1.67 and RR = 1.98, 95% 0 = 1.07 to 3.66, respectively) among men reporting excessive use of multivitamins (more than seven times per week) when compared with never users.

(From Michael Leitzman, et al. "Multivitamin Use and Risk of Prostate Cancer in the National Institutes of Health-AARP Diet and Health Study." *Journal of the National Cancer Institute* 99.10 (16 May 2007): 754–764.

Anyone can immediately recognize the differences between these two pieces of writing. Obviously, the *USA Today* coverage is general in nature, employs simple vocabulary and no technical terms, and is therefore easy to follow. The abstract, on the other hand, with its highly specialized content and terminology, is much more challenging. Even the titles of the two articles reflect these contrasts. The reason for the differences is that a mass-circulation newspaper like *USA Today* is intended for the general public, whereas a professional periodical like the *Journal of the National Cancer Institute* is written specifically for highly educated experts. Both articles cover the same material, and the purpose of both is to inform. But the two publications are targeted at entirely different audiences; hence the dissimilarity. This contrast makes sense. For the newspaper piece to be significantly more specialized, or for the abstract to be any less so, would be inappropriate. Each is well suited to its readership.

Workplace communications are governed by this same dynamic. An e-mail, memo, letter, report, or oral presentation must be tailored to its intended audience; otherwise, it probably won't achieve the desired results. Therefore, ask yourself the following questions before attempting to prepare any sort of formal communication:

- Am I writing to one person or more than one?
- What are their job titles and/or areas of responsibility?
- What do they already know about the specific situation?
- Why do they need this information?
- What do I want them to do as a result of receiving it?
- What factors might influence their response?

Because these questions are closely related, the answers will sometimes overlap. A good starting point for sorting them out is to classify your audience by level: layperson, expert, or executive. The layperson does not possess significant prior knowledge of the field, whereas an expert obviously does. An executive reader has decision-making power and, one hopes, considerable expertise as well. By profiling your readers or listeners in this way, you'll come to see the subject of your planned communication from your audience's viewpoint as well as your own. You'll be better able to state the purpose of your communication, provide necessary details, cite meaningful examples, achieve the correct level of formality, and avert possible misunderstandings, thereby achieving your desired outcome.

In identifying your audience, remember that workplace communications fall into four broad categories:

- *Upward communication:* Intended for those above you in the hierarchy. (Example: An e-mail reply to a question from your supervisor.)

- *Lateral communication:* Intended for those at your own level in the hierarchy. (Example: A voice mail to a co-worker with whom you're collaborating.)

- *Downward communication:* Intended for those below you in the hierarchy. (Example: An oral reminder to an intern you've been assigned to train.)

- *Outward communication:* Intended for those outside your workplace. (Example: A letter to someone at a company with which you do business.)

These differences will influence your communications in many ways, particularly in determining format. For in-house communications (the first three categories) the memo was traditionally the preferred written medium. Now the memo has largely been replaced by e-mail. For outward communications, such as correspondence with clients, customers, or the general public, the standard business letter has been the norm. Business letters are either mailed or transmitted by fax machine. Even for outward communications, though, e-mail is often the best choice because of its speed and efficiency. If a more formal document is required, a confirmation letter can always be sent later.

Tone

Your hierarchical relationship to your reader will play a major role in determining the *tone* of your communication as well. This is especially true when you're attempting to convey "bad news" (the denial of a request from an employee whom you supervise, for example) or to suggest that staff members adopt some new or different procedure. Although such messages can be phrased in a firm, straightforward manner, a harsh voice or belligerent attitude is seldom productive.

The workplace is essentially a set of individuals and relationships, busy people working together to accomplish a common goal: the mission of the business, organization, or agency. A high level of cooperation and collective commitment is needed for this to happen. Ideally, each person exerts a genuine effort to foster a climate of shared enthusiasm and commitment. When co-workers become defensive or resentful, morale problems inevitably develop, undermining productivity. In such a situation, everyone loses.

Therefore, do not try to sound tough or demanding when writing about potentially sensitive issues. Instead, appeal to the reader's sense of fairness and cooperation. Phrase your sentences in a nonthreatening way, emphasizing the reader's point of view by using a reader-centered (rather than a writer-centered) perspective. For obvious reasons, this approach should govern your correspondence intended for readers outside the workplace as well.

Here are some examples of how to creatively change a writer-centered perspective into a reader-centered perspective:

Writer-Centered Perspective	Reader-Centered Perspective
If I can answer any questions, I'll be happy to do so.	If you have any questions, please ask.
We shipped the order this morning.	Your order was shipped this morning.
I'm happy to report that . . .	You'll be glad to know that . . .

Notice that changing *I* and *we* to *you* and *your* personalizes the communication. Focusing on the reader is also known as the "you" approach. Another important element of the you approach is the use of *please, thank you,* and other polite terms.

Now consider Figures 1.1 and 1.2. Both e-mails have the same purpose, to change a specific behavior, and both address the same audience.

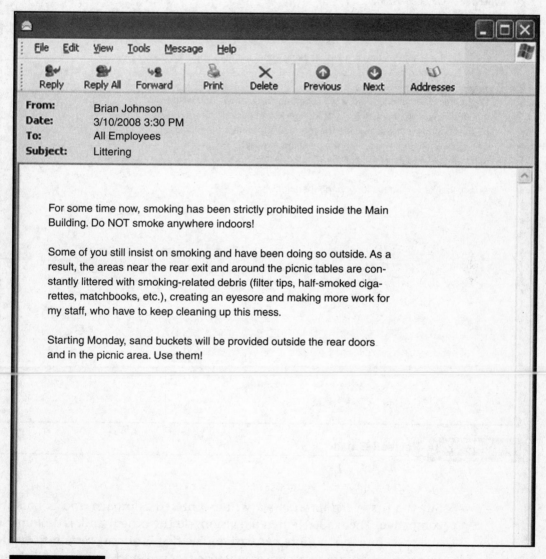

File   Edit   View   Tools   Message   Help

Reply   Reply All   Forward   Print   Delete   Previous   Next   Addresses

From:	Brian Johnson
Date:	3/10/2008 3:30 PM
To:	All Employees
Subject:	Littering

For some time now, smoking has been strictly prohibited inside the Main Building. Do NOT smoke anywhere indoors!

Some of you still insist on smoking and have been doing so outside. As a result, the areas near the rear exit and around the picnic tables are constantly littered with smoking-related debris (filter tips, half-smoked cigarettes, matchbooks, etc.), creating an eyesore and making more work for my staff, who have to keep cleaning up this mess.

Starting Monday, sand buckets will be provided outside the rear doors and in the picnic area. Use them!

FIGURE 1.1   Original E-mail

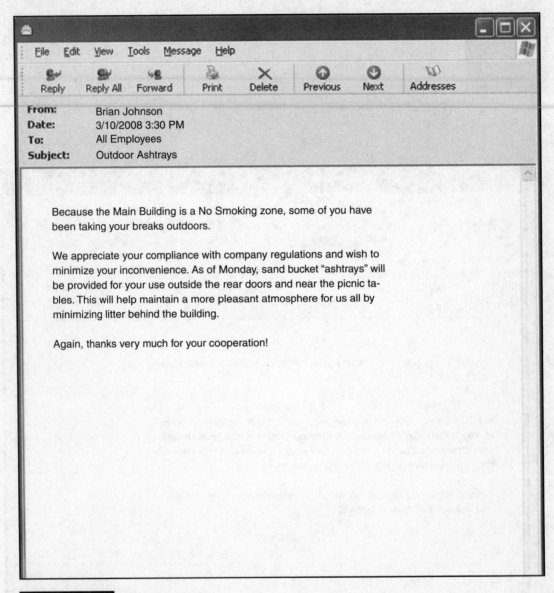

File   Edit   View   Tools   Message   Help

Reply   Reply All   Forward   Print   Delete   Previous   Next   Addresses

From:	Brian Johnson
Date:	3/10/2008 3:30 PM
To:	All Employees
Subject:	Outdoor Ashtrays

Because the Main Building is a No Smoking zone, some of you have been taking your breaks outdoors.

We appreciate your compliance with company regulations and wish to minimize your inconvenience. As of Monday, sand bucket "ashtrays" will be provided for your use outside the rear doors and near the picnic tables. This will help maintain a more pleasant atmosphere for us all by minimizing litter behind the building.

Again, thanks very much for your cooperation!

FIGURE 1.2   **Revised E-mail**

But the first version adopts a writer-centered approach and is harshly combative. The reader-centered revision, on the other hand, is diplomatic and therefore much more persuasive. The first is almost certain to create resentment and hard feelings, whereas the second is far more likely to achieve the desired results.

Tech Tips

A slangy, vernacular style is out of place in workplace writing, as are expletives and any other coarse or vulgar language. Something that may seem clever or humorous to you may not amuse your reader and will probably appear foolish to anyone reviewing the correspondence later on. Keep this in mind when sending e-mail, a medium that seems to encourage a looser, more playful manner of interaction. Typical of this tendency are e-mail emoticons, silly "faces" created by combining punctuation marks, like this:

: -)	: - (	; -)
Smile	Frown	Wink

Although intended to reinforce meaning, such devices just distract or annoy most serious readers, undermining the writer's credibility.

In a similar vein you should avoid overdependence on abbreviations and acronyms (words composed of the initial letters of a phrase or expression). Probably the most familiar are ASAP (as soon as possible), FYI (for your information), FAQ (frequently asked questions), NRN (no reply necessary), and SASE (self-addressed, stamped envelope). Although such well-known acronyms can be useful, a great many others—far less obvious—have hatched in Internet chat rooms and other informal contexts such as instant messaging. Although inventive, most are inappropriate for the workplace because they may not be readily understood—especially by older workers and those for whom English is not their native language. Here are ten examples.

BTW: by the way	IRL: in real life
FWIW: for what it's worth	OTOH: on the other hand
HAND: have a nice day	TMOT: trust me on this
IMHO: in my humble opinion	TTYTT: to tell you the truth
IOW: in other words	WADR: with all due respect

At the same time, there exist innumerable technical acronyms that are specific to particular businesses and occupations, and are therefore quite useful to workers in those fields. Such acronyms as ADC (aid to dependent children), CAD (computed assisted design), and PVC (polyvinyl chloride) are just a few examples among countless others that facilitate efficient dialogue among employees familiar with those terms. As with so many aspects of workplace communications, the use of acronyms is largely governed by considerations of audience, purpose, and tone.

Note: Among the many Web sites devoted to acronyms, Acronym Finder is one of the most comprehensive. See www.acronymfinder.com/.

In most settings you can adopt a somewhat more casual manner with your equals and with those below you than you can with those above you in the chain of command or with persons outside the organization. But in any case avoid an excessively conversational style. Even when the situation is not particularly troublesome, and even when your reader is well known to you, remember that "business is business." Although you need not sound stuffy, it is important to maintain a certain level of formality. Accordingly, you should never allow personal matters to appear in workplace correspondence. Consider, for example, Figure 1.3, an e-mail in which the writer has obviously violated this rule. Although the writer's tone toward his supervisor is appropriately respectful, the content should be far less detailed, as in the revised version shown in Figure 1.4.

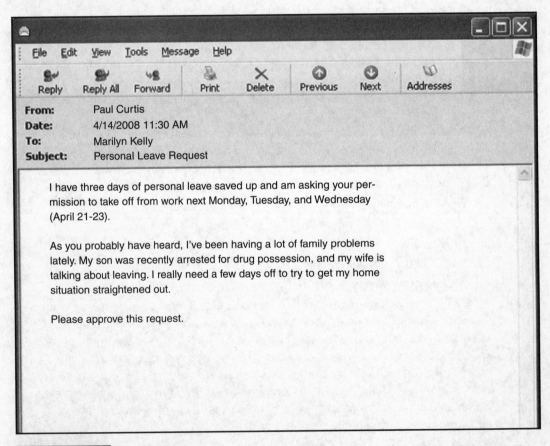

| **FIGURE 1.3** | **Original E-mail** |

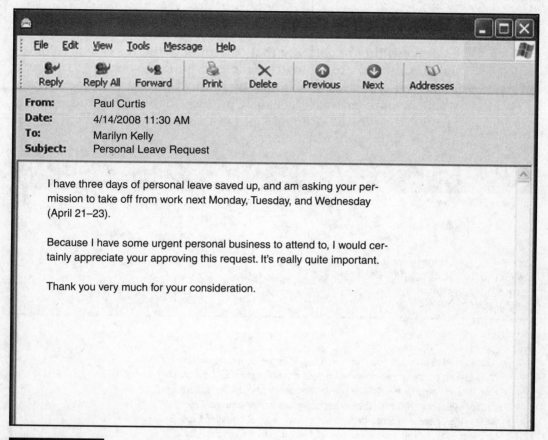

From: Paul Curtis
Date: 4/14/2008 11:30 AM
To: Marilyn Kelly
Subject: Personal Leave Request

I have three days of personal leave saved up, and am asking your permission to take off from work next Monday, Tuesday, and Wednesday (April 21–23).

Because I have some urgent personal business to attend to, I would certainly appreciate your approving this request. It's really quite important.

Thank you very much for your consideration.

FIGURE 1.4 **Revised E-mail**

A sensitive situation awaits you when you must convey unpleasant information or request assistance or cooperation from superiors. Although you may sometimes yearn for a more democratic arrangement, every workplace has a pecking order that you must take into account as you choose your words. Hierarchy exists because some individuals—by virtue of greater experience, education, or access to information—are in fact better positioned to lead. Although this system sometimes functions imperfectly, the supervisor, department head, or other person in charge will respond better to subordinates whose communications reflect an understanding of this basic reality. Essentially, the rules for writing to a person higher on the ladder are the same as for writing to someone on a lower rung. Be focused and self-assured, but use the you approach, encouraging the reader to see the advantage in accepting your recommendation or granting your request.

An especially polite tone is advisable when addressing those who outrank you. Acknowledge that the final decision is theirs and that you are fully willing to abide by that determination. This can be achieved either through "softening" words and phrases (*perhaps, with your permission, if you wish*) or simply by stating outright that you'll accept whatever outcome may develop. Consider, for example, the e-mail in Figures 1.5 and 1.6. Although both say essentially the same thing, the

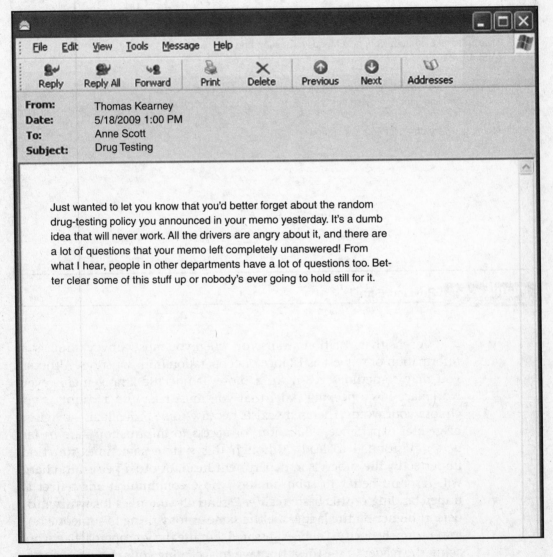

FIGURE 1.5   Original E-mail

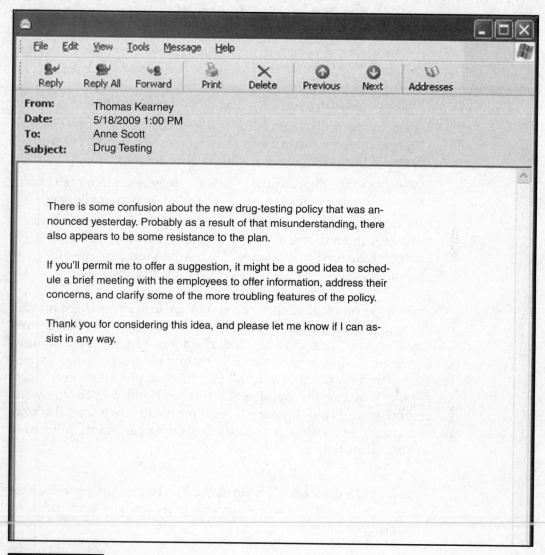

FIGURE 1.6   Revised E-mail

first is completely inappropriate in tone, so much so that it would likely result in negative personal consequences for the writer. The second would be much better received because it properly reflects the nature of the professional relationship between writer and reader.

Communicating with customers or clients also requires a great deal of sensitivity and tact. When justifying a price increase, denying a claim, or apologizing for a delay, you will probably create an unpleasant climate unless you present the facts in an unantagonistic manner. Always strive for the most upbeat, reader-centered wording you can devise. Here are some examples of how to rephrase negative content in more positive, reader-centered terms:

Negative Wording	Positive Wording
We cannot process your claim because the necessary forms have not been completed.	Your claim can be processed as soon as you complete the necessary forms.
We do not take phone calls after 3:00 p.m. on Fridays.	You may reach us by telephone until 3:00 p.m. on Fridays.
We closed your case because we never received the information requested in our letter of April 2.	Your case will be reactivated as soon as you provide the information requested in our April 2 letter.

When the problem has been caused by an error or oversight on your part, be sure to apologize. However, do not state specifically what the mistake was, or your letter may be used as evidence against you should a lawsuit ensue. Simply acknowledge that a mistake has occurred, express regret, explain how the situation will be corrected, and close on a conciliatory note. Consider, for example, the letter in Figure 1.7. The body and conclusion are fine, but the introduction practically invites legal action. Here's a suggested revision of the letter's opening paragraph, phrased in less incriminating terms:

> Thank you for purchasing our product and for taking the time to contact us about it. We apologize for the unsatisfactory condition of your Superior microwave dinner.

Moreover, given the serious nature of the complaint, the customer services representative should certainly have made a stronger effort to establish a tone of sincerely apologetic concern. As it stands, this letter seems abrupt and rather impersonal—certainly not what the context requires. (For a much better handling of this kind of situation, see the adjustment letter in Figure 3.7.)

This is not to suggest, however, that workplace communications should attempt to falsify reality or dodge responsibility. On the contrary, there is a moral imperative to uphold strict ethical standards. The Enron scandal and other corporate misdeeds have put ethical questions under

Superior Foods, Inc.

135 Grove St., Atlanta, GA 30300 • (324) 555-1234

October 13, 2008

Mr. Philip Updike
246 Alton St.
Atlanta, GA 30300

Dear Mr. Updike:

We are sorry that you found a piece of glass in your Superior microwave dinner. Please accept our assurances that this is a very unusual incident.

Here are three coupons redeemable at your local grocery store for complimentary Superior dinners of your choice.

We hope you will continue to enjoy our fine products.

Sincerely,

John Roth

John Roth
Customer Services Dept.

Enclosures (3)

FIGURE 1.7 **Letter to Customer**

the spotlight and greatly increased the public appetite for investigative reporting by the media. The Merriam-Webster Online Dictionary defines ethics as "the discipline dealing with what is good or bad and with moral duty and obligation." Reduced to its essentials, ethics involves choosing honesty over dishonesty, requiring us to act with integrity even when there would be short-term gains for behaving otherwise. Ethical communication must therefore be honest and fair to everyone involved in the exchange.

By their nature, workplace communications can greatly affect people's lives. Accordingly, customers and clients, investors, taxpayers, and workers themselves should be able to treat such materials as accurate, reliable, and trustworthy—in short, ethical. But those documents fail the ethics test if corrupted by any of the following tactics:

- **Suppression of information:** The outright burying of data to hide inconvenient truths. (Example: A company fails to reveal product-testing results that indicate potential danger to consumers.)
- **Falsification or fabrication:** Changing or simply inventing data to support a desired outcome. (Example: A company boasts of a fictitious enterprise to lure investors into supporting a new venture.)
- **Overstatement or understatement:** Exaggerating the positive aspects of a situation or downplaying negative aspects to create the desired impression. (Example: A public-opinion survey describes 55 percent of the respondents as a "substantial majority" or 45 percent as "a small percentage.")
- **Selective misquoting:** Deleting words from quoted material to distort the meaning. (Example: A supervisor changes a report's conclusion that "this proposal will seem feasible only to workers unfamiliar with the situation" to "this proposal will seem feasible . . . to workers.")
- **Subjective wording:** Using terms deliberately chosen for their ambiguity. (Example: A company advertises "customary service charges," knowing that "customary" is open to broad interpretation.)
- **Conflict of interest:** Exploiting behind-the-scenes connections to influence decision making. (Example: A board member of a community agency encourages the agency to hire her company for paid services rather than soliciting bids.)
- **Withholding information:** Refusing to share relevant data with co-workers. (Example: A computer-savvy employee provides

misleading answers about new software to make a recently hired co-worker appear incompetent.)
- **Plagiarism:** Taking credit for someone else's ideas, findings, or written material. (Example: An employee assigned to prepare a report submits a similar report written by someone at another company and downloaded from the Internet.)

Workers must weigh the consequences of their actions, considering their moral obligations. If this is done in good faith, practices such as those outlined in the preceding list will surely be avoided. Decisions can get complicated, however, when obligations to self and others come into conflict. Workers often feel pressure to compromise personal ethical beliefs to achieve company goals. All things being equal, a worker's primary obligation is to self—to remain employed. But if the employer permits or requires actions that the employee considers immoral, an ethical dilemma is created, forcing the worker to choose among two or more unsatisfactory alternatives.

What if, for example, an employee discovers that the company is habitually ignoring Occupational Safety and Health Administration (OSHA) or Environmental Protection Agency (EPA) standards? As everyone knows, whistle-blowing can incur heavy penalties: ostracism, undesirable work assignments, poor performance reviews—or even termination. Although the Sarbanes-Oxley Act of 2002 prohibits such retribution, it's quite difficult to actually prove retaliation unless the worker is prepared for potentially lengthy and expensive legal combat with no guarantee of success and the added threat of countersuit. And even if the attempt does succeed, the worker must then return to an even more hostile climate. Should the person seek employment elsewhere, blacklisting may already have sabotaged the job search. Not everyone who battles large companies emerges as heroically as the legendary Erin Brockovich, whose victory over Pacific Gas & Electric was portrayed by actress Julia Roberts in the 2000 Hollywood film named for this environmental activist.

There are no easy resolutions to ethical dilemmas, but we all must be guided by conscience. Obviously, this can involve some difficult decisions. By determining your purpose, analyzing your audience, and considering the moral dimensions of the situation, you will achieve the correct tone for any communication. As we have seen, this is crucial for dealing with potentially resistive readers (especially those above you in the workplace hierarchy) and when rectifying errors for which you are accountable. In all instances, however, a courteous, positive, reader-centered, and ethical approach gets the best results.

Exercises

■ **EXERCISE 1.1**

Revise each of the following three communications to achieve a tone more appropriate to the purpose and audience.

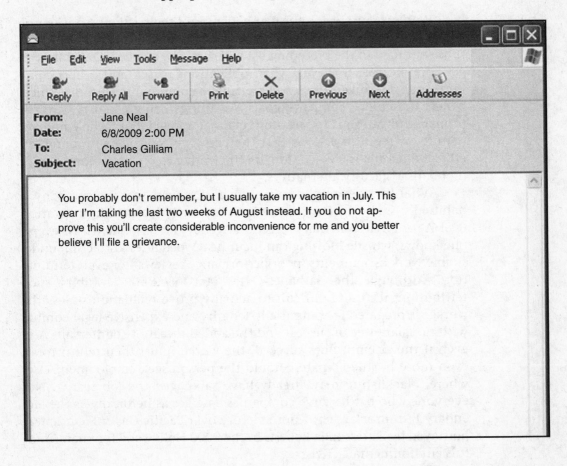

File   Edit   View   Tools   Message   Help

Reply   Reply All   Forward   Print   Delete   Previous   Next   Addresses

From: Jane Neal
Date: 6/8/2009 2:00 PM
To: Charles Gilliam
Subject: Vacation

You probably don't remember, but I usually take my vacation in July. This year I'm taking the last two weeks of August instead. If you do not approve this you'll create considerable inconvenience for me and you better believe I'll file a grievance.

■ **EXERCISE 1.1** **Continued**

COUNTY DEPARTMENT OF SOCIAL SERVICES

MEMO

DATE: March 17, 2008

TO: All Caseworkers

FROM: Cheryl Alston, Case Supervisor *CA*

SUBJECT: Goofing Off

A lot of you seem to think that this is a country club and are spending entirely too much time in the break room! As you well know, you're entitled to one <u>15-minute</u> break in the morning and another in the afternoon. The rest of the time you're supposed to be AT YOUR DESK unless signed out for fieldwork.

■ **EXERCISE 1.1**   Continued

County Community College

MEMORANDUM

DATE: May 4, 2009

TO: All Employees

FROM: Charles Rigney, Chief of *CR*
            Security

SUBJECT: Burglarized Vehicles

Recently, there's been a rash of burglaries in the faculty/staff parking lot.
Items such as CD players, cellular phones, and even a personal computer have
been reported missing from vehicles.

After investigating, however, we've learned that several of these vehicles had
been left unlocked. Don't be stupid! Always lock your car or else be prepared
to get ripped off. My staff can't be everywhere at once, and if you set yourself
up to be victimized, it's not our fault.

■ **EXERCISE 1.2**

Revise each of the following three letters to achieve a tone more appropriate to the purpose and audience.

Bancroft's in the Mall

The Turnpike Mall • Turnpike East • Augusta, Maine 04330

February 18, 2008

Ms. Barbara Wilson
365 Grove St.
Augusta, ME 04330

Dear Ms. Wilson:

Your Bancroft's charge account is $650.55 overdue. We must receive a payment immediately.

If we do not receive a minimum payment of $50 within three days, we will refer your account to a collection agency and your credit rating will be permanently compromised.

Send a payment at once!

Sincerely,

Michael Modoski

Michael Modoski
Credit Department

■ **EXERCISE 1.2**   **Continued**

Southeast Insurance Company

Southeast Industrial Park   Tallahassee, FL 32301
Telephone: (850) 555-0123   FAX: (850) 555-3210

November 5, 2009

Mr. Francis Tedeschi
214 Summit Avenue
Tallahassee, FL 32301

Dear Mr. Tedeschi:

This is to acknowledge receipt of your 10/30/09 claim.

Insured persons entitled to benefits under the Tallahassee Manufacturing Co. plan effective December 1, 2005, are required to execute statements of claims for medical-surgical expense benefits only in the manner specifically mandated in your certificate holder's handbook.

Your claim has been quite improperly executed, as you have neglected to procure the Physician's Statement of Services Rendered. The information contained therein is prerequisite to any consideration of your claim.

Enclosed is the necessary form. See that it's filled out and returned to us without delay, or your claim cannot be processed.

Yours truly,

Ann Jurkiewicz

Ann Jurkiewicz
Claims Adjustor

Enclosure

■ **EXERCISE 1.2**   Continued

DEPARTMENT OF SOCIAL SERVICES

County Administration Building   Easton, NJ 07300
                                                             (201) 555-0123

November 10, 2008

Easton Savings Bank
36 Bank Street
Easton, NJ 07300

Re: Charles Mangan (Social Security # 000-00-0000)

To Whom It May Concern:

The above individual has applied for Medical Assistance. This Department requires that a 30-month banking history accompany all such applications. You must send us the necessary information immediately.

Provide a listing of each month's average balance for the period of March 1, 2006, to November 1, 2008, along with verification of all closed or transferred accounts during that period.

This directive is made pursuant to New Jersey State Law, which mandates that all banking organizations must furnish such information to authorized representatives of the Department of Social Services to verify eligibility for any form of Public Assistance.

Sincerely,

Mary Louise Martin

Mary Louise Martin
Caseworker

■ **EXERCISE 1.3**

Revise each of the following three e-mails to eliminate inappropriate tone and/or content.

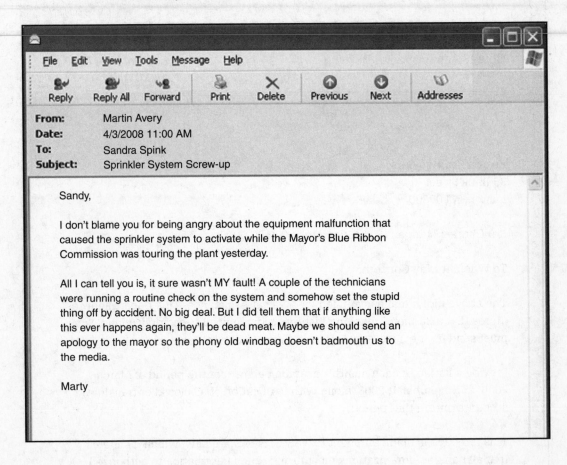

File   Edit   View   Tools   Message   Help

Reply   Reply All   Forward   Print   Delete   Previous   Next   Addresses

From: Martin Avery
Date: 4/3/2008 11:00 AM
To: Sandra Spink
Subject: Sprinkler System Screw-up

Sandy,

I don't blame you for being angry about the equipment malfunction that caused the sprinkler system to activate while the Mayor's Blue Ribbon Commission was touring the plant yesterday.

All I can tell you is, it sure wasn't MY fault! A couple of the technicians were running a routine check on the system and somehow set the stupid thing off by accident. No big deal. But I did tell them that if anything like this ever happens again, they'll be dead meat. Maybe we should send an apology to the mayor so the phony old windbag doesn't badmouth us to the media.

Marty

■ **EXERCISE 1.3**   Continued

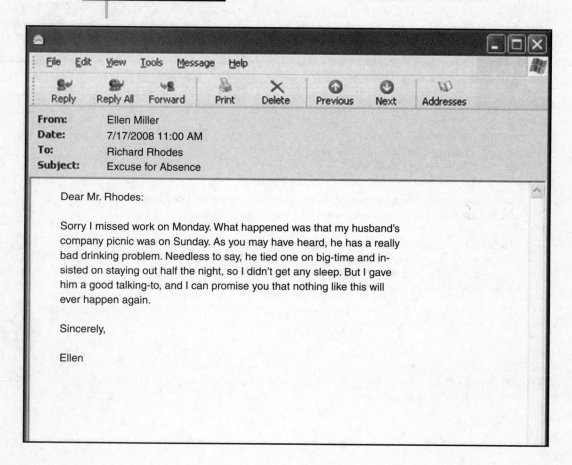

File Edit View Tools Message Help

Reply   Reply All   Forward   Print   Delete   Previous   Next   Addresses

From: Ellen Miller
Date: 7/17/2008 11:00 AM
To: Richard Rhodes
Subject: Excuse for Absence

Dear Mr. Rhodes:

Sorry I missed work on Monday. What happened was that my husband's company picnic was on Sunday. As you may have heard, he has a really bad drinking problem. Needless to say, he tied one on big-time and insisted on staying out half the night, so I didn't get any sleep. But I gave him a good talking-to, and I can promise you that nothing like this will ever happen again.

Sincerely,

Ellen

■ **EXERCISE 1.3**   Continued

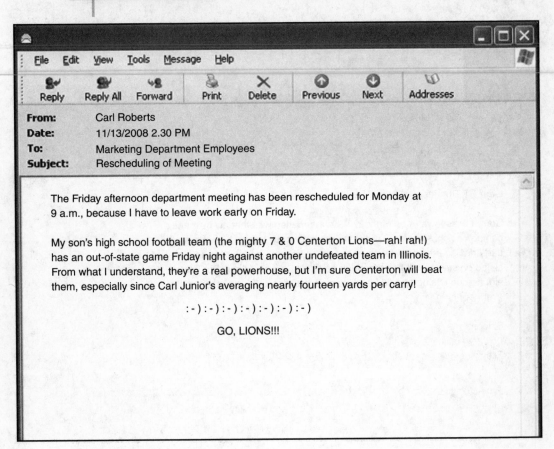

File   Edit   View   Tools   Message   Help

Reply   Reply All   Forward   Print   Delete   Previous   Next   Addresses

From: Carl Roberts
Date: 11/13/2008 2.30 PM
To: Marketing Department Employees
Subject: Rescheduling of Meeting

The Friday afternoon department meeting has been rescheduled for Monday at 9 a.m., because I have to leave work early on Friday.

My son's high school football team (the mighty 7 & 0 Centerton Lions—rah! rah!) has an out-of-state game Friday night against another undefeated team in Illinois. From what I understand, they're a real powerhouse, but I'm sure Centerton will beat them, especially since Carl Junior's averaging nearly fourteen yards per carry!

:-):-):-):-):-):-):-)

GO, LIONS!!!

■ **EXERCISE 1.4**

Revise each of the following three letters to eliminate wording that might create legal liability.

Fin & Feather Pet Supplies

133 Court Street   Olympia, WA 98501

January 15, 2009

Mr. Robert Ryan
352 Stegman Street
Olympia, WA 98501

Dear Mr. Ryan:

We have received your letter of January 3, and we regret that the heating unit we sold you malfunctioned, killing your tropical fish worth $1,500.

Because the unit was purchased more than three years ago, however, our storewide warranty is no longer in effect, and we are therefore unable to accept any responsibility for your loss. Nevertheless, we are enclosing a Fin & Feather discount coupon good for $20 toward the purchase of a replacement unit or another product of your choice.

We look forward to serving you in the future!

Sincerely,

Sandra Kouvel

Sandra Kouvel
Store Manager

Enclosure

APPLIANCE WORLD

521 Scott Street   Ames, Iowa 50010   (515) 555-1234

February 20, 2008

Ms. Christine Nguyen
230 Fairview Street
Ames, Iowa 50010

Dear Ms. Nguyen:

Thank you for your recent letter about the faulty toaster oven you purchased at Appliance World. We are glad to hear that the fire it caused resulted in only minor damages to your apartment.

If you bring the unit in, we'll gladly exchange it for a more reliable one. Customer satisfaction is our #1 priority!

We are happy to assist you with all your appliance needs.

Yours truly,

Peter Keane

Peter Keane
Store Manager

■ **EXERCISE 1.4**   Continued

HIGH ROLLER
BIKES & BOARDS

516 Bridge Street ■ **Phoenix, AZ 85001**

August 17, 2009

Mr. Patrick Casey
252 Sheridan Street
Phoenix, AZ 85001

Dear Mr. Casey:

We are sorry that the bicycle tire we sold you burst during normal use, causing personal injury resulting in lingering lower back pain.

Certainly we will install a replacement tire free of charge if you simply bring your bicycle into our shop any weekday during the hours of 9 a.m. to 5 p.m.

Thank you for purchasing your bicycle supplies at High Roller!

Sincerely,

Monica Lamb

Monica Lamb
Store Manager

2

Memos and E-mail

Learning Objective   When you complete this chapter you'll be able to use basic format and organization patterns to write effective memos and e-mail messages.

 Memos
Format
E-mail
Checklist: Evaluating a Memo or E-mail

Exercises

Of all the forms of written communication used in the workplace, memos and e-mail are certainly among the most common. Any large corporation, agency, or other organization generates thousands of such documents daily. Even in a small setting, they are fundamental to office procedure. Focusing on both format and content, and exploring some of the effects of recent technological advances, this chapter explains how to handle memos and e-mail.

Memos

Traditionally, the memo was a vehicle for internal or "intramural" communication—a message from someone at Company X to someone else at Company X. The memo may be written to one person or to a group, but it has almost always been a form of in-house correspondence.

The writer and reader of a memo may be well acquainted. They may even have had lunch together. Indeed, the contents of the memo may already be known to all parties involved in the exchange. Although the usual purpose of a memo is to inform, often its function is to create a written record of a request or other message previously communicated in person, over the phone, or through the grapevine.

Accordingly, a memo is usually quite direct in approach. It should come to the point quickly and not ramble on. A common error is to obscure the central issue and confuse the reader with irrelevant details. A good memo focuses sharply, zooming in on what the reader needs to know. Depending on the subject, a memo should make its point in three or four short paragraphs: a concise introduction, a middle paragraph or two conveying the details, and perhaps a brief conclusion. If the message is quite simple, however, you should get to the point quickly. Some memos are as short as one paragraph, or even one sentence. Like so many other features of workplace communications, memo length is determined by purpose and audience.

Format

A memo has essentially one basic format. Although minor variations do exist, practically all memos share certain standard format features:

- The word *Memo, Memorandum,* or some equivalent term at or near the top of the page.

- The TO line, enabling the memo to be "addressed," and the FROM line, enabling it to be "signed." When creating a memo, always use the recipient's full name, title, and/or department. This not only ensures that the memo will reach its intended destination but also creates a more complete record for anyone reviewing the file later. For the same reason, use your own full name, title, and/or department in the FROM line.

- The DATE line

- The SUBJECT line, identifying the topic. Like a newspaper headline, but even more concisely, the SUBJECT line orients and prepares the reader for what is to follow. To write a good subject line, answer this question: "In no more than three words, what is this memo really about?"

- Of course, the message or content of the memo. As explained earlier, three or four paragraphs should be sufficient.

The memo in Figure 2.1 embodies all these features and provides an opportunity to explore further the principle of *tone* introduced in Chapter 1.

The personnel manager has picked her words carefully to avoid sounding bossy. She says "You *may want* to send him a . . . card," not "You *should* send him a . . . card," even though that's what she really means. As discussed in Chapter 1, a tactful writer can soften a recommendation, a request, or even a command simply by phrasing it in a diplomatic way. In this situation an employee's decision whether to send a card is strictly a matter of personal choice, so the memo's gentle tone is particularly appropriate. But the same strategy can also be used when conveying important directives you definitely expect the reader to follow.

For the sake of convenience, most word-processing programs include at least one preformatted memo form, called a template. The template automatically generates formatted headings and inserts the date. The writer simply fills in the blanks. Microsoft Word, the most widely used software program, provides several memo templates, one of which is reproduced in Figure 2.2.

E-mail

Because an e-mail is essentially just an electronic memo, practically everything that's already been said here about traditional memos applies to e-mail as well. Indeed, e-mail has nearly replaced the memo altogether, especially in situations where speed of delivery is important, confidentiality is not required, and the message is brief.

By now almost everyone is famliar with how to use e-mail. Typically, a worker logs on to the system by typing his or her user name and a secure

CITY MANUFACTURING CO.

MEMORANDUM

DATE: May 9, 2008

TO: All Employees

FROM: Susan Lemley, Manager SL
            Personnel Department

SUBJECT: James Mahan

As many of you already know, James Mahan of the Maintenance Department was admitted to Memorial Hospital over the weekend and is scheduled to undergo surgery on Tuesday.

Although Jim will not be receiving visitors or phone calls for a while, you may want to send him a "Get Well" card to boost his spirits. He's in Room 325.

We'll keep you posted about Jim's progress.

FIGURE 2.1   Basic Memo Format

password that prevents unauthorized access. To read new e-mail stored in the inbox, the worker clicks the mouse to access each message. Depending on one's preferences, messages can then be deleted, saved for future reference, printed, answered, or forwarded—or a combination of these options. To respond to a message the writer clicks on the appropriate prompt (in Microsoft Outlook it's Reply) and inserts the new message above the existing one. To create an entirely new e-mail, the writer clicks on the appropriate prompt (in Microsoft Outlook it's New), causing a blank template to appear on the screen, ready to be completed. When the writer finishes the message, a click of the mouse sends it to as many other users as the writer wishes—one or everyone—depending on how the To line has been addressed. The new e-mail is also stored in the writer's electronic Sent file and can be kept there indefinitely for future reference. Figure 2.3

Company Name Here

Memo

To: [Click **here** and type name]

From: [Click **here** and type name]

CC: [Click **here** and type name]

Date: 4/23/2007

Re: [Click **here** and type subject]

How to Use This Memo Template

Select text you would like to replace, and type your memo. Use styles such as Heading 1-3 and Body Text in the Style control on the Formatting toolbar. To save changes to this template for future use, choose Save As from the File menu. In the Save As Type box, choose Document Template. Next time you want to use it, choose New from the File menu, and then double-click your template.

FIGURE 2.2   **Microsoft Word's Professional Memo Template**

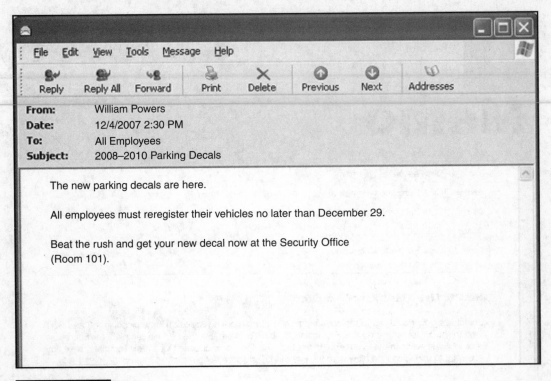

is a typical e-mail memo, similar to those you saw in Chapter 1.

There are good reasons e-mail has been so widely adopted since becoming generally available in the 1990s. On the most obvious level, it's incomparably faster than traditional correspondence. In the past, communicating by memo or letter involved at least five distinct steps:

1. Drafting
2. Typing (usually by a secretary)
3. Proofreading and initialing by the writer
4. Photocopying for the writer's file
5. Routing to the intended reader

Depending on office workload and clerical staffing levels, this process could be very time-consuming. With e-mail, however, all five steps are compressed into one, permitting speedy communication. Additionally, e-mail allows for rapid-fire exchanges, and the most recent transmittal can reproduce a complete record of all that has gone before, as shown in Figure 2.4.

Unfortunately, however, e-mail can also create some problems. One

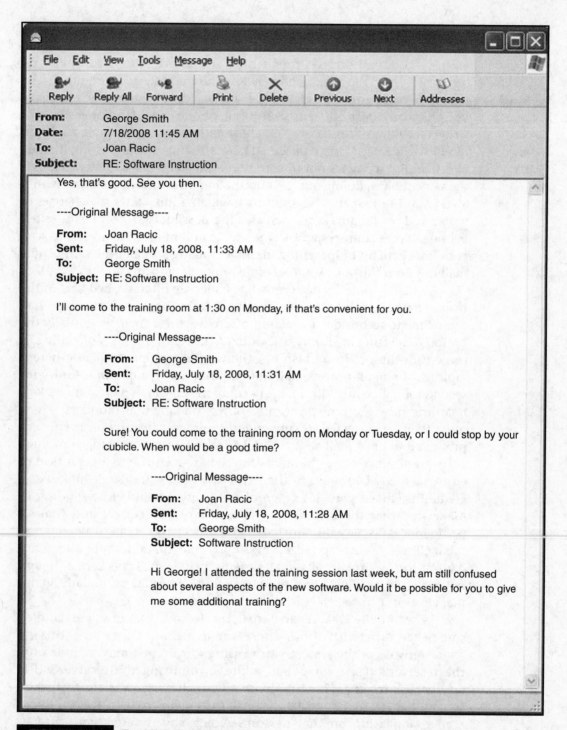

File   Edit   View   Tools   Message   Help

Reply   Reply All   Forward   Print   Delete   Previous   Next   Addresses

From: George Smith
Date: 7/18/2008 11:45 AM
To: Joan Racic
Subject: RE: Software Instruction

Yes, that's good. See you then.

----Original Message----

From: Joan Racic
Sent: Friday, July 18, 2008, 11:33 AM
To: George Smith
Subject: RE: Software Instruction

I'll come to the training room at 1:30 on Monday, if that's convenient for you.

----Original Message----

From: George Smith
Sent: Friday, July 18, 2008, 11:31 AM
To: Joan Racic
Subject: RE: Software Instruction

Sure! You could come to the training room on Monday or Tuesday, or I could stop by your cubicle. When would be a good time?

----Original Message----

From: Joan Racic
Sent: Friday, July 18, 2008, 11:28 AM
To: George Smith
Subject: Software Instruction

Hi George! I attended the training session last week, but am still confused about several aspects of the new software. Would it be possible for you to give me some additional training?

FIGURE 2.4   E-mail Correspondence

major drawback is that the very ease with which e-mail can be generated encourages overuse. In the past a writer would not bother to send a memo without good reason; too much time and effort were involved to do otherwise. Now, though, much needless correspondence is produced. The situation represented in Figure 2.4, for example, could probably have been handled more efficiently with one phone call. Many of yesterday's writers would wait until complete information on a given topic had been received, organized, and considered before acting on it or passing it along to others. But today it's not uncommon for many e-mails to be written on the same subject, doling out the information piecemeal, sometimes within a very short time span. The resulting fragmentation wastes the energies of writer and reader alike and increases the possibility of confusion, often because of premature response. One way to minimize this danger is to scan your entire menu of incoming messages, taking special note of multiple mailings from the same source, before responding to any.

Similarly, e-mails about sensitive issues are often dashed off "in the heat of battle," without sufficient reflection. In the past most writers had some time to reconsider a situation before reacting. There was usually the option of revising or simply discarding a memo if, upon proofreading, it came to seem a bit too harsh or otherwise inappropriate. The inherent rapidity of e-mail, however, all but eliminates any such opportunity for second thoughts. In addition, hasty composition causes a great many keyboarding miscues, omissions, and other fundamental blunders. These must then be corrected in subsequent messages, creating an inefficient proliferation of "e-mail about e-mail." Indeed, hurried writing combined with the absence of a secretarial "filter" has given rise to a great deal of embarrassingly bad prose in the workplace. You risk ridicule and loss of credibility unless you closely proofread every e-mail before sending it. Make sure that the information is necessary and correct and that all pertinent details have been included. Be particularly careful to avoid typos, misspellings, faulty capitalization, sloppy punctuation, and basic grammatical errors. Virtually all e-mail systems include spell-checkers; although not foolproof, they help minimize typos and misspellings. Similarly, grammar checkers can detect basic sentence problems.

When you're creating an e-mail, the To and From lines are handled somewhat differently from those on a memo. Depending on the characteristics of the system you're using, the To line may include only the receiver's name (or e-mail address), omitting the receiver's title and/or department. This is because an e-mail message is electronically transmitted (rather than being physically delivered) to the intended reader, appearing on that person's screen shortly after you send it. Likewise, your name (or e-mail address) is automatically activated as

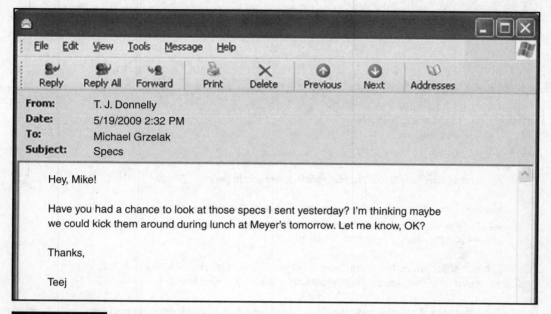

File	Edit	View	Tools	Message	Help

Reply   Reply All   Forward   Print   Delete   Previous   Next   Addresses

From: T. J. Donnelly
Date: 5/19/2009 2:32 PM
To: Michael Grzelak
Subject: Specs

Hey, Mike!

Have you had a chance to look at those specs I sent yesterday? I'm thinking maybe we could kick them around during lunch at Meyer's tomorrow. Let me know, OK?

Thanks,

Teej

FIGURE 2.5   **Informal E-mail**

soon as you log on to the system, thereby eliminating the need for you to type it in on each document you create.

Be aware that although the To and From lines on an e-mail eliminate the need for a letter-style salutation ("Dear Ms. Bernstein") or complimentary close ("Yours truly"), most writers employ these features when using e-mail, to make their messages seem less abrupt and impersonal. The relative formality or informality of these greetings and sign-offs depends on the relationship between writer and reader. In any case, if your own e-mail name and address do not fully reveal your identity, you *must* include a complimentary close to inform your readers who you are. Most e-mail systems enable you to create a "signature file" for this purpose. Figures 2.5 and 2.6 provide examples.

Understand also that e-mail is not private. Recent court decisions—some involving high-profile government scandals—have confirmed the employer's right to monitor or inspect workers' e-mail (and Internet activity). Indeed, it's not uncommon for workers to be fired for impropriety in this regard. A good rule of thumb is, "Don't say it in an e-mail unless you'd have no problem with it appearing on the front page of your company newsletter." In some situations a given message may be entirely appropriate but may contain highly sensitive information. In such cases the best choice may be a paper memo personally delivered in a sealed envelope.

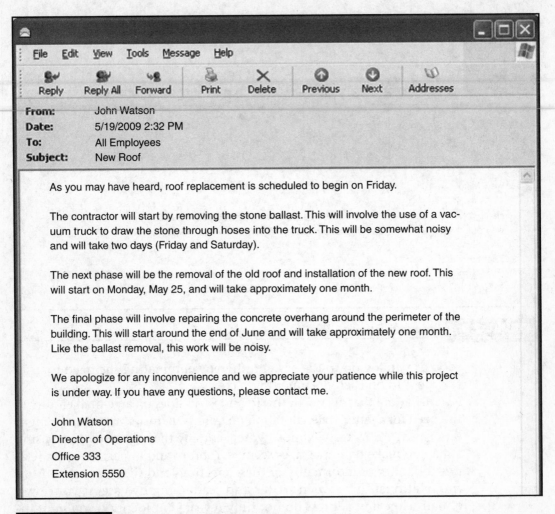

As you may have heard, roof replacement is scheduled to begin on Friday.

The contractor will start by removing the stone ballast. This will involve the use of a vacuum truck to draw the stone through hoses into the truck. This will be somewhat noisy and will take two days (Friday and Saturday).

The next phase will be the removal of the old roof and installation of the new roof. This will start on Monday, May 25, and will take approximately one month.

The final phase will involve repairing the concrete overhang around the perimeter of the building. This will start around the end of June and will take approximately one month. Like the ballast removal, this work will be noisy.

We apologize for any inconvenience and we appreciate your patience while this project is under way. If you have any questions, please contact me.

John Watson
Director of Operations
Office 333
Extension 5550

FIGURE 2.6 **Formal E-mail with Signature File**

As mentioned in Chapter 1, the company e-mail network is no place for personal messages or an excessively conversational style. Many employers provide a separate e-mail "bulletin board" on which workers can post and access announcements about garage or vehicle sales, car-pooling, unwanted theater and sports tickets, and the like. Such matters are appropriate only as bulletin board content.

Now that nearly all organizations are on-line, e-mail is no longer just an intramural communications medium; indeed, it's beginning to rival the business letter as the major form of correspondence across company boundaries. When you're sending e-mail to readers at other locations, tone takes on even greater importance than usual. Because the writer and

Tech Tips

Despite its seemingly informal, spontaneous nature, e-mail is no less "official" and permanent than a memo printed on paper. It's important, therefore, to use this medium thoughtfully, efficiently, and responsibly. These guidelines will help:

- New computer viruses crop up constantly. Although most workplaces use spam filters to weed out junk mail and potentially troublesome material, some dangerous clutter does find its way through. Guard against it by never opening attachments from unknown or suspicious sources; simply delete.

- Resist the temptation to forward chain letters, silly jokes, political rants, pornographic images, and the like. This not only wastes people's time, but in certain circumstances can also be hazardous to your professional health.

- Never forward legitimate e-mail to other readers without the original writer's knowledge and permission. The message may have been intended for you alone.

- Create new e-mail only when necessary, sending only to the person(s) needing it; resist the urge to mass-mail. Similarly, when responding to a mass-mailing, do not click Reply All unless there's a valid reason to do so; reply only to the sender.

- Remember that e-mail is only partially able to convey "tone of voice." For this reason voice mail or actual conversation is often preferable, allowing your reasoning and feelings to be understood more accurately. This is especially true in complicated or delicate situations, particularly those involving negative messages—the denial of a request, for example.

- Follow the normal rules governing capitalization, spelling, punctuation, and grammar. There's a mistaken notion that writing becomes easier to read if "unrestricted" by conventional standards. In actuality the opposite is true. Because of its nontraditional appearance, unusual text is much more difficult for the reader to process.

- If no response is required from your reader, say so. In a related vein, you should not feel obliged to reply to every routine message you receive. If a reply is necessary, however, you should answer promptly—within a day or two at most.

- Some readers routinely ignore attachments, so don't create one if you can build the information into the body of the e-mail, where it's more likely to be read. If that's not practical, provide a one- or two-sentence summary in the body of the e-mail to prompt the reader to open the attachment. Because very large attachments can clog readers' accounts, it's better to send hard copy of such material.

- When you're engaged in a lengthy back-and-forth exchange, the situation under discussion often evolves. In such circumstances it's wise to continuously revise the Subject line to reflect that fact.

- Never attempt to communicate when angry. Observe the standard rules of e-mail etiquette. Avoid "flaming" (openly hostile or abusive comments, whether directed at the reader or at a third party). The fact that you're communicating electronically does not exempt you from accepted norms of workplace courtesy.

NOTE: For more information on e-mail etiquette (sometimes called netiquette), you can consult these Web sites:

- www.fau.edu/netiquette/net/culture.html
- www.linfield.edu/policy/netiquette.html
- www.albion.com/netiquette/

the reader probably do not know each other personally, a higher level of courteous formality is in order. Additionally, the subject matter is often more involved than that of in-house correspondence, so e-mail sent outside the workplace is commonly longer and more fully developed than messages intended for co-workers. And outside e-mail nearly always includes a letter-style salutation and complimentary close unless the writer and the reader have established an ongoing professional relationship.

To sum up, e-mail is no different from any other form of workplace communication in requiring close attention to audience, purpose, and tone—not to mention ethical considerations. Just as you would after composing a conventional memo on paper, assess your e-mail by consulting the checklist on page 45.

 # Exercises

■ EXERCISE 2.1

You're the assistant to the personnel manager of a metals fabrication plant. Monday is Labor Day, and most of the 300 employees will be given a paid holiday. The company is under pressure, however, to meet a deadline. Therefore, a skeleton force of 40—all in the production department—will be needed to work on the holiday. Those who volunteer

✓ Checklist   Evaluating a Memo or E-mail

A good memo or e-mail

—— Follows standard format;

—— Includes certain features:

☐ Date line (appears automatically in e-mail)

☐ To line, which includes the name and often the title and/or department of the receiver

☐ From line, which includes the name (appears automatically in e-mail) and often the title and/or department of the sender; on a paper memo, the From line must be initialed by the writer before the memo is sent.

☐ Subject line, which is a clear, accurate, but brief statement of what the memo is about

—— Is organized into paragraphs (one is often enough) covering the subject fully in an orderly way;

—— Includes no inappropriate content;

—— Uses clear, simple language;

—— Maintains an appropriate tone, neither too formal nor too conversational;

—— Contains no typos or mechanical errors in spelling, capitalization, punctuation, or grammar.

will have the option of being paid overtime at the standard time-and-a-half rate or receiving two vacation days. If fewer than 40 employees volunteer, others will be assigned to work on the basis of seniority, with the most recently hired employees chosen first. The personnel manager has asked you to alert affected employees. Write an e-mail.

■ EXERCISE 2.2

You're a secretary at a regional office of a state agency. Normal working hours for civil service employees in your state are 8:30 a.m. to 4:30 p.m., with a lunch break from 12:00 to 12:30 p.m. During the summer, however, the hours are 8:30 a.m. to 4:00 p.m., with lunch unchanged. Summer hours are in effect from July 1 to September 2. It is now mid-June, and the busy office supervisor has asked you to remind employees of the summer schedule. Write a memo to be posted on the main bulletin board and send an e-mail as well.

■ **EXERCISE 2.3**

You work in the lumber yard of a building supplies company. Every year on the July 4 weekend, the town sponsors the Liberty Run, a 10K (6.2 mile) road race. This year, for the first time, local businesses have been invited to enter five-member teams to compete for the Corporate Cup. The team with the best combined time takes the trophy. There will be no prize money involved but much good publicity for the winners. Because you recently ran the Boston Marathon, the company president wants you to recruit and organize a team. It's now April 21. Better get started. Write an e-mail.

■ **EXERCISE 2.4**

You're an office worker at a large paper products company that has just installed an upgraded computer system. Many employees are having difficulty with the new software. The manufacturer's representatives will be on-site all next week to provide training. Because you are studying computer technology, you've been asked to serve as liaison. You must inform your co-workers about the training, which will be delivered in Conference Room 3 from Monday through Thursday in eight half-day sessions (9:00 a.m. to 12:00 p.m. and 1:00 to 4:00 p.m.), organized alphabetically by workers' last names, as follows: A–B, C–E, F–I, J–M, N–P, Q–SL, SM–T, and U–Z. Workers unable to attend must sign up for one of two make-up sessions that will be held on Friday. You must ensure that everyone understands all these requirements. Write a memo to be posted on all bulletin boards and send an e-mail as well.

■ **EXERCISE 2.5**

You're the manager of the employee cafeteria at a printing company. For many years the cafeteria has provided excellent service, offering breakfast from 7:00 to 8:30 a.m. and lunch from 11:00 a.m. to 2:00 p.m. It also serves as a break room, selling coffee, soft drinks, and snacks all day. But the cafeteria is badly in need of modernization. Work is scheduled to begin next Wednesday. Naturally, the cafeteria will have to be closed while renovations are in progress. Employees will still be able to have lunch and breaks, however, because temporary facilities are being set up in Room 101 of Building B, a now-vacant area formerly used for storage. The temporary cafeteria will provide all the usual services except for breakfast. Obviously, employees need to know about the situation. Write an e-mail.

■ EXERCISE 2.6

You're the security chief at a manufacturing company that makes small metal hand tools. The plant employs roughly one hundred people. Management has told you that many tools have disappeared. According to company records, the plant produces approximately fifty thousand per day, but far fewer are actually being shipped out. After double-checking the figures to ensure their accuracy, you have concluded that pilferage is the only possible explanation. A metal detector positioned at the employee exit near the time clock would catch anyone trying to smuggle tools out of the factory. Because the purchase cost of a metal detector is prohibitive, you have decided to rent one. Anyone caught stealing will immediately be fired, and a note to that effect will become part of the individual's personnel file. You don't want to create an atmosphere of hostility, but you do need to inform the employees about these developments. Write a memo to be posted on the main bulletin board and send an e-mail as well.

■ EXERCISE 2.7

You're a caseworker at a new county agency that assists troubled youths by placing them in group homes run by the agency. There are five boys or girls per home, supervised by specially trained counselors. You find this job rewarding, although it involves more paperwork than you'd prefer. Yesterday, for example, the agency psychiatrist recommended a medication change for a boy named Eli Bradley, who resides at Group Home #6. The boy has been diagnosed as hyperactive and has been receiving a daily dosage of 30 mg of Ritalin (one 10-mg tablet in the morning, one at noon, and one at bedtime). The doctor has decided to increase the dosage to 35 mg daily by changing the 10-mg morning tablet to a 15-mg morning tablet. You have no reason to question the doctor's judgment, but you must inform the boy's counselors. Send an e-mail.

■ EXERCISE 2.8

You're the production manager for a computer parts manufacturer. Last month four machines had excessive downtime. The company's production of Part #Z43 has dropped. Two of your best customers have complained about late shipments of Part #Z43. One customer has canceled a standing order and is now buying the part from your principal competitor. For the past two months the company's production of Part #Y01 has also been declining. To discuss the situation, all production supervisors will meet in Conference Room G, in the west wing of the main building, at 10:00 a.m. next Monday. Each supervisor should bring to the meeting up-to-date figures on costs, equipment, personnel, and so on. You must inform the production supervisors about the meeting. Send an e-mail.

■ **EXERCISE 2.9**

Proofread and rewrite the following memo, correcting all errors.

Memorial Hospital

MEMORANDUM

DATE: September 8, 2008

TO: All Employes

FROM: Roger Sammon, Clerk
               Medical Recrods Department

SUBJECT: Patricia Klosek

As many of you allready know. Patricia Klosik from the Medical records Depratment is retiring next month. After more then thirty years of faithfull service to Memorial hospital.

A party is being planed in her honor. It will be at seven oclock on friday October 17 at big Joes Resturant tickets are $35 per person whitch includes a buffay diner and a donation toward a gift.

If you plan to atend please let me no by the end of this week try to get you're check to me by Oct 10

■ **EXERCISE 2.10**

Proofread and rewrite the following e-mail, correcting all errors.

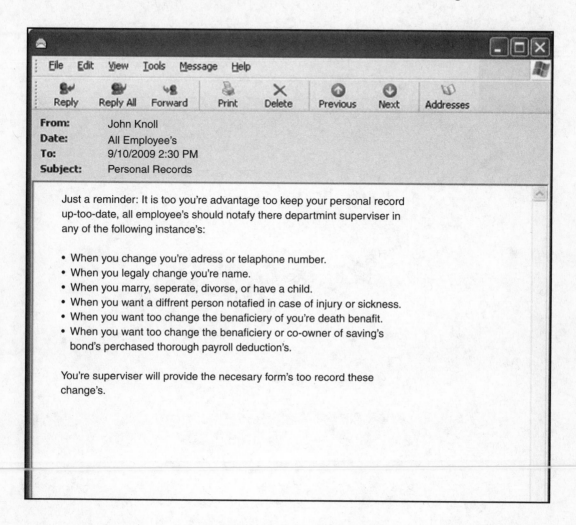

From: John Knoll
Date: All Employee's
To: 9/10/2009 2:30 PM
Subject: Personal Records

Just a reminder: It is too you're advantage too keep your personal record up-too-date, all employee's should notafy there departmint superviser in any of the following instance's:

• When you change you're adress or telaphone number.
• When you legaly change you're name.
• When you marry, seperate, divorse, or have a child.
• When you want a diffrent person notafied in case of injury or sickness.
• When you want too change the benaficiery of you're death benafit.
• When you want too change the benaficiery or co-owner of saving's bond's perchased thorough payroll deduction's.

You're superviser will provide the necesary form's too record these change's.

3

Business Letters

■ **Letters**
   Formats
   Checklist: Evaluating a Letter
■ **Exercises**

Unlike memos, business letters are typically used for *external* communication, a message from someone at Company X to someone elsewhere—a customer or client, perhaps, or a counterpart at Company Y. As mentioned in Chapter 2, however, e-mail is now often used in situations that in the past would have required letters, and this trend is increasing. Nevertheless, countless letters are still written every day, for an enormous variety of reasons. Some of the more typical purposes of a letter are to do the following:

- Purchase a product or service (order)
- Request payment (collection)
- Voice a complaint (claim)
- Ask for information (inquiry)
- Sell a product or service (sales)
- Respond to a complaint (adjustment)
- Thank someone (acknowledgment)

Figures 3.1 through 3.8 provide examples of letters serving these needs.

Formats

Regardless of purpose, a letter can be formatted in various ways. The three most common formats are the modified block style, the modified block style with indented paragraphs, and the full block style.

Modified Block Style

As shown in Figures 3.1 through 3.3, the date, the complimentary close, and the sender's identification begin at the center of the page. If the sender's address is not preprinted on company letterhead (as it is in each of the examples), it should begin at the center of the page, above the date. All other lines (including the first line of each paragraph) are flush with the left margin.

Modified Block Style with Indented Paragraphs

As shown in Figures 3.4 and 3.5, the date, the complimentary close, and the sender's identification begin at the center of the page. Again, if the sender's address is not preprinted on company letterhead, it should begin at the center of the page, above the date. The first line of each paragraph is indented five spaces. All other lines are flush with the left margin.

Full Block Style

As shown in Figures 3.6 through 3.9 and 3.12 and 3.13, every line (including the first line of each paragraph) is flush with the left margin.

Southton High School

62 Academy Street, Southton, GA 30300
Telephone (404) 555-1234 · Fax (404) 555-4321

July 10, 2009

Value-Rite Office Supplies
462 Decatur Street
Atlanta, GA 30300

Dear Value-Rite:

It's time once again for Southton High to order a shipment of custom-printed, spiral-bound notebooks for use by our students.

You may charge the following order to our account (#2468).

Catalog #	Quantity	Description	Unit Cost	Total
471	300	100 pages	$1.00	$300
472	200	250 pages	2.00	400
473	100	350 pages	3.00	300
			Subtotal	$1,000
			Tax (5%)	50
			Shipping	30
			Total	$1,080

Please provide blue covers with the gold SHS logo (which you have on file) and ship as promptly as possible.

Sincerely,

Karl Bradbury

Karl Bradbury, Vice Principal

FIGURE 3.1   **Order Letter in Modified Block Style**

Greene's

New Acres Mall   Tallahassee, FL 32301

June 16, 2008

Mr. William Britton
55-A Jackson Road
Tallahassee, FL 32301

Dear Mr. Britton:

We appreciate your continued patronage of Greene's. We note, however, that your charge account is now $565.31 overdue, and that we have not received your monthly payment since April.

If you have recently sent in your payment, please ignore this friendly reminder. If not, we would appreciate a minimum remittance of $50.00 at your earliest convenience.

If you have any questions about your account, please call me at 555-0123, Ext. 123.

Sincerely,

Heather Sutcliffe

Heather Sutcliffe
Credit Services Department

FIGURE 3.2   **Collection Letter in Modified Block Style**

Jane's Homestyle Restaura...

239 Northrop Square   Seattle, WA 98100   (206) 555-1234

October 29, 2008

Mr. Joseph Chen, Director
Sales & Service Department
Ace Technologies Corporation
1168 Crosstown Turnpike
Seattle, WA 98100

Dear Mr. Chen:

I purchased the Ace Cash Register System 3000 for my three restaurants in December 2007 and have experienced continuous problems with the video monitors since then.

As recently as September of this year, another of the monitors had to be sent in for repairs. Yesterday afternoon that same unit failed again. This occurrence is not uncommon, as you can see by the nine repair invoices I have enclosed for your reference.

Given the many problems we have had with these monitors, I am requesting that you replace them, free of charge. Please call me about this as soon as possible.

Sincerely,

Jane Pelham

Jane Pelham, Owner

Enclosures

FIGURE 3.3   **Corporate Claim Letter in Modified Block Style**

The Weekly News

P.O. Box 123

Littleton, New York 13300

Telephone (315) 555-1234 • Fax (315) 555-4321

February 24, 2009

Chief Joseph Kealy
Littleton Police Department
911 Main Street
Littleton, NY 13300

Dear Chief Kealy:

It is our understanding that a Littleton resident, Mr. Alex Booth, is the subject of an investigation by your department, with the assistance of the county district attorney. In keeping with the provisions of the New York Freedom of Information Law, I am requesting information about Mr. Booth's arrest.

This information is needed to provide our readership with accurate news coverage of the events leading to Mr. Booth's current situation. The *Weekly News* prides itself on fair, accurate, and objective reporting, and we are counting on your assistance as we seek to uphold that tradition.

Because the police blotter is by law a matter of public record, we will appreciate your full cooperation.

Sincerely,

Nancy Muller

Nancy Muller, Reporter

FIGURE 3.4 **Inquiry Letter in Modified Block Style with Indented Paragraphs**

Fashion First

254 Sunset Blvd, Weston, CA 95800 • telephone (916) 555-1234

March 3, 2008

Ms. Sarah Levy
643 Glenwood Avenue
Weston, CA 95800

Dear Ms. Levy:

As a preferred customer and holder of our special Gold Card, you won't
want to miss our annual Savings Spectacular.

All the fine clothing pictured in the enclosed brochure has been marked
down a full 25%! To take advantage of these incredible bargains, you need
only complete the order form on the back cover of the brochure. Or if you
prefer, you may simply telephone your order. Our operators are standing by.

Purchases totaling $300 or more are entitled to another 10% off! But you
must act quickly! The sale—open to Gold Card customers exclusively—ends
on March 10. Order now!

Sincerely,

Jorgé Figueroa

Jorgé Figueroa, Manager
Customer Services Department

Enclosure

FIGURE 3.5 **Sales Letter in Modified Block Style with Indented Paragraphs**

41 Allan Court
Tucson, AZ 86700
June 30, 2008

Consumer Relations Department
Superior Foods, Inc.
135 Grove Street
Atlanta, GA 30300

Dear Superior Foods:

Superior microwave dinners are excellent products that I have purchased
regularly for many years. Recently, however, I had an unsettling experience
with one of these meals.

While enjoying a serving of Pasta Alfredo, I discovered in the food what appeared to be a thick splinter of wood. I'm sure this is an isolated incident, but
I thought your quality control department would want to know about it.

I've enclosed the splinter, taped to the product wrapper, along with the sales
receipt for the dinner. May I please be reimbursed $4.98 for the cost?

Sincerely,

George Eaglefeather

George Eaglefeather

Enclosures

FIGURE 3.6   **Consumer Claim Letter in Full Block Style**

Superior Foods, Inc.

135 Grove St., Atlanta, GA 30300 • (324) 555-1234

July 7, 2008

Mr. George Eaglefeather
41 Allan Court
Tucson, AZ 86700

Dear Mr. Eaglefeather:

Thank you for purchasing our product and for taking the time to contact us about it. We apologize for the unsatisfactory condition of your Pasta Alfredo dinner.

Quality is of paramount importance to all of us at Superior Foods, and great care is taken in the preparation and packaging of all our products. Our quality assurance staff has been notified of the problem you reported. Although Superior Foods does not issue cash refunds, we have enclosed three coupons redeemable at your grocery for complimentary Superior dinners of your choice.

We appreciate this opportunity to be of service, and we hope you will continue to enjoy our products.

Sincerely,

John Roth

John Roth
Customer Services Department

Enclosures (3)

FIGURE 3.7   **Adjustment Letter in Full Block Style**

VALUE-RITE OFFICE SUPPLIES

462 Decatur Street • Atlanta, GA 30300 • (404) 555-1234

March 19, 2008

Ms. Helen Reynard, Owner
Reynard's Auto Palace
Central Highway
Atlanta, GA 30300

Dear Ms. Reynard:

For the past 10 years, Value-Rite Office Supplies has purchased all our delivery vans from your dealership, and we have relied on your service department for routine maintenance and necessary repairs. During that time I have been repeatedly impressed by the professionalism of your employees, especially Jarel Carter, who staffs the service desk.

Both in person and on the telephone, Jarel has always been exceptionally knowledgeable, helpful, and courteous and is always willing to go the extra mile to ensure customer satisfaction. Just last week, for example, he interrupted his lunch break to get me some information about a part that has been on back order.

If you can continue to attract employees of Jarel's caliber, you shouldn't have any difficulty remaining the area's #1 dealership. Be sure to keep him in mind the next time you're considering merit raises!

Sincerely,

Gary Richie

Gary Richie, Owner

FIGURE 3.8   **Acknowledgment Letter in Full Block Style**

Company Name Here   [Click **here** and type return address]

April 3, 2007

[Click **here** and type recipient's address]

Dear Sir or Madam:

Type your letter here. For more details on modifying this letter template, double-click ⊠. To return to this letter, use the Window menu.

Sincerely,

[Click **here** and type your name]
[Click **here** and type job title]

FIGURE 3.9   **Microsoft Word's Professional Letter Template in Full Block Style**

The three formats share several features: all are single-spaced throughout (except between the separate elements, where double-spacing is used), are centered on the page, and are framed by margins of 1 to 1½ inches. All three formats are in common use, with the modified block style with indented paragraphs considered the most traditional format (and rather old-fashioned). Full block style, on the other hand, is the most contemporary and is rapidly becoming the norm. Regardless of its format, however, every letter includes certain essential components that are set forth on the page in the following sequence:

1. Writer's address (often preprinted on letterhead) at the top of the page

2. Date (like e-mail, letters sent by fax are automatically imprinted with the exact time of transmission as well)

3. Inside address (the full name, title, and address of the receiver)

4. Salutation, followed by a colon (avoid gender-biased salutations such as "Dear Sir" or "Gentlemen")

5. Body of the letter, using the three-part approach outlined later in this chapter

6. Complimentary close ("Sincerely" is best), followed by a comma

7. Writer's signature

8. Writer's name and title beneath the signature

9. Enclosure line, if necessary, to indicate item(s) accompanying the letter

Along with these standard components, all business letters—irrespective of format—also embrace the same three-part organization:

1. A brief introductory paragraph establishing context (by referring to previous correspondence, perhaps, or by orienting the reader in some other way) and stating the letter's purpose concisely

2. A middle section (as many paragraphs as needed) conveying the content of the message by providing all necessary details, presented in the most logical sequence

3. A brief concluding paragraph politely requesting action, thanking the reader, or providing any additional information pertinent to the situation

Table 3.1 provides guidance in applying this three-part approach in each of the basic letter-writing situations.

TABLE 3.1 Letter Content Guidelines

Letter Type	Introduction	Middle Paragraphs	Conclusion
Order (Fig. 3.1)	Establish that this is indeed an order letter, and state what you want to purchase.	Provide all relevant details about your order (product numbers, prices, quantities, method of payment, etc.). A table is often the best format for presenting this information.	Thank the reader in advance for filling the order. If you must have the product or service by a certain date, specify it. Make sure you've provided all the information the reader will need to ship the order (address, billing address, method of delivery).
Collection (Fig. 3.2)	Open with a polite but firm reminder that the reader's payment is overdue. (In a second or third collection letter, the tone of the introduction can be more urgent.)	If you have not already done so in the introduction, provide all the relevant details about how much is owed, when it was due, and when it must be paid to avoid penalty, but acknowledge the possibility of error at your end.	Repeat the payment request and encourage the reader to contact you with any concerns or to discuss payment options. Make sure you've provided all the information the reader will need to respond (address, phone number, e-mail address). It's a good idea to include a stamped, self-addressed envelope.
Claim (Figs. 3.3, 3.6)	Provide some background information, but come quickly to the point, identifying the problem.	Politely provide all relevant details about what has gone wrong and what you want the reader to do about it. If appropriate, provide copies of bills, receipts, contracts, etc.	Thank the reader in advance for correcting the problem and make sure you've provided all the information the reader will need to contact you (address, phone number, e-mail address).
Inquiry (Fig. 3.4)	Briefly explain the reason for your inquiry, and clearly identify what you are inquiring about.	Provide all relevant details about your inquiry. Concretely specify what you want to know, why the reader should	Thank the reader in advance for complying with your request. If you must have a reply by a certain date,

(continued on next page)

TABLE 3.1 *(continued)*

Letter Type	Introduction	Middle Paragraphs	Conclusion
		provide this information, and what you'll use it for. If you have more than one question, create a bulleted list.	specify it. Make sure you've provided all the information the reader will need to reply (address, phone number, e-mail address). It's a good idea to provide a stamped, self-addressed envelope.
Sales (Fig. 3.5)	Get the reader's attention, perhaps by asking a question, describing a situation, presenting an interesting fact, or using a quotation (the same strategies explained in Chapter 9 for opening a speech), and state what you're selling.	Provide all relevant details about the product or service you're selling and create an incentive by explaining to the reader the advantages of purchasing.	Thank the reader in advance for becoming a customer and make sure you've provided all the information the reader will need to place an order (price list or catalog, order form, address, Web site, phone number, e-mail address).
Adjustment (Fig. 3.7)	Thank the reader for bringing the problem to your attention, and, if the complaint is justified, apologize.	If the complaint is justified, explain what you'll do to fix the problem. If not, tactfully explain why you must deny the claim.	Thank the reader again for writing to you and provide reassurances that everything will be satisfactory in the future.
Acknowledgment (Figs. 3.8, 3.12, 3.13)	Briefly explain why you are writing the acknowledgment and identify the person, group, or situation you're commending.	Provide all relevant details about why the person, group, or situation deserves commendation.	Conclusions vary greatly depending on the nature of the situation. Commonly, you'll thank the reader for considering the remarks and invite a reply. In such cases, make sure you've provided all the information the reader will need to contact you (address, phone number, e-mail address).

Tech Tips

Letters and other documents are often sent by a facsimile (fax) machine—basically, a scanner with a modem that converts documents into digital data that is then transmitted over telephone lines to the receiver's fax machine, which prints out hard copy. Like e-mail, this technology has the obvious advantage of speed; a letter that might take two or three days to arrive by conventional mail can be received instantaneously by fax.

But whenever you fax anything, you must fax a cover memo along with it. In this memo you should include any additional information that might be necessary to orient the reader and indicate how many pages (including the cover memo itself) you have included in the transmission so that the reader will know if there's anything that was sent but not received. You should also include your fax number, telephone number, and e-mail address, so that the reader has the option of replying. Here's an example:

DONROC, INC.
36 Clinton St., Collegeville, NY 13323
FAX

DATE: November 14, 2008 (3:15 p.m.)

TO: John Lapinski, Main Office Comptroller (fax #212-123-4567)

FROM: George Smith, Branch Office Manager (fax #212-891-0111)
           Telephone (212)555-2595, e-mail gsrls@sarge.com

SUBJECT: Cosgrove Letter

PAGES: 2

Here's Michael Cosgrove's letter of November 10. Let's discuss this at Thursday's meeting.

As with memos and letters, Microsoft Word provides three fax templates, one of which is shown in Figure 3.10.

Although the "fax machine to fax machine" scenario is the most common, computer software now permits interface between fax machines and computers. Another option, of course, is to send the cover memo as an e-mail, with the accompanying document scanned in as an attachment. With so many workplace computers equipped with scanners, fax machines may eventually be rendered obsolete, especially because computer printers produce better hard copy. At least for now, though, the fax machine remains a useful device.

[Click **here** and type return address and phone and fax numbers]

Company Name Here

To:	[Click **here** and type name]	**From:**	[Click **here** and type name]
Fax:	[Click **here** and type fax number]	**Pages:**	[Click **here** and type # of pages]
Phone:	[Click **here** and type phone number]	**Date:**	1/21/2005
Re:	[Click **here** and type subject of fax]	**CC:**	[Click **here** and type name]

☐ **Urgent**   ☐ **For Review**   ☐ **Please Comment**   ☐ **Please Reply**   ☐ **Please Recycle**

● **Comments:** Select this text and delete it or replace it with your own. To save changes to this template for future use, choose Save As from the File menu. In the Save As Type box, choose Document Template. Next time you want to use it, choose New from the File menu, and then double-click your template.

FIGURE 3.10   **Microsoft Word's Professional Fax Template**

A fairly recent development in letter writing is the open punctuation system, in which the colon after the salutation and the comma after the complimentary close are omitted. Figure 3.12 illustrates this variation, which is gaining widespread acceptance. A more radical change is the trend toward a fully abbreviated, "no punctuation, all capitals" approach to the inside address, as shown in Figure 3.13. This derives from the U.S. Postal Service recommendation that envelopes be so addressed to facilitate computerized scanning and sorting. Because the inside address has traditionally matched the address on the envelope, such a feature may well become standard, at least for letters sent by conventional mail rather than by electronic means. Indeed, many companies using "window" envelopes have already adopted this style. Figure 3.11 lists standard abbreviations used in letter writing.

Alabama	AL	Kentucky	KY	Ohio	OH
Alaska	AK	Louisiana	LA	Oklahoma	OK
Arizona	AZ	Maine	ME	Oregon	OR
Arkansas	AR	Maryland	MD	Pennsylvania	PA
California	CA	Massachusetts	MA	Puerto Rico	PR
Colorado	CO	Michigan	MI	Rhode Island	RI
Connecticut	CT	Minnesota	MN	South Carolina	SC
Delaware	DE	Mississippi	MS	South Dakota	SD
District of Columbia	DC	Missouri	MO	Tennessee	TN
		Montana	MT	Texas	TX
Florida	FL	Nebraska	NE	Utah	UT
Georgia	GA	Nevada	NV	Vermont	VT
Hawaii	HI	New Hampshire	NH	Virginia	VA
Idaho	ID	New Jersey	NJ	Washington	WA
Illinois	IL	New Mexico	NM	West Virginia	WV
Indiana	IN	New York	NY	Wisconsin	WI
Iowa	IA	North Carolina	NC	Wyoming	WY
Kansas	KS	North Dakota	ND		

Avenue	AVE	Expressway	EXPY	Parkway	PKWY
Boulevard	BLVD	Freeway	FWY	Road	RD
Circle	CIR	Highway	HWY	Square	SQ
Court	CT	Lane	LN	Street	ST
Turnpike	TPKE				

North	N	West	W	Southwest	SW
East	E	Northeast	NE	Northwest	NW
South	S	Southeast	SE		

Room	RM	Suite	STE	Apartment	APT

FIGURE 3.11 **Standard Abbreviations**

Source: U.S. Postal Service.

VALUE-RITE OFFICE SUPPLIES

462 Decatur Street • Atlanta, GA 30300 • (404) 555-1234

March 19, 2008

Ms. Helen Reynard, Owner
Reynard's Auto Palace
Central Highway
Atlanta, GA 30300

Dear Ms. Reynard

For the past 10 years, Value-Rite Office Supplies has purchased all our delivery vans from your dealership, and we have relied on your service department for routine maintenance and necessary repairs. During that time I have been repeatedly impressed by the professionalism of your employees, especially Jarel Carter, who staffs the service desk.

Both in person and on the telephone, Jarel has always been exceptionally knowledgeable, helpful, and courteous and is always willing to go the extra mile to ensure customer satisfaction. Just last week, for example, he interrupted his lunch break to get me some information about a part that has been on back order.

If you can continue to attract employees of Jarel's caliber, you shouldn't have any difficulty remaining the area's #1 dealership. Be sure to keep him in mind the next time you're considering merit raises!

Sincerely

Gary Richie

Gary Richie, Owner

FIGURE 3.12   **Acknowledgment Letter in Full Block Style with Open Punctuation**

VALUE-RITE OFFICE SUPPLIES

462 Decatur Street • Atlanta, GA 30300 • (404) 555-1234

March 19, 2008

MS HELEN REYNARD
REYNARDS AUTO PALACE
CENTRAL HIGHWAY
ATLANTA GA 30300

Dear Ms. Reynard:

For the past 10 years, Value-Rite Office Supplies has purchased all our delivery vans from your dealership, and we have relied on your service department for routine maintenance and necessary repairs. During that time I have been repeatedly impressed by the professionalism of your employees, especially Jarel Carter, who staffs the service desk.

Both in person and on the telephone, Jarel has always been exceptionally knowledgeable, helpful, and courteous and is always willing to go the extra mile to ensure customer satisfaction. Just last week, for example, he interrupted his lunch break to get me some information about a part that has been on back order.

If you can continue to attract employees of Jarel's caliber, you shouldn't have any difficulty remaining the area's #1 dealership. Be sure to keep him in mind the next time you're considering merit raises!

Sincerely,

Gary Richie

Gary Richie, Owner

FIGURE 3.13 **Acknowledgment Letter in Full Block Style with Capitalized Inside Address**

As mentioned earlier, more and more companies are communicating with each other by e-mail and other forms of electronic messaging rather than by business letter. The letter is still preferred, however, for more formal exchanges, especially those in which speed of delivery is not a major factor. In situations involving individual customers and clients (some of whom may still rely on conventional mail), the business letter is also the best choice. At least for the immediate future, therefore, the letter will continue to be a major form of workplace correspondence, although its role will almost certainly undergo further redefinition as various forms of electronic communication become increasingly widespread.

Like all successful communication, a good letter must employ an appropriate tone. Obviously, a letter is a more formal kind of communication than an in-house memo or e-mail because it's more public. Accordingly, a letter should uphold the image of the sender's company or organization by reflecting a high degree of professionalism. However, though a letter's style should be polished, the language should be natural and easy to understand. The key to achieving a readable style—in a letter or in anything else you write—is to understand that writing should not sound pompous or "official." Rather, it should sound much like ordinary speech—shined up just a bit. Whatever you do, avoid stilted, old-fashioned business clichés. Strive instead for direct, conversational phrasing. One way to achieve this is to use active rather than passive verbs. Instead of saying, for example, "Your report has been received," it's better to say "We have received your report." Here's a list of overly bureaucratic constructions, paired with "plain English" alternatives:

Cliché	Alternative
As per your request	As you requested
Attached please find	Here is
At this point in time	Now
In lieu of	Instead of
In the event that	If
Please be advised that X	X
Pursuant to our agreement	As we agreed
Until such time as	Until
We are in receipt of	We have received
We regret to advise you that X	Regrettably, X

If you have a clear understanding of your letter's purpose and have analyzed your audience, you should experience little difficulty achieving the appropriate tone for the situation. In addition, if you have written your letter following one of the three standard formats described earlier, and if you have used clear, accessible, and mechanically correct language, your correspondence will likely accomplish its objectives. As noted earlier, you must scrupulously avoid typos and mechanical errors in memos and e-mails. This is equally important when you compose letters intended for outside readers, who will take their business elsewhere if they perceive you as careless or incompetent. Always proofread carefully, making every effort to ensure that your work is error-free, and consult the following checklist.

✓ Checklist   Evaluating a Letter

A good letter

—— Follows a standard letter format (full block is best);

—— Includes certain features:
   ☐ Sender's complete address
   ☐ Date
   ☐ Receiver's full name and complete address
   ☐ Salutation, followed by a colon
   ☐ Complimentary close ("Sincerely" is best), followed by a comma
   ☐ Sender's signature and full name
   ☐ Enclosure notation, if necessary

—— Is organized into paragraphs, covering the subject fully in an orderly way:
   ☐ First paragraph establishes context and states the purpose
   ☐ Middle paragraphs provide all necessary details
   ☐ Last paragraph politely achieves closure

—— Includes no inappropriate content;

—— Uses clear, simple language;

—— Maintains an appropriate tone, neither too formal nor too conversational;

—— Contains no typos or mechanical errors in spelling, capitalization, punctuation, or grammar.

Exercises

■ **EXERCISE 3.1**

For ten days, save all the business letters you receive. Even though the bulk of them will be junk mail, make a list identifying the *purpose* of each. Prepare a brief oral presentation explaining which letter is the best and which is the worst, and why. (It may be helpful to create overhead transparencies or distribute photocopies to the class, assuming the letters do not contain confidential information.)

■ **EXERCISE 3.2**

A consumer product that you especially like is suddenly no longer available in retail stores in your area. Write the manufacturer an inquiry letter requesting information about the product and how to place an order.

■ **EXERCISE 3.3**

Proceeding as if you've received the information requested in Exercise 3.2, write a letter ordering the product.

■ **EXERCISE 3.4**

Pretend you've received the product ordered in Exercise 3.3, but it's somehow unsatisfactory. Write the manufacturer a claim letter expressing dissatisfaction and requesting an exchange or a refund.

■ **EXERCISE 3.5**

Team up with a classmate, exchange the claim letters you each wrote in response to Exercise 3.4, and write adjustment letters to each other.

■ **EXERCISE 3.6**

Write a claim letter expressing dissatisfaction with some product or service that you have actually been disappointed with in the recent past. After the letter has been returned to you with your instructor's corrections, you should then actually mail your claim letter and see if you receive a reply or perhaps even some form of compensation.

■ **EXERCISE 3.7**

Write an acknowledgment letter to the editor of either your campus newspaper or a regional daily, expressing your approval of some meaningful contribution made by a local person or organization.

■ **EXERCISE 3.8**

The writer of this form letter appears to have no knowledge of standard styles of letter layout. Rewrite the letter, adjusting and correcting irregularities.

Centerton High School

100 School Street   Centerton, Iowa 50300

January 14, 2008

Dear Classmate,

Remember when the Centerton football team beat City Vocational 7–6 for the County Championship in '97? Or when the Honors Math Club went all the way to the finals in statewide competition? Or when Mr. Fisk lost his eyeglasses and accidentally went into the women's lavatory at the highway rest area during the class trip? It's hard to believe, but this spring will mark the 10th anniversary of our graduation from good old Centerton High! To celebrate this landmark, a Class of '98 committee—myself included—is working on a special reunion event starting at 6:00 p.m. on Saturday, May 10, at the Union Hall on Main Street. Husbands, wives, and "dates" are of course welcome in addition to the grads. Cost is $70 per person, which includes buffet dinner, cash bar, reunion T-shirt and a DJ playing all our favorite songs from the good old days. Mr. Fisk and many of our other teachers—some now retired—are also being invited to attend (free of charge). Please try to make it—the reunion won't be the same without you. You can complete the enclosed preregistration form indicating your intention to attend and your T-shirt size. We'd also like payment (or at least a $30/person deposit) at this time. Hope to see you at the reunion!

Yours truly, *Jane Hermanski (Class of '98)*, CHS Guidance Counselor

---

■ **EXERCISE 3.9**

The writer of this letter has adopted a highly artificial and self-important style. Rewrite the letter to convey the message in "plain English."

COUNTY DEPARTMENT OF SOCIAL SERVICES

County Building, Northton, MN 55100

November 9, 2009

Ms. Sally Cramdon
359 Roberts Road
Northton, MN 55100

Dear Ms. Cramdon:

We are in receipt of your pay stubs and your letter of 5 November 2009 and have ascertained a determination re: your application for food stamp eligibility.

Enclosed please find photocopy of food stamp budget sheet prepared by this office on above date, counterindicating eligibility at this point in time. Per county eligibility stipulations, it is our judgment that your level of fiscal solvency exceeds permissible criteria for a household the size of your own (four persons).

In the subsequent event that your remuneration should decrease, and remain at the decreased level for a period of thirty (30) calendar days or more, please do not hesitate to petition this office for a reassessment of your eligibility status at that juncture.

Very truly yours,

William Hanlon

William Hanlon
Casework Aide

■ **EXERCISE 3.10**

The writer of this letter has committed a great many fundamental blunders, typos, and mechanical errors. Rewrite the letter, fixing all problems.

20/20 Optical Supply, Inc.

North Side Plaza   Northweston, WA 98501

August 11, 2008

Service Manger
Northweston Plumbing
23 Reynolds street
Northweston, Wa 98501

Dear Northwesern Plumbing;

Last week your worker's installed a new 50-gallon hot water heater in the basement of are North Side Plazza retail store, now the heater is leaking all over the floor.

Every time I call your phone number I get a recording thet say's you will return my call but you never do. As this has been going on for more than a weak I must ensist that you either call imediatley or send a service person. I'm getting tried of moping up water!!!

Please see to this at your very earlyest convience!

Your's truely

Robert Creech

Robert Creech
Store Manger

4

Effective Visuals: Tables, Graphs, Charts, and Illustrations

Learning Objective When you complete this chapter, you'll be able to enhance your written and oral reports with effective visual elements such as tables, graphs, charts, and pictures.

People often communicate without the benefit of written or spoken language—through gestures and facial expressions, for example, and of course by means of diagrams, pictures, and signs. Consider the familiar displays shown here:

Workplace communications make extensive use of visual aids along with text. Proposals, manuals, instructions, and reports of all kinds contain numerous illustrations to capture and hold people's attention and help convey information. To function successfully in today's increasingly sophisticated workplace, an employee must be well acquainted with these visual elements. This chapter begins with a brief overview of basic principles governing the use of visuals. It then explores the four main categories of visuals—tables, graphs, charts, and illustrations—and explains the principal features and applications of each.

Principles of Effective Visuals

Until the 1980s, inserting visuals of any kind into a document was a fairly cumbersome process. Blank space would have to be provided so that tables, graphs, and charts could be created by hand and pasted in. Then the result would be photocopied to create the finished page. Unless trained in illustration, persons responsible for creating documents that required actual drawings faced a particularly challenging task. Therefore, most would purchase clip art files—collections of pre-packaged illustrations suitable for a broad range of situations.

With the widespread adoption of word-processing programs, however, it was suddenly much easier to create and insert tables, graphs, and charts "on the fly," just by activating those programs' graphics capabilities. With today's software packages you can assemble data on a spreadsheet, for example, and then display it in whatever format is most suitable. For drawings and photographs you can choose from the vast array of electronic clip art now readily available. Computer technology produces highly polished results while encouraging a great deal of experimentation with various design features. Like computerized text, graphics stored electronically have the added advantage of easy revision if your data change.

Ironically, the one potential drawback of computer-generated graphics derives from the same versatility that makes these programs so exciting to work with. Inexperienced users can become carried away with the many options at their disposal, creating cluttered, overly elaborate visuals that confuse rather than illustrate. As with writing and page design, simpler is better. Always bear in mind that visuals should never be introduced simply for their own sake, to "decorate" a document. Theoretically, every visual should be able to stand alone, but its true purpose is to clarify the text it accompanies.

Like good writing, effective visuals are simple, clear, and easy to understand. It's also very important to choose the most appropriate *type* of visual for the task at hand. When using any kind of visual aid, however, you must observe the following fundamental rules:

- Number and title every visual in your document sequentially, with outside sources clearly identified. If the document contains only one visual, you can omit the number. Titling a visual is much like writing a subject line for a memo or e-mail. The title should be brief, accurate, and informative. To write a good title, answer this question: In just a few words, what does this visual depict? The number, title, and source usually appear *beneath* the visual rather than above. (Tables are the exception to this rule; they are often numbered and labeled *above*.)

- Any information you provide in a visual you must first discuss in the text. The text should refer the reader to the visual (for example, "See Figure 5"), and the visual should be positioned logically, as soon as possible *after* the reference.

- Present all visuals in an appealing manner. Each visual should be surrounded by ample white space, not crowded by the text or squeezed in between other visuals.

- Clearly label all elements of the visual and provide a "key" whenever necessary to show scale, direction, and the like. Labels must be easy to read, with their terms matching those used in the text; you cannot call something "x" in the text and label it "y" in the visual if you expect the reader to find it easily.

- When visuals accompany instructions, the point of view in the visuals must be the same as that of the reader performing the illustrated procedure. For example, an overhead view might be confusing if the reader will be approaching the task head-on.

- A visual should never omit, distort, or otherwise manipulate information to deceive or mislead the reader. Because the purpose of a visual is to reinforce the meaning of your text, any visual you include is subject to the same ethical standards of honesty and accuracy that your text must meet.

- Avoid spelling mistakes, poor grammar, inconsistent formatting, or other blunders in the labels, key, title, or other text accompanying a visual. Nothing undermines the credibility of a visual faster than a careless error.

Tables

The purpose of tables is to portray statistical and other information for easy comparison. Tables consist of horizontal rows and vertical columns in which the data are presented. The top row, which holds the column headings, is called the boxhead; the leftmost column, which holds the row headings, is called the stub. This arrangement permits ready access to information that would be exceptionally difficult to sort out if it were presented only as text. A convenient example is the league standings that appear on the sports pages of most newspapers, enabling fans to determine at a glance the ranking, won/lost records, and other information pertaining to team performance.

Consider, for instance, the following paragraph, which is so full of statistical detail that it is impossible to retain it all.

Boston finished the 2007 season in first place in the American League East, with a record of 96 wins and 66 losses, for a .593 percentage. New York was in second place, 2 games behind, with 94 wins and 68 losses, for a .580 percentage. Toronto was third, 13 games behind, with 83 wins and 79 losses, for a .512 percentage. Next was Baltimore, 27 games behind, with 69 wins and 93 losses, for a .426 percentage. Tampa Bay was last, 30 games behind, with 66 wins and 96 losses, for a .407 percentage.

Certainly, this would be far better presented in table format, as in Figure 4.1.

Team	Won	Lost	Percentage	Games Behind
Boston	96	66	.593	—
New York	94	68	.580	2
Toronto	83	79	.512	13
Baltimore	69	93	.426	27
Tampa Bay	66	96	.407	30

FIGURE 4.1   Table Showing Final 2007 Standings of American League East Baseball Teams

Violation	Mandatory Fine	Maximum Jail Term	Mandatory Action Against License
DRIVING WHILE INTOXICATED First violation	$500–$1,000	1 year	Revoked at least 6 months
2 violations in 5 years	$1,000–$5,000	4 years	Revoked at least 1 year
3 or more violations in 10 years	$2,000–$10,000	7 years	Revoked at least 1 year
DRIVING WHILE ABILITY IMPAIRED First violation	$300–$500	15 days	Suspended 90 days
2 violations in 5 years	$500–$750	30 days	Revoked at least 6 months
3 or more violations in 10 years	$750–$1,500	180 days	Revoked at least 1 year if current violation occurred within 5 years of previous violation

Source: New York State Department of Motor Vehicles.

FIGURE 4.2 Table Showing Penalties for Selected Driving Offenses in New York

Sometimes a table includes subdivisions within categories. In such cases you can use various design options to avoid confusion. In Figure 4.2, for example, the violation category headings are capitalized, and the categories are separated by a double horizontal rule.

Graphs

Graphs are used to display statistical trends, changes, and comparisons. There are essentially two kinds: line graphs and bar graphs.

Line Graphs

The primary purpose of line graphs is to portray change over time. A line graph is created by plotting points along horizontal and vertical axes (the x-axis and y-axis, respectively), and then joining the points by means of straight lines. The horizontal axis identifies the categories of information that are being compared (the fixed, or independent, variables—usually, chronological intervals), whereas the vertical axis identifies the incremental values that are being compared (the dependent variables). Figure 4.3 is a graph of a company's annual profits during a 10-year period.

Additional lines can be added for purposes of comparison, but each line must appear different to avoid confusion. For example, one line can be solid and another broken, or lines can be drawn in contrasting colors, as in Figure 4.4, which compares the annual profits of two competing companies during a 10-year period. Notice the key, which indicates that the darker line represents Company A and the lighter line represents Company B.

FIGURE 4.3

Line Graph Showing Profits of Company A, 1998–2007

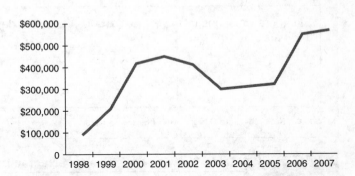

FIGURE 4.4

Line Graph Showing Profits of Company A and Company B, 1998–2007

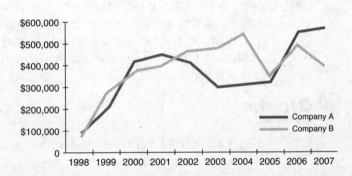

Bar Graphs

Another useful tool for comparing data is the bar graph. Like line graphs, bar graphs consist of horizontal and vertical axes that depict the dependent and independent variables. But which axis depicts which variable is determined by whether the bars are horizontal or vertical. If the bars are vertical, the vertical axis identifies the dependent variables, and the horizontal axis identifies the independent variables. Figure 4.5, for example, is a vertical bar graph that portrays income differences among persons with various levels of education.

If the bars are horizontal, the arrangement is reversed, with the horizontal axis showing the dependent variables and the vertical axis showing the independent variables. A horizontal bar graph is useful for accommodating many bars and offers the added advantage of permitting the independent variables to be labeled horizontally if those labels are relatively lengthy. This feature is helpful, for example, in Figure 4.6.

To create comparisons within categories of information in a bar graph, each bar can be presented alongside an accompanying bar or

FIGURE 4.5

Vertical Bar Graph Showing Mean 2004 Earnings by Educational Level

Source: U.S. Census Bureau, www.census.gov/population/www/socdemo/educ-attn.html.

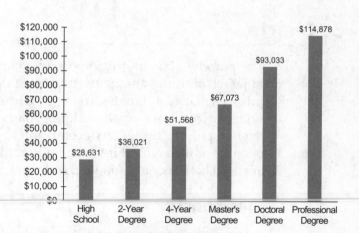

FIGURE 4.6

Horizontal Bar Graph Showing Average Total Stopping Distance at 55 mph

Source: Driver's Manual (Albany: New York State Department of Motor Vehicles, 2006), 103.

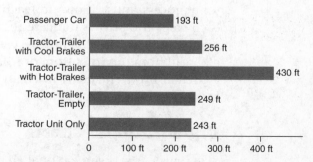

Distance based on a study of average braking distances by the Insurance Institute for Highway Safety.

FIGURE 4.7

**Vertical Bar Graph
Showing Workdays Lost
to Injuries and Illness,
2003–2005**

Source: U.S. Department of
Labor, Bureau of Labor Statistics,
www.bls.gov/iif/home.htm.

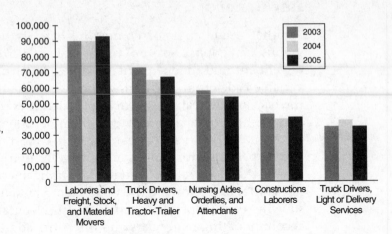

two, but the additional bar(s) must be colored or shaded differently to avoid confusion. Figure 4.7 is illustrative. Notice the key, which shows which shade represents which year.

Charts

The purpose of a chart is to portray quantitative, cause-and-effect, and other relationships among the component parts of a unified whole. Comprising squares, rectangles, triangles, circles, and other geometric shapes linked by plain or arrowhead lines, charts can depict the steps in a production process, the chain of command in an organization, and other sequential or hierarchical interactions. Among the principal kinds of charts are flowcharts, organizational charts, circle charts, and Gantt charts.

Flowcharts

A flowchart is typically used to portray the steps through which work (or a process) must "flow" to reach completion. The chart clearly labels each step, and arrows indicate the sequence of the steps so that someone unfamiliar with the process can easily follow it. Flowcharts are usually read from top to bottom or from left to right, although some depict a circular flow. The chart in Figure 4.8, for example, shows how a successful bill is signed into law.

Organizational Charts

Like flowcharts, organizational charts consist of labeled boxes linked by lines or arrows. Organizational charts portray chains of command

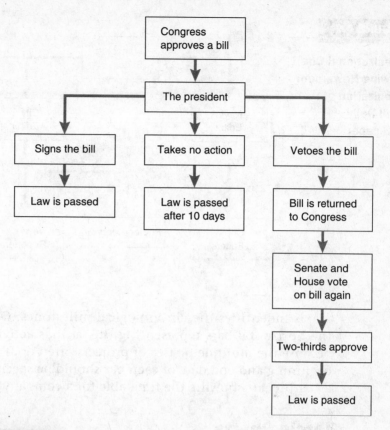

FIGURE 4.8   **Flowchart Showing How a Bill Is Signed into Law**

within businesses, agencies, and other collective bodies, indicating who has authority over whom and suggesting the relationships among various functional areas or components within the organization. Not surprisingly, the most powerful positions are placed at the top and the least powerful at the bottom. Those on the same horizontal level are at approximately equal levels of responsibility. Figure 4.9, for example, shows the newsroom organization of a small daily newspaper.

Gantt Charts

Named after the mechanical engineer Henry Gantt (1861–1919), who invented them, Gantt charts are essentially time-line charts that depict the schedule of necessary activities from start to finish of a project. Often used in proposals (see Chapter 11), they resemble bar graphs. The y-axis identifies the steps in the project, whereas the

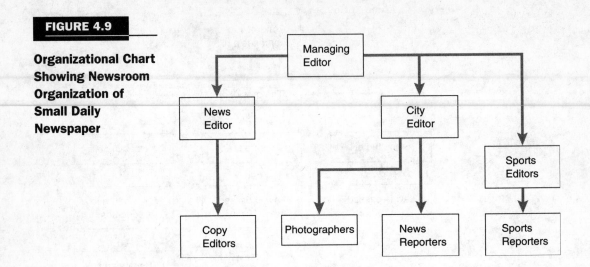

FIGURE 4.9

Organizational Chart
Showing Newsroom
Organization of
Small Daily
Newspaper

x-axis indentifies the chronological milestones. Obviously, some of the horizontal bars representing the various activities may overlap, because the mulitple phases of projects often do. For this reason, the beginning and end date of each bar should be specified. Figure 4.10 is a Gantt chart showing the timetable for a company's expansion.

Circle Charts

Among the most familiar of all visual devices, circle (or pie) charts are often used to show the percentage distribution of money. As such, they are helpful in analyzing relative costs and profits. Their more general application is simply to depict relationships among parts within statistical wholes. In that broader context, they facilitate such tasks as risk analysis, needs assessment, and resource allocation.

Each segment of a circle chart resembles a slice of pie and constitutes a percentage. For maximum effectiveness, the pie should include at least three but no more than seven slices. (To limit the number of slices without omitting data, several small percentages can be lumped together under the heading of "Other.") As if the pie were a clock face, the biggest slice usually begins at 12 o'clock, with the slices getting progressively smaller as they continue clockwise around the circle. Each slice is labeled, showing its percentage of the total. (Obviously, the slices must add up to 100 percent.) A key must be provided to identify what each slice represents. Figure 4.11 shows the costs of attending a residential community college for one semester.

FIGURE 4.10

Gantt Chart Showing Timetable for Company's Expansion

	March	April	May	June
Purchase Adjacent Building	3/1–31 ▬			
Renovate Building		4/1–5/31 ▬▬▬		
Purchase Equipment & Furnishings			5/1–31 ▬	
Install Equipment & Furnishings				6/1–20 ▬
Hire Additional Workers			5/1–31 ▬	
Train Additional Workers				6/1–20 ▬
Open Expansion				6/21 ▬

FIGURE 4.11

Circle Chart Showing Cost of Attending Residential Community College for One Semester

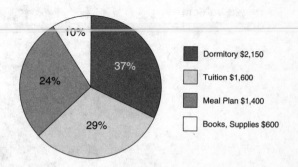

10%

37%

24%

29%

Dormitory $2,150

Tuition $1,600

Meal Plan $1,400

Books, Supplies $600

Illustrations

Illustrations—be they photographs, drawings, or diagrams—are another highly effective form of visual aid. Each type has certain advantages. As with so many aspects of workplace communications, which type you choose depends on your purpose and your audience.

Photographs

A photograph is an exact representation; its main virtue, therefore, is strict accuracy. Of course, Adobe Photoshop and other editing programs can be used to alter images. Nevertheless, photos are often required in certain kinds of documents, such as licenses, passports, accident reports (especially for insurance purposes), and patent applications. Photos are often used in law enforcement, whether to warn the public of fugitive criminals depicted in "Most Wanted" posters or to document the scene of a crime or accident. Figure 4.12, for example, is a photograph documenting vehicle damage following a collision.

Ideally, photos should be taken by trained professionals. Even an amateur, however, can create reasonably useful photos by observing the following fundamental guidelines:

FIGURE 4.12

**Photograph Documenting
Damaged Vehicle**

- Use a good digital camera.

- Ensure that the light source, whether natural (the sun) or artificial (floodlamp or other electrically generated light), is behind you; avoid shooting *into* the light.

- Stand close enough to your subject to eliminate surroundings, unless they are relevant.

- Try to focus on the most significant part of your subject to minimize unwanted detail. (By using Adobe Photoshop, you can crop out unwanted detail and enlarge the remaining image.)

- To provide a sense of scale in photographs of unfamiliar objects, include a familiar object within the picture. In photos of small objects, for example, a coin or paper clip works well. In photos of very large objects, a human figure is helpful.

- Hold the camera absolutely still while taking the picture. If possible, mount the camera on a tripod and use an automatic shutter release.

Drawings

The purpose of most drawings—whether freehand or computer-generated—is to create clear, realistic depictions of objects under discussion. The main advantage is that in a drawing you can easily omit unwanted detail and portray only what is most relevant (see Figure 4.13). In addition, a drawing can clarify information it depicts by simplifying, enlarging, or otherwise emphasizing key features. One obvious example of this is a type of drawing called a floor plan, which—like a map—is much clearer and more informative than an overhead photo (see Figure 4.14).

Other useful applications are the exploded view, which is often used in assembly instructions (see Figure 4.15), and the cross section, or cutaway view, which provides visual access to the interior workings of mechanisms and other objects (see Figure 4.16). Moreover, drawings can be combined with tables, graphs, and charts to create pictographs that enliven otherwise routine documents. For example, in Figure 4.17, depictions of vehicles have been added to the horizontal bar graph to create an attention-getting effect.

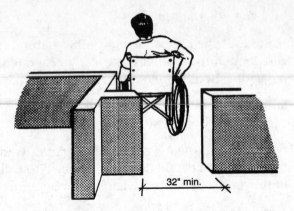

Removing the turnstile to provide an accessible passageway

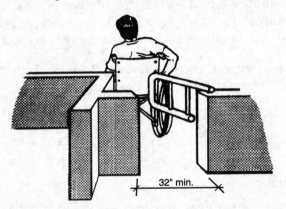

An example of an accessible gate

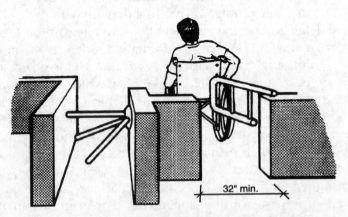

An accessible gate provided adjacent to a turnstile

FIGURE 4.13 **Drawings Showing Wheelchair-Accessible Entrances**

Source: ADA Guide for Small Businesses (Washington, DC: U.S. Small Business Administration and Department of Justice, 1997), 9.

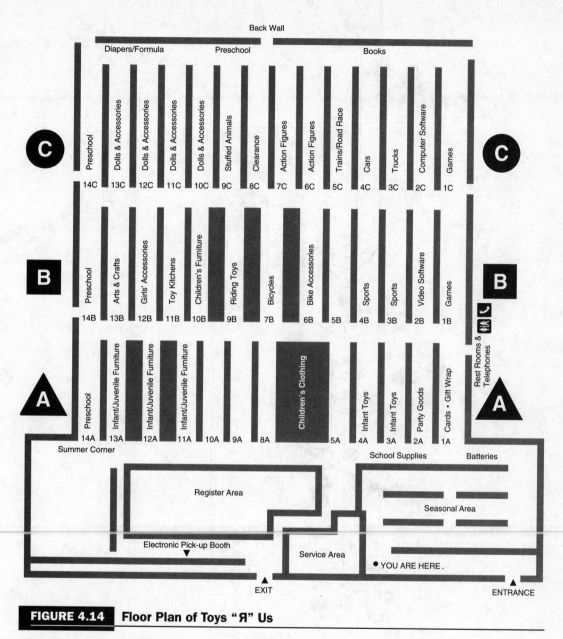

FIGURE 4.14   **Floor Plan of Toys "Я" Us**

Source: Toys "Я" Us Store Directory.

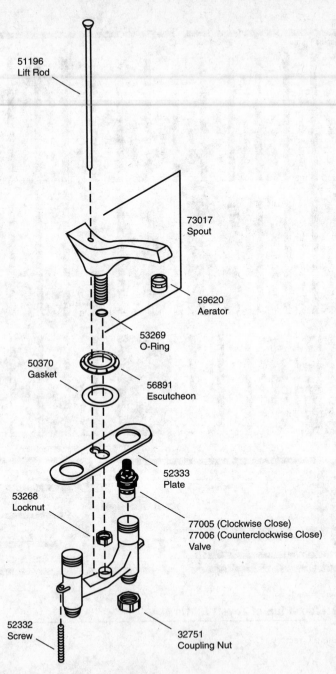

51196
Lift Rod

73017
Spout

59620
Aerator

53269
O-Ring

50370
Gasket

56891
Escutcheon

52333
Plate

53268
Locknut

77005 (Clockwise Close)
77006 (Counterclockwise Close)
Valve

52332
Screw

32751
Coupling Nut

FIGURE 4.15   **Exploded View of Kohler Faucet Assembly**

Source: Drawing Courtesy of Kohler Co.

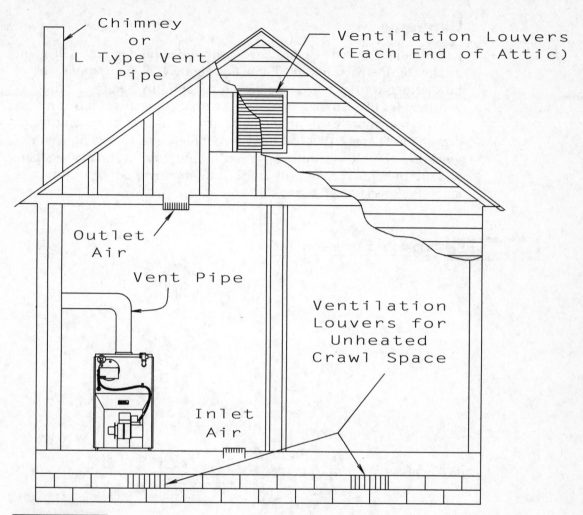

FIGURE 4.16 **Cutaway View Showing Ventilation Requirements for Gas-Fired Boiler**

Source: Drawing courtesy of ECR International.

FIGURE 4.17

Pictograph Showing Average Stopping Distances at 55 mph

Source: Driver's Manual (Albany: New York State Department of Motor Vehicles, 2006), 103.

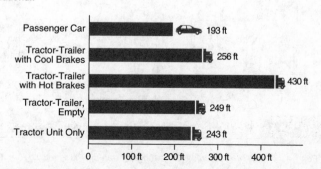

Distance based on a study of average braking distances by the Insurance Institute for Highway Safety.

Diagrams

Just as a drawing can be considered a simplified photograph, a diagram can be considered a simplified drawing. Figure 4.18, for example, shows how a three-way switch is wired. Even though this is not what the real wiring looks like, anyone conversant with electrical symbols can read the diagram more easily than the realistic—and far more complex—drawing in Figure 4.19. Most diagrams—blueprints, for example, or engineering graphics—require advanced familiarity on the reader's part and are therefore useful only in documents intended for technicians and other specialists.

FIGURE 4.18 **Diagram of a Three-Way Switch**

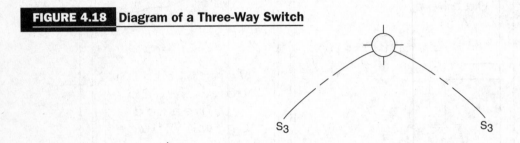

FIGURE 4.19 **Realistic Drawing of a Three-Way Switch**

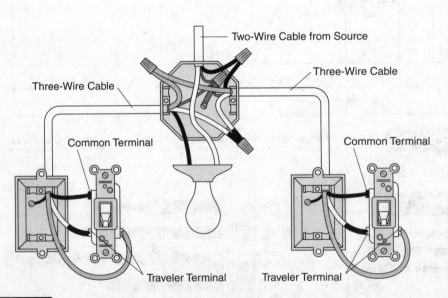

Source: Reader's Digest New Complete Do-It-Yourself Manual (Pleasantville, NY: Reader's Digest Association, 1991), 253.

During the 1990s whole companies sprang into existence for the sole purpose of producing electronic clip art packages—generic graphics for specific applications. At this point, electronic clip art has almost completely replaced hard-copy drawings, partially because the electronic versions can easily be enhanced, enlarged, reduced, or otherwise modified to suit anyone's needs.

Like traditional clip art packages, these collections sort the images into categories by topic, thereby simplifying the task of finding what you need. You still cut and paste the images into documents, but now you do it all electronically, much faster and with far less effort.

One especially useful form of clip art is the icon, a simple image with all nonessential detail removed. An icon instantaneously conveys a specific idea visually. The icons for no smoking, wheelchair access, and restrooms at the beginning of this chapter are good examples. Others would be the toolbar icons that appear on most word-processing screens: To print a document, you simply click on the printer icon; to delete a document, you drag it to the trash can icon; and so on.

You can purchase clip art separately in disk form or as a component of word-processing software. Disks can include background designs, individual images, stock photographs, and type fonts. Packages intended for use in preparing oral or on-line presentations commonly feature live-action video, sound effects, and music clips. Purchasing the package entitles you to free use without paying royalty fees.

Electronic clip art is available from mail-order catalogs, local retail stores, and on-line sources such as Microsoft Network, America Online, CompuServe, and Prodigy. Perhaps the most popular of the royalty-free Web sites, however, is Google images. Bulletin board systems greatly expand the range of available images by enabling users to share files.

Like all graphics, however, you should not use clip art excessively. You risk trivializing your work unless you exercise selectivity and restraint. Clip art is a highly useful option, but—as with written text—less is often more.

A good visual

____ is the most appropriate choice—table, graph, chart, or picture—for a particular communication;

____ is numbered and titled, with the source (if any) identified;

____ occupies the best possible position within the document, immediately after the text it clarifies;

____ does not appear crowded, with enough white space surrounding it to ensure effective page design;

____ includes clear, accurate labels that plainly identify all elements;

____ includes a key if necessary for further clarification;

____ maintains consistency with all relevant text in terms of wording, point of view, and so on;

____ upholds strict standards of accuracy;

____ contains no typos or mechanical errors in spelling, capitalization, punctuation, or grammar.

Exercises

■ EXERCISE 4.1

Choosing from Column B, identify the most appropriate kind of visual for depicting each item in Column A.

Column A	Column B
Registration procedure at your college	Table
Interest-rate fluctuations during the past 10 years	Photograph
Inner workings of a steam boiler	Line graph
Structure of the U.S. Executive Branch	Bar graph
Average salaries of six selected occupations	Cutaway view
Uniform numbers, names, ages, hometowns, heights/weights, and playing positions of the members of a college football team	Diagram
	Flowchart
House for sale	Exploded view
Percentage distribution of your college's student body by major	Organizational chart
	Pie chart
Automobile steering mechanism	
Circuitry of an electronic calculator	

■ EXERCISE 4.2

Create a table showing the current cost per gallon for regular and high octane of three major brands of gasoline. Include self-serve and full-service variables, if applicable.

■ EXERCISE 4.3

Create a line graph showing your favorite professional sports team's place in the league standings for the past 10 seasons.

■ EXERCISE 4.4

Building on the information in Exercise 4.3, create a double-line graph comparing your favorite professional sports team's place in the league standings for the past 10 seasons to that of one other team.

■ EXERCISE 4.5

Create a bar graph showing the total population of the New England states.

■ EXERCISE 4.6

Write a two- or three-page report explaining a process related to your field of study or employment. Include a flowchart depicting that process.

■ EXERCISE 4.7

Write a two- or three-page report about a club or other group to which you belong. Include a chart showing its organizational structure.

■ EXERCISE 4.8

Create a circle graph showing how you spend your money in a typical month.

■ EXERCISE 4.9

Create drawings of any three of the following: a flashlight (cutaway), an electric plug (exploded), the route from your home to your college (map), three different kinds of hammer, and the floor plan of a place where you have worked.

■ EXERCISE 4.10

Find and photocopy or otherwise reproduce an example of each kind of visual discussed in this chapter. Write a booklet report that incorporates the visuals and evaluates them for clarity and effectiveness.

5

Short Reports: Page Design, Formats, and Types

Learning Objective   When you complete this chapter, you'll be able to apply the basic principles of page design and format to write effective short reports of various kinds.

■ **Page Design**

■ **Report Formats: Memo, Letter, and Booklet**

■ **Types of Reports**

Exercises

Like e-mails and letters, reports are an important form of on-the-job communications, can be internal or external documents, and follow certain standard conventions. In several respects, however, reports are quite different from e-mails and letters.

For example, a report is rarely just a written account of information the reader already knows. Nearly always, the report's subject matter is new information. The reader may be acquainted with the general outline of the situation the report explores but not with the details. Very often, in fact, the reader will have specifically requested the report to get those details. Reports exist for the very purpose of communicating needed information that's too complicated for an e-mail or letter. Stated in the simplest terms, there are essentially two kinds of reports: short and long. This chapter focuses on the former, discussing the basic principles of page design, short-report formats, and several common types of short reports.

Page Design

As we have seen, the physical characteristics of memos, e-mails, and letters are largely determined by established guidelines that vary only slightly. But reports, though also subject to certain conventions, are to a much greater degree the creation of individual writers who determine not only their content but also their physical appearance. This is significant because our ability to comprehend what we read is greatly influenced by its physical arrangement on the page or screen. A report, therefore, should never *look* difficult or intimidating. Consider, for example, Figure 5.1, which has been adapted from a safety manual for railroad employees.

The passage is nearly unreadable in its present state. To make it more visually appealing, the first step is to insert more space between the lines and use both uppercase and lowercase letters (see Figure 5.2).

Certainly, the revised page is far more legible. It can be improved still further, however, by organizing the content into paragraphs and adopting a ragged right margin (see Figure 5.3).

The use of varied spacing, lists, and boldface headings, as well as some minor editing, will make the content emerge even more clearly. Obviously, Figure 5.4 is easier to read than the earlier versions. Such revision is worthwhile and not particularly difficult if the following fundamental principles of effective page design are observed.

ELECTRIC SHOCK

ELECTRIC SHOCK IS NOT ALWAYS FATAL, AND RARELY IS IT IMMEDIATELY FATAL. IT MAY ONLY STUN THE VICTIM AND MOMENTARILY ARREST BREATHING. IN CASES OF ELECTRIC SHOCK, BREAK CONTACT, RESTORE THE VICTIM'S BREATHING BY MEANS OF ARTIFICIAL RESPIRATION, AND MAINTAIN WARMTH. TO AVOID RECEIVING A SHOCK YOURSELF, EXERCISE EXTREME CAUTION WHEN AT-TEMPTING TO RELEASE THE VICTIM FROM CONTACT WITH A LIVE CON-DUCTOR. MANY PERSONS, BY THEIR LACK OF KNOWLEDGE OF SUCH MATTERS, HAVE BEEN SEVERELY SHOCKED OR BURNED WHEN ATTEMPTING TO RESCUE A CO-WORKER. TO RELEASE A VICTIM FROM CONTACT WITH LIVE CONDUCTORS KNOWN TO BE 750 VOLTS OR LESS, DO NOT TOUCH THE CONDUCTOR, AND DO NOT TOUCH THE VICTIM OR THE VICTIM'S BARE SKIN IF THE VICTIM IS IN CONTACT WITH THE LIVE CONDUCTOR. INSTEAD, USE A PIECE OF DRY, NONCONDUCTING MATERIAL SUCH AS A PIECE OF WOOD, ROPE, OR RUBBER HOSE TO PUSH OR PULL THE LIVE CONDUCTOR AWAY FROM THE VICTIM. THE LIVE CONDUCTOR CAN ALSO BE HANDLED SAFELY WITH RUBBER GLOVES. IF THE VICTIM'S CLOTHES ARE DRY, THE VICTIM CAN BE DRAGGED AWAY FROM THE LIVE CONDUCTOR BY GRASPING THE CLOTHES—NOT THE BARE SKIN. IN SO DOING, THE RESCUER SHOULD STAND ON A DRY BOARD AND USE ONLY ONE HAND. DO NOT STAND IN A PUDDLE OR ON DAMP OR WET GROUND. TO RELEASE A VICTIM FROM CONTACT WITH LIVE CONDUCTORS OF UNKNOWN VOLTAGE OR MORE THAN 750 VOLTS . . .

FIGURE 5.1   **Poor Page Design**

- *Legible type:* Although many different typefaces and type sizes exist, most readers respond best to 12-point type using both up-percase and lowercase letters, like this text. Anything smaller or larger is difficult to read, as is the all-capitals approach; such op-tions are useful only in major headings or to emphasize a partic-ular word or phrase.

ELECTRIC SHOCK

Electric shock is not always fatal, and rarely is it immediately fatal. It may only stun the victim and momentarily arrest breathing. In cases of electric shock, break contact, restore the victim's breathing by means of artificial respiration, and maintain warmth. To avoid receiving a shock yourself, exercise extreme caution when attempting to release the victim from contact with a live conductor. Many persons, by their lack of knowledge of such matters, have been severely shocked or burned when attempting to rescue a co-worker. To release a victim from contact with live conductors known to be 750 volts or less, do not touch the conductor, and do not touch the victim or the victim's bare skin if the victim is in contact with the live conductor. Instead, use a piece of dry, nonconducting material such as a piece of wood, rope, or rubber hose to push or pull the live conductor away from the victim. The live conductor can also be handled safely with rubber gloves. If the victim's clothes are dry, the victim can be dragged away from the live conductor by grasping the clothes—not the bare skin. In so doing, the rescuer should stand on a dry board and use only one hand. Do not stand in a puddle or on damp or wet ground. To release a victim from contact with live conductors of unknown voltage or more than 750 volts . . .

FIGURE 5.2   Revised Page

- *Generous margins:* Text should be framed by white space. The top and bottom margins should both be at least 1 inch and the side margins 1.25 inches. If the report is to be bound, the left margin should be 2 inches. (If the report is to be duplicated

ELECTRIC SHOCK

Electric shock is not always fatal, and rarely is it immediately fatal. It may only stun the victim and momentarily arrest breathing. In cases of electric shock, break contact, restore the victim's breathing by means of artificial respiration, and maintain warmth. To avoid receiving a shock yourself, exercise extreme caution when attempting to release the victim from contact with a live conductor. Many persons, by their lack of knowledge of such matters, have been severely shocked or burned when attempting to rescue a co-worker.

To release a victim from contact with live conductors known to be 750 volts or less, do not touch the conductor, and do not touch the victim or the victim's bare skin if the victim is in contact with the live conductor. Instead, use a piece of dry, nonconducting material such as a piece of wood, rope, or rubber hose to push or pull the live conductor away from the victim. The live conductor can also be handled safely with rubber gloves. If the victim's clothes are dry, the victim can be dragged away from the live conductor by grasping the clothes—not the bare skin. In so doing, the rescuer should stand on a dry board and use only one hand. Do not stand in a puddle or on damp or wet ground.

To release a victim from contact with live conductors of unknown voltage or more than 750 volts . . .

FIGURE 5.3   **Second Revision**

back-to-back before binding, the 2-inch margin should be on the *right* side of the even-numbered pages.) The right margin should not be justified; this improves legibility by creating length variation from line to line.

ELECTRIC SHOCK

Electric shock is not always fatal, and is rarely immediately fatal. It may only stun the victim and momentarily arrest breathing. In cases of electric shock, do three things:

1. Break contact.
2. Restore breathing by artificial respiration.
3. Maintain warmth.

To avoid receiving a shock yourself, exercise extreme caution when attempting to release the victim from contact with a live conductor. Many persons, lacking knowledge of such matters, have been severely shocked or burned attempting to rescue a co-worker.

Release victim from contact with live conductors known to be 750 volts or less:

- Do not touch the live conductor.
- Do not touch the victim or the victim's bare skin while the victim is in contact with the live conductor.
- Instead, use a piece of DRY, nonconducting material such as a piece of wood, rope, or rubber hose to push or pull the live conductor away from the victim. The live conductor may be handled safely with rubber gloves.
- If the victim's clothes are dry, the victim can be dragged away from the live conductor by grasping the clothing—not the bare skin. In so doing, the rescuer should stand on a dry board and . . .

FIGURE 5.4   **Third Revision**

- ***Textual divisions:*** Long, unbroken passages of text are very difficult to follow with attention, which is why the practice of dividing text into paragraphs was adopted centuries ago. In most workplace writing, paragraphs should not exceed five or six sentences and should be plainly separated by ample white space. If the paragraphs are single-spaced, insert double-spacing between them; if the paragraphs are double-spaced, use triple-spacing between them. To further organize content, group related paragraphs within a report into separate sections that logically reflect the internal organization of the report's information. Like the individual paragraphs, these sections should be plainly separated by proportionately greater spacing.

- ***Headings:*** Separate sections of text should be labeled with meaningful headings that further clarify content and allow the reader to skim the report for specific aspects of its subject matter. Ordinarily, a heading consists of a word or phrase, *not* a complete sentence. (Instructional materials, however, sometimes use *questions* as headings.) The position of a heading is determined by its relative importance. A major heading is set in boldface caps and centered,

LIKE THIS

A secondary heading is set either in uppercase letters or in both uppercase and lowercase, is flush with the margin, and can be set in boldface print,

LIKE THIS

or

Like This

A subtopic heading is run into the text, separated by a period or a colon, and is sometimes indented. Set in both uppercase and lowercase letters, it can be set in bold print,

Like This. These recommendations are based on those in *The Gregg Reference Manual,* the most widely recognized authority on such matters.

Obviously, these principles are flexible, and various approaches to heading design and placement are used, some of them quite elaborate. Among the most helpful recommendations in *Gregg* is to limit a report to no more than three levels of headings.

Thanks to computerized word processing, nearly every workplace writer now has access to many page design features that in the past were available only through commercial print shops. As we've already seen, options such as varied spacing and type size, boldface print, capitalization, and underlining can make your documents appear much more professional. In addition, pages can be formatted in columns or other spatial arrangements.

Used selectively, these features enhance the design of a page not only by signaling major divisions and subdivisions within the content but also by creating emphasis with highlighted key words and phrases. In addition, many software packages are equipped with ready-made report templates and other features such as headers and automatic page numbering for multipage documents, and these can be adapted to the individual writer's needs.

Even more versatile are the many DTP (desktop publishing) programs now available. These programs take electronic word processing to the next level and are therefore ideal for creating documents that are more elaborate, such as newsletters, brochures, and manuals. By imitating traditional print-shop techniques, which required a drafting table, scissors, paste, rulers, compasses, and the like, DTP programs enable you to draw complex layouts right on the page. You can rotate bits of text to any angle, curve text, and wrap text around irregularly shaped graphics. Graphics can be enlarged, reduced, or cropped. In addition, DTP programs provide a vast range of fonts and permit very tiny gradations in spacing and type size. Interfaced with standard word-processing and graphic-design software, a good optical scanner, and a high-resolution laser printer, a DTP program such as Adobe InDesign can produce excellent, professional-quality results.

Remember to exercise restraint and maintain consistency in using these tools. Keep your page design relatively simple. It's very easy to get carried away and end up creating a messy and confusing document, especially if you're still relatively new to this technology. Like visual elements, page design options should never function simply as decoration but as aids to your reader's understanding. The key is to experiment with your software and thoroughly familiarize yourself with its capabilities. Soon you'll develop a more accurate sense of which page design features might genuinely help your reader.

- *Lists:* Sometimes a list is more effective than a conventional paragraph. If the purpose of the list is to indicate a definite order of importance, the items in the list should be *numbered* in descending order, with the most important item first, and the least important last. Similarly, if the list's purpose is to indicate a chronological sequence of events or actions (as in a procedures manual), the items should be numbered in sequential order. Numbers are not necessary, however, in a list of approximately equal items. In those cases, bullets (solid black dots, like those used in this section), asterisks, or dashes will suffice.

Report Formats: Memo, Letter, and Booklet

Many companies and organizations prepare short reports by using the fill-in-the-blanks approach typified by the form reproduced in Figure 5.5. As we have seen, however, computer technology now enables individual writers to personally design the pages of their reports. A customized report can usually be categorized into one of three report formats: memo, letter, or booklet.

Typically used for in-house purposes, the **memo report** is similar to the conventional memo but is longer (two pages or more) and is therefore divided into labeled sections. The **letter report**—typically sent to an outside reader—is formatted like a conventional business letter, except that the letter report is divided into labeled sections, much like a memo report. The **booklet report** resembles a short term paper and includes a title page. It too is divided into labeled sections. It is also accompanied by a cover memo (for in-house reports) or cover letter (for reports sent to outside readers). Much like the opening paragraph of a memo report or letter report, the cover memo or letter serves to orient the reader by establishing context and explaining the purpose and scope of the booklet report.

Both memo reports and booklet reports often contain visuals; letter reports sometimes do. Figures 5.6–5.16 illustrate the three formats. Written by a fictitious health inspector and his supervisor, these examples use easily understood subject matter. The three report formats can be adapted to any workplace situation, however, simply by changing the headings (and, of course, the text) to suit the subject at hand.

EMPLOYEE ACCIDENT/FORM A

TO BE COMPLETED BY EMPLOYEE

Name _____ Home address _____

Social Security no._____ Date of birth _____

Sex __M__ __F__ Department in which you work _____

Accident date _____ Day of week _____ Time ____ a.m. ____ p.m.

Date accident was reported _____ To whom _____

Location of accident _____ Witnesses _____

Description of accident (what you were doing, what equipment you

were using, etc.)

_____

_____

_____

Description of injury (include nature of injury and body part)

_____

_____

_____

Did you receive medical care on premises? _____ Describe _____

_____

If you are being treated:

Name and address of physician: _____

Name and address of hospital: _____

Do you have a second job? _____

EMPLOYEE'S SIGNATURE _____ Date: _____

TO BE COMPLETED BY COMPANY NURSE

Above employee came to me on _____ regarding the above injury.

Comments:

_____

_____

_____

NURSE'S SIGNATURE _____ Date: _____

FIGURE 5.5   **Employee Accident Report Form**

Monroe County Health Department

MEMORANDUM

DATE: February 4, 2008

TO: Marjorie Witkowski, Supervisor

FROM: Richard Vaughan, Senior Inspector

SUBJECT: Restaurant Inspections

As you requested, here are the results of my most recent inspections of food service establishments in the county, along with a week-by-week statistical summary of inspections during January.

UNSATISFACTORY

The following establishments were found to be in substantial violation of the sanitary code.

Big Daddy's Steak House
431 Grand Avenue, Conover Falls
Inspected January 28, 2008

Toxic chemicals (antifreeze, can of ant/roach killer) found on premises. Potentially hazardous foods not kept at or above 140 degrees F during hot holding. Food not protected—buckets of food stored on floor in cooler, food not covered in coolers. Raw meat stored over prepared foods in cooler. Food

FIGURE 5.6   **Memo Report, Page 1**

2

build-up in storage room refrigerator. Canned goods in poor condition (dented, rusted). Bowl used as flour scoop. Box of paper towels improperly stored on floor. Nonfood contact surfaces not easily cleanable. Cardboard used as liner on food storage shelves. Restroom missing hand wash sign. Light fixture missing shield and end caps. Kitchen ceiling tiles missing. No 2006 permit on display.

Employee Cafeteria, Paragon Insurance Co.
Airport Road, Cedarville
Inspected January 30, 2008

Potentially hazardous foods not kept at or below 45 degrees F during cold holding. Potentially hazardous foods not kept at or above 140 degrees F during hot holding. Single-service napkins stored on kitchen floor.

Roma Pizzeria
38 Crowley Street, Dunkirk
Inspected January 31, 2008

Worker serving pizza slices with bare hands. Potentially hazardous foods not kept at or above 140 degrees F during hot holding. Food not protected— uncovered food in freezer, salt bucket not labeled. Hair improperly restrained— hats, nets/visors required. In-use utensils stored on paper plate. Employee (delivery driver) smoking in kitchen.

SATISFACTORY

The following establishments were found to be in essential compliance with the sanitary code, although some violations were noted.

Imperial Wok
618 Rogers Street, Cooperton
Inspected January 31, 2008

Potentially hazardous foods not kept at or above 140 degrees F during hot holding. Food not protected—jars of juice stored on kitchen floor. Improper use of utensils—scoop stored handle down in flour.

FIGURE 5.7   **Memo Report, Page 2**

3

Cuzzie's Pub
39 Railroad Street, Monroe
Inspected January 31, 2008

Unshielded light fixture in walk-in cooler. No hand soap in restroom.

NO VIOLATIONS

The following establishments were found to be in full compliance with the sanitary code.

Conover Falls Coffee House
17 Village Green East, Conover Falls
Inspected January 28, 2008

Mister Eight Ball
49 Clinton Street, Dunkirk
Inspected January 31, 2008

SUMMARY OF JANUARY 2006 INSPECTIONS

	Unsatisfactory	Satisfactory	No Violations
Jan. 7–11	3	2	2
Jan. 14–18	5	0	1
Jan. 21–25	2	3	2
Jan. 28–31	3	2	2
Totals	13	7	7

FIGURE 5.8 **Memo Report, Page 3**

Monroe County Health Department

County Office Building ✦ **Court House Square**
Monroe, Wyoming 82001 ✦ **(307) 555-1200**

February 4, 2008

Mr. Daniel Runninghorse, Editor
The Monroe Daily Observer
687 Harpur Street
Monroe, WY 82001

Dear Mr. Runninghorse:

As you may know, the County Health Department conducts ongoing, unannounced inspections of food service establishments to ensure their compliance with state codes, rules, and regulations. Since the findings of these inspections are a matter of public record, the Monroe Daily Observer has in the past printed that information in its entirety. Now that you have become the editor of the Observer, we would like you to continue this practice, which we regard as a valuable service to the community and a validation of our efforts here at the department.

Here are the results of recent inspections, as well as a week-by-week statistical summary of all inspections during January.

UNSATISFACTORY

The following establishments were found to be in substantial violation of the sanitary code.

Big Daddy's Steak House
431 Grand Avenue, Conover Falls
Inspected January 28, 2008

Toxic chemicals (antifreeze, can of ant/roach killer) found on premises. Potentially hazardous foods not kept at or above 140 degrees F during hot holding. Food not protected—buckets of food stored on floor in cooler, food not

---

FIGURE 5.9   Letter Report, Page 1

2

covered in coolers. Raw meat stored over prepared foods in cooler. Food build-up in storage room refrigerator. Canned goods in poor condition (dented, rusted). Bowl used as flour scoop. Box of paper towels improperly stored on floor. Nonfood contact surfaces not easily cleanable. Cardboard used as liner on food storage shelves. Restroom missing hand wash sign. Light fixture missing shield and end caps. Kitchen ceiling tiles missing. No 2006 permit on display.

Employee Cafeteria, Paragon Insurance Co.
Airport Road, Cedarville
Inspected January 30, 2008

Potentially hazardous foods not kept at or below 45 degrees F during cold holding. Potentially hazardous foods not kept at or above 140 degrees F during hot holding. Single-service napkins stored on kitchen floor.

Roma Pizzeria
38 Crowley Street, Dunkirk
Inspected January 31, 2008

Worker serving pizza slices with bare hands. Potentially hazardous foods not kept at or above 140 degrees F during hot holding. Food not protected—uncovered food in freezer, salt bucket not labeled. Hair improperly restrained—hats, nets/visors required. In-use utensils stored on paper plate. Employee (delivery driver) smoking in kitchen.

SATISFACTORY

The following establishments were found to be in essential compliance with the sanitary code, although some violations were noted.

Imperial Wok
618 Rogers Street, Cooperton
Inspected January 31, 2008

Potentially hazardous foods not kept at or above 140 degrees F during hot holding. Food not protected—jars of juice stored on kitchen floor. Improper use of utensils—scoop stored handle down in flour.

FIGURE 5.10   Letter Report, Page 2

3

Cuzzie's Pub
39 Railroad Street, Monroe
Inspected January 31, 2008

Unshielded light fixture in walk-in cooler. No hand soap in restroom.

NO VIOLATIONS

The following establishments were found to be in full compliance with the sanitary code.

Conover Falls Coffee House
17 Village Green East, Conover Falls
Inspected January 28, 2008

Mister Eight Ball
49 Clinton Street, Dunkirk
Inspected January 31, 2008

SUMMARY OF JANUARY 2006 INSPECTIONS

	Unsatisfactory	Satisfactory	No Violations
Jan. 7–11	3	2	2
Jan. 14–18	5	0	1
Jan. 21–25	2	3	2
Jan. 28–31	3	2	2
Totals	13	7	7

Please feel free to call me at your convenience if you have questions regarding these inspections or any other matters relating to the Monroe County Health Department. Unless I hear otherwise, I will continue to provide inspection results on a weekly basis.

Sincerely,

Marjorie Witkowski

Marjorie Witkowski
Supervisor

FIGURE 5.11 **Letter Report, Page 3**

Monroe County Health Department

MEMORANDUM

DATE: February 11, 2008

TO: Janet Butler, Commissioner

FROM: Marjorie Witkowski, Supervisor

SUBJECT: Inspections Report

As you requested, here is a complete report on the results of Richard Vaughan's inspections of food service establishments in the county during late January, along with a week-by-week statistical summary of his inspections during that month.

FIGURE 5.12   Booklet Report, Cover Memo

**INSPECTIONS OF FOOD SERVICE ESTABLISHMENTS
IN MONROE COUNTY, WYOMING
JANUARY 27–31, 2008**

Report Submitted to

Janet Butler
Commissioner of Public Health

by

Marjorie Witkowski
Supervisor, County Health Department

February 11, 2008

FIGURE 5.13   **Booklet Report, Title Page**

INTRODUCTION

In keeping with its mandate to safeguard the public welfare, the Monroe County Health Department conducts ongoing, unannounced inspections of the county's food service establishments to ensure their compliance with state codes, rules, and regulations. This report provides the results of seven inspections conducted by Senior Inspector Richard Vaughan during the period of January 27–31 of this year, along with a week-by-week statistical summary of Mr. Vaughan's 26 total inspections during January.

UNSATISFACTORY

The following establishments were found to be in substantial violation of the sanitary code.

Big Daddy's Steak House
431 Grand Avenue, Conover Falls
Inspected January 28, 2008

Toxic chemicals (antifreeze, can of ant/roach killer) found on premises. Potentially hazardous foods not kept at or above 140 degrees F during hot holding. Food not protected—buckets of food stored on floor in cooler, food not covered in coolers. Raw meat stored over prepared foods in cooler. Food build-up in storage room refrigerator. Canned goods in poor condition (dented, rusted). Bowl used as flour scoop. Box of paper towels improperly stored on floor. Nonfood contact surfaces not easily cleanable. Cardboard used as liner on food storage shelves. Restroom missing hand wash sign. Light fixture missing shield and end caps. Kitchen ceiling tiles missing. No 2008 permit on display.

Employee Cafeteria, Paragon Insurance Co.
Airport Road, Cedarville
Inspected January 30, 2008

Potentially hazardous foods not kept at or below 45 degrees F during cold holding. Potentially hazardous foods not kept at or above 140 degrees F during hot holding. Single-service napkins stored on kitchen floor.

FIGURE 5.14   **Booklet Report, Page 1**

2

Roma Pizzeria
38 Crowley Street, Dunkirk
Inspected January 31, 2008

Worker serving pizza slices with bare hands. Potentially hazardous foods not kept at or above 140 degrees F during hot holding. Food not protected—uncovered food in freezer, salt bucket not labeled. Hair improperly restrained—hats, nets/visors required. In-use utensils stored on paper plate. Employee (delivery driver) smoking in kitchen.

SATISFACTORY

The following establishments were found to be in essential compliance with the sanitary code, although some violations were noted.

Imperial Wok
618 Rogers Street, Cooperton
Inspected January 31, 2008

Potentially hazardous foods not kept at or above 140 degrees F during hot holding. Food not protected—jars of juice stored on kitchen floor. Improper use of utensils—scoop stored handle down in flour.

Cuzzie's Pub
39 Railroad Street, Monroe
Inspected January 31, 2008

Unshielded light fixture in walk-in cooler. No hand soap in restroom.

NO VIOLATIONS

The following establishments were found to be in full compliance with the sanitary code.

Conover Falls Coffee House
17 Village Green East, Conover Falls
Inspected January 28, 2008

FIGURE 5.15   Booklet Report, Page 2

3

Mister Eight Ball
49 Clinton Street, Dunkirk
Inspected January 31, 2008

SUMMARY OF JANUARY 2008 INSPECTIONS

	Unsatisfactory	Satisfactory	No Violations
Jan. 7–11	3	2	2
Jan. 14–18	5	0	1
Jan. 21–25	2	3	2
Jan. 28–31		2	
Totals		7	

FIGURE 5.16   Booklet Report, Page 3

Types of Reports

Like e-mails and letters, workplace reports are written in all kinds of situations for an enormous variety of reasons. Many reports are in a sense unique because they are written in response to one-time occurrences. On the other hand, it's not uncommon for a given report to be part of an ongoing series of weekly, monthly, or annual reports on the same subject. Generally, reports can be classified into several broad categories, but the most common categories are as follows:

- *Incident report:* Explains the circumstances surrounding a troublesome occurrence such as an accident, fire, equipment malfunction, or security breach.

- *Progress report:* Outlines the status of an ongoing project or undertaking.

- *Recommendation report:* Urges that certain procedures be adopted (or rejected).

- *Travel report:* Identifies the purpose and summarizes the results of business-related travel.

Of course, an individual report can serve more than one purpose; overlap is not uncommon. An incident report, for example, may well conclude with a recommendations section intended to minimize the likelihood of recurrence. In every situation the writer must consider the purpose and intended audience for the report. Content, language, tone, degree of detail, and overall approach must be appropriate to the circumstances, and the report headings, formatting, visuals, and other features must suit the role of the particular report. The following pages discuss the four common report types in detail.

Incident Report

An incident report creates a written record of a troublesome occurrence. The report is written either by the person involved in the incident or by the person in charge of the area where it took place. Such a report may be needed to satisfy government regulations, to guard against legal liability, or to draw attention to unsafe or otherwise unsatisfactory conditions in need of correction. Accordingly, an incident report must provide a thorough description of the occurrence and, if possible, an explanation of the cause(s). In addition, it often includes a section of recommendations for corrective measures.

When describing the incident, always provide complete details:

- Names and job titles of all persons involved, including onlookers
- Step-by-step narrative description of the incident
- Exact location of the incident
- Date and exact time of each major development
- Clear identification of any equipment or machinery involved
- Detailed description of any medical intervention required, including names of ambulance services and personnel, nurses, physicians, hospitals, or clinics
- Reliable statements (quotation or paraphrase) from persons involved
- Outcome of the incident

To avoid liability when discussing possible causes, use qualifiers such as *perhaps, maybe, possibly,* and *it appears.* Do not report the comments of witnesses and those involved as if those observations were verified facts; often they are grossly inaccurate. Attribute all such comments to their sources, and identify them as speculation only. Furthermore, exclude any comments unrelated to the immediate incident. Although you're ethically required to be as complete and accurate as possible, don't create an unnecessarily suspicious climate by relying on secondhand accounts or reporting verbatim the remarks of persons who are obviously angry or distraught, as in this example:

Ronald Perkins suffered a severed index finger when his left hand became caught in a drill press after he tripped on some wood that another employee had carelessly left on the floor near the machine. According to Perkins, this was "pretty typical of how things are always done around here."

A more objective phrasing might look something like this:

Ronald Perkins suffered a severed index finger when his left hand became caught in a drill press. Perkins said he had tripped on wood that was lying on the floor near the machine.

Similarly, the recommendations section of an incident report should not seek to assign blame or highlight incompetence but to encourage the adoption of measures that will decrease the likelihood of repeated problems. Consider, for example, the incident report in Figures 5.17–5.18, prepared in memo format.

Southeast Insurance Company

MEMORANDUM

DATE: October 16, 2009

TO: Jonathan Purdy
               Physical Plant Supervisor

FROM: Bonnie Cardillo
               Nurse

SUBJECT: Incident Report

John Fitzsimmons, a claims adjuster, slipped and fell in the front lobby of the building, striking his head and momentarily losing consciousness.

DESCRIPTION OF INCIDENT

At approximately 2:55 p.m. on Thursday, October 15, Fitzsimmons was returning from his break when he slipped and fell in the front lobby, striking his head on the stone floor and momentarily losing consciousness. According to Beverly Barrett, the receptionist, the floor had just been mopped and was still wet. She paged Mike Moore, the security officer, who in turn paged me. When I arrived at approximately 3:00 p.m., Fitzsimmons had revived. I immediately checked his vital signs, which were normal. He refused further medical attention and returned to work. I advised him to contact me if he experienced any subsequent discomfort, but to my knowledge there has been none.

FIGURE 5.17   Incident Report (Memo Format), Page 1

2

RECOMMENDATIONS

Two ideas come to mind.

Perhaps we should remind all employees to contact me first (rather than Security) in situations involving personal injury. The sooner I'm contacted, the sooner I can respond. Obviously, time can be an important factor if the problem is serious.

To prevent other occurrences of this nature, perhaps the maintenance staff should be provided with large, brightly colored warning signs alerting employees and the public alike to the presence of wet floors. I see these signs in use at the mall, the hospital, and elsewhere, and they do not appear expensive. I have noted also that many are bilingual, bearing both the English warning "Caution: Wet Floor" and the Spanish "Cuidado: Piso Mojado." No doubt they can be ordered from any of the catalogs regularly received by your office.

FIGURE 5.18 **Incident Report (Memo Format), Page 2**

Progress Report

A progress report provides information about the status of an ongoing project or activity that must be monitored to ensure successful completion within a specified period. Sometimes called status reports or periodic reports, progress reports are submitted either upon completion of key stages of a project or at regular, preestablished intervals—quarterly, monthly, weekly, or sometimes as often as every day. They are written by the individual(s) directly responsible for the success of the undertaking. The readers of these reports are usually in the management sector of the organization, however, and may not be familiar with the technical details of the situation. Rather, their priority is successful completion of the project within established cost guidelines. Therefore, the information in a progress report tends to be more general than specific, and the language tends to be far less technical than that of other kinds of reports.

Most progress reports include the following components:

- *Introduction:* Provides context and background, identifying the project, reviewing its objectives, and alerting the reader to any new developments since the previous progress report.

- *Work completed:* Summarizes accomplishments to date. This section can be organized in either of two ways: If the report deals with one major task, a chronological approach is advisable; if it deals with several related projects, the report should have subdivisions by task.

- *Work remaining:* Summarizes all uncompleted tasks, emphasizing what is expected to be accomplished first.

- *Problems:* Identifies any delays, cost overruns, or other unanticipated difficulties. If all is well, or if the problems are of no particular consequence, this section may be omitted.

- *Conclusion:* Summarizes the status of the project and recommends solutions to any major problems.

If properly prepared and promptly submitted, progress reports can be invaluable in enabling management to make necessary adjustments to meet deadlines, avert crises, and prevent unnecessary expense. Figures 5.19–5.22 present a progress report on capital projects, prepared in booklet format with a cover memo.

FALLKILL INDUSTRIES, INC.

MEMORANDUM

DATE: November 10, 2008

TO: Judith Ayres
             Accounting Department

FROM: John Daly
             Physical Plant

SUBJECT: Progress Report on Capital Projects

As requested, here is the progress report on the five capital projects identified as high-priority items at last spring's long-range planning meeting:

- Replacement of front elevator in Main Building
- Replacement of all windows in Main Building
- Installation of new fire alarm system in all buildings
- Installation of emergency lighting system in all buildings
- Renovation of "B" Building basement

Please contact me if you have any questions.

FIGURE 5.19   **Progress Report (Booklet Format), Cover Memo**

FALLKILL INDUSTRIES, INC.

PROGRESS REPORT

on

CAPITAL PROJECTS

by

John Daly
Physical Plant

Submitted to

Judith Ayres
Accounting Department

November 10, 2008

FIGURE 5.20 Progress Report (Booklet Format), Title Page

INTRODUCTION

Fallkill Industries, Inc. is currently involved in several major capital projects that were identified as high-priority items at last spring's long-range planning meeting: replacement of the front elevator and all windows in the Main Building, installation of a new fire alarm system and emergency lighting system in all buildings, and renovation of the "B" Building basement. Progress has been made on all of these projects, although there have been a few problems.

WORK COMPLETED

Elevator Replacement
Equipment has been ordered from Uptown Elevator. The pump has arrived and is in storage. We have asked Uptown for a construction schedule.

Window Replacement
Entrance and window wall: KlearVue Window Co. has completed this job, but it is unsatisfactory. See "Problems" section below. Other windows: Architect has approved submittal package, and Cavan Glass Co. is preparing shop drawings. Architect has sent Cavan Glass Co. a letter stating that work must begin no later than April 3, with completion in July.

Fire Alarm System
First submittal package from Alert-All, Ltd. was reviewed by architect and rejected. A second package was accepted. The alarm system is on order.

Emergency Lighting System
BriteLite, Inc. has begun installation in the Main Building. They will proceed on a building-by-building basis, completing one before moving on to another.

Basement Renovation
First submittal package from Innovation Renovation was reviewed by architect and rejected. Innovation Renovation is preparing a second package to reduce HVAC costs. Work will begin in June.

FIGURE 5.21   **Progress Report (Booklet Format), Page 1**

2

WORK REMAINING

Elevator Replacement
Construction schedule must be received from Uptown Elevator. Work must begin.

Window Replacement
Entrance and window wall: Problems with KlearVue Window Co. must be resolved. See "Problems" section below. Other windows: Shop drawings must be received from Cavan Glass Co. and approved. Work must begin.

Fire Alarm System
System must be received. Work must begin. Work will be completed during downtime (10 p.m. to 6 a.m.) to minimize disruption.

Emergency Lighting System
BriteLite, Inc. must complete installation in the Main Building, then move on to other buildings. Bulk of this work will be done during downtime.

Basement Renovation
Final submittal package must be received from Innovation Renovation and approved. Work must begin.

PROBLEMS

Window Replacement
Entrance and window wall: KlearVue Window Co. is still responsible for replacing one window that has a defect in the glass. In addition, the architect refuses to accept three of the five large panes in the window wall due to excessive distortion in the glass. The architect has sent several letters to KlearVue but has received no response. The remaining balance on this contract ($18,750) is therefore being held, pending resolution of these problems.

CONCLUSION

Although none of the five capital projects targeted at the spring meeting has in fact been satisfactorily completed, all but one are moving forward through expected channels. The one troublesome item—the unsatisfactory windows—should be resolved. If KlearVue continues to ignore the architect's inquiries, perhaps our attorneys should attempt to get a response.

FIGURE 5.22   **Progress Report (Booklet Format), Page 2**

Recommendation Report

A recommendation report assesses a troublesome or unsatisfactory situation, identifies a solution to the problem, and persuades decision makers to pursue a particular course of action that will improve matters. Such reports are sometimes unsolicited. Generally, however, a recommendation report is written by a knowledgeable employee who has been specifically assigned the task. As with most kinds of reports, the content can vary greatly depending on the nature of the business or organization and on the nature of the situation at hand. In nearly all cases, however, recommendation reports are intended to enhance the quality of products or services, maximize profits, reduce costs, or improve working conditions.

In the case of a solicited report, the writer should attempt to get a written request from the individual who wants the report and then carefully study it to determine the exact parameters of the situation in question. If unsure of any aspect of the assignment, the writer should seek clarification before continuing. As discussed in Chapter 1, it's vital to establish a firm sense of purpose and audience before you attempt to compose any workplace writing. A clear and focused written request—or the discussion generated by the lack of one—will provide guidance in this regard.

Because recommendation reports are persuasive in nature, they are in several respects trickier to write—and to live with afterward—than reports intended primarily to record factual information. Tact is of great importance. Because your report essentially is designed to bring about an improvement in existing conditions or procedures, you should guard against appearing overly critical of the present circumstances. Focus more on what *will be* than on what *is*. Emphasize solutions rather than problems. Do not assign blame for present difficulties except in the most extreme cases. A very helpful strategy in writing recommendation reports is to request input from co-workers, whose perspective may give you a more comprehensive understanding of the situation you're assessing.

Recommendation reports are structured in various ways, but almost all include three basic components:

- *Problem:* Identifies not only the problem itself but also, if possible, its causes and its relative urgency.

- *Solution:* Sets forth a recommendation and explains how it will be implemented; also clearly states the advantages of the recommendation, including relevant data on costs, timing, and the like.

- **Discussion:** Summarizes briefly the report's key points and politely urges the adoption of its recommendation.

Figure 5.23 and 5.24 present a recommendation report prepared in letter format. The report focuses on enabling a feed manufacturing company to avert fiscal problems by cutting costs at one of its mills.

Travel Report

There are two kinds of travel reports: field reports and trip reports. The purpose of both is to create a record of—and, by implication, justification for—an employee's work-related travel. The travel may be directly related to the performance of routine duties (a field visit to a customer or client, for example) or it may be part of the employee's ongoing professional development (such as a trip to a convention, trade show, or off-site training session). Submitted to the employee's immediate supervisor, a travel report not only describes the employee activity made possible by traveling but also assesses the activity's value and relevance to the organization.

Travel reports are usually structured as follows:

- **Introduction:** Provides all basic information, including destination, purpose of travel, arrival and departure dates and time, and mode of travel (personal car, company car, train, plane).

- **Description of activity/service performed:** Not an itinerary but rather a selectively detailed account. The degree of detail is greater if readers other than the supervisor will have access to the report and expect to learn something from it. In the case of a field report, any problems encountered should be detailed, along with corrective actions taken.

- **Cost accounting:** Usually required for nonroutine travel. The employee accounts for all money spent, especially if the employer provides reimbursement.

- **Discussion:** An assessment of the usefulness of the travel and, if applicable, recommendations regarding the feasibility of other such travel in the future. In the case of a field report, suggestions are sometimes made based on the particulars of the situation.

Figures 5.25 and 5.26 present the two kinds of travel reports, both in memo format.

COOPER & SONS FEED COMPANY

"Serving Livestock Breeders Since 1932"

Des Moines Mill   •   State Highway, Des Moines, IA 50300   •   (515) 555-1234

February 12, 2009

Ms. Mary Cooper, CEO
Cooper & Sons Feed Company
Main Office
427 Cosgrove Street
Des Moines, IA 50300

Dear Ms. Cooper:

Here is the report you requested, outlining a proposed expense management
plan that will enable the Des Moines Mill to cut costs.

PROBLEM

Because of the recent closings of several large family-run farms in the
surrounding area, our profit margin has shrunk. We must therefore reduce
the Des Moines Mill's annual operating budget by at least $70,000 for it to
remain viable.

SOLUTION

Inventory Reduction
Reduce inventory by $50,000, thereby creating savings on 10% interest expense.
Saving: $5,000.

Elimination of Hourly Position
Based on seniority, eliminate one customer service position, distributing re-
sponsibilities between the two remaining employees.
Saving: $15,500 in wages plus $2,500 in benefits; total, $18,000.

FIGURE 5.23   **Recommendation Report (Letter Format), Page 1**

2

Elimination of Salaried Position
Eliminate plant manager position, distributing responsibilities between the two assistant managers.

Saving: $36,320 in salary plus $7,264 in benefits; total, $43,584.

Reduction of Remill Costs
Each load returned from farm for remill costs an average of $165 and creates 3.5 hours of overtime work. Lowering our error rate from 2 per month to 1 per month will save $1,980 annually. In addition, this will raise the ingredient value we capture on these feeds by 50% (6 ton/month × 12 months × $100 increased value) or $7,200.

Saving: total, $9,200.

DISCUSSION

Adoption of the above measures will result in a total annual savings of $75,784. This more than meets the requirements.

The principal negative impact will be on personnel, and we regret the necessity of eliminating the two positions. It should be noted, however, that the situation could be much worse. The hourly customer service employee can be rehired after the scheduled retirement of another customer service worker next year. Also, the retrenched plant manager can be offered a comparable position at the Cooper & Sons mill in Northton, where business is booming and several openings currently exist.

Therefore, the above measures should be implemented as soon as possible to ensure the continued cost-effectiveness of the Des Moines Mill.

Thank you for considering these recommendations. I appreciate having the opportunity to provide input that may be helpful in the company's decision-making process.

Sincerely,

John Svenson

John Svenson
Operations Assistant

FIGURE 5.24   **Recommendation Report (Letter Format), Page 2**

ACE TECHNOLOGIES CORP.

MEMORANDUM

DATE: November 17, 2008

TO: Joseph Chen, Director
            Sales & Service

FROM: Thomas Higgins
            Service Technician

SUBJECT: Travel to Jane's Homestyle Restaurant (Account #2468)

INTRODUCTION

On Monday, November 10, I traveled by company truck to Jane's Homestyle
Restaurant in Seattle to investigate the owner's complaint regarding
malfunctioning video monitors (Ace Cash Register System 2000). I left the
plant at 9:00 a.m. and was back by 10:30 a.m.

SERVICE PERFORMED

All three video monitors were functioning erratically. When I examined them,
however, the problem turned out to be very simple. Because of how the
Jane's Homestyle Restaurant counter area is designed, the keypad must be
positioned farther away from the monitor than usual. As a result, the 15" cable
(part #012) that creates the interface between the two units is not quite long
enough to stay firmly in place, making the connection unstable.

After explaining the problem to the restaurant manager, I provided a
temporary "quick fix" by duct-taping the connections. When I returned to the
plant, I instructed the shipping department to send the restaurant three
20" replacement cables (part #123) by overnight delivery.

DISCUSSION

This incident demonstrates the need for thorough testing of systems when
they're installed, taking into account the environments where they'll be used.
We might check whether other customers have experienced similar difficulties. Maybe all System 2000 units should be installed with longer cable.

FIGURE 5.25   **Field Report (Memo Format)**

ACE TECHNOLOGIES CORP.

MEMORANDUM

DATE: November 17, 2008

TO: Floyd Danvers, Director
            Human Resources

FROM: Thomas Higgins
            Service Technician

SUBJECT: Travel to Northweston Marriott for Seminar

INTRODUCTION

On Thursday, November 6, and Friday, November 7, I traveled by company car to the Northweston Marriott to attend a seminar entitled "Workplace Communications: The Basics," presented by a corporate training consultant, Dr. George J. Searles. I left the plant at 8 a.m. and was back by 5 p.m. both days.

ACTIVITIES

The seminar consisted of four half-day sessions, as follows:

- Workplace Communications Overview (Thursday a.m.)
- Review of Mechanics (Thursday p.m.)
- Memos and Letters (Friday a.m.)
- Reports (Friday p.m.)

There were 21 participants from a variety of local businesses and organizations, and the sessions were a blend of lecture and discussion, with emphasis on clear, concise writing. The instructor distributed numerous handouts that illustrated the points under consideration.

COSTS

The program cost $800, paid by the company. Aside from two days' lunch allowance ($30 total) and use of the company car (38 miles total), there were no other expenses.

DISCUSSION

This was a very worthwhile program. I learned a lot from it. Since it would be quite difficult, however, to summarize the content here, I've appended a complete set of the handouts distributed by the instructor. As you will see when you examine these materials, the focus of the program was quite practical and hands-on. I recommend that other employees be encouraged to attend the next time this program is offered in our area.

FIGURE 5.26   **Trip Report (Memo Format)**

 **Checklist   Evaluating a Memo Report**

A good memo report

—— follows standard memo report format;

—— includes certain features:

  ☐ To line, which provides the name and often the title and/or department of the receiver

  ☐ From line, which provides the name (provided automatically on e-mail) and often the title and/or department of the sender

  ☐ Date line (provided automatically on e-mail)

  ☐ Subject line, which provides a clear, accurate, but brief indication of what the memo report is about

—— is organized into separate, labeled sections, covering the subject fully in an orderly way;

—— includes no inappropriate content;

—— uses clear, simple language;

—— maintains an appropriate tone, neither too formal nor too conversational;

—— employs effective visuals—tables, graphs, charts, and the like—where necessary to clarify the text;

—— contains no typos or mechanical errors in spelling, capitalization, punctuation, or grammar.

 # Exercises

■ EXERCISE 5.1

Write a report either to your supervisor at work or to the campus safety committee at your college fully describing the circumstances surrounding an accident or injury you've experienced at work or at college and the results of that mishap. Include suggestions about how similar situations might be avoided in the future. Use the memo report format, and include visuals if appropriate.

☑ Checklist   Evaluating a Letter Report

A good letter report

___ follows a standard letter format (full block is best);

___ includes certain features:

   ☐ Sender's complete address

   ☐ Date

   ☐ Receiver's full name and complete address

   ☐ Salutation, followed by a colon

   ☐ Complimentary close ("Sincerely" is best), followed by a comma

   ☐ Sender's signature and full name

   ☐ Enclosure notation, if necessary

___ is organized into paragraphs, covering the subject fully in an orderly way:

   ☐ First paragraph establishes context and states the purpose

   ☐ Middle paragraphs constitute the report, separated into labeled sections that provide all necessary details

   ☐ Last paragraph politely achieves closure

___ includes no inappropriate content;

___ uses clear, simple language;

___ maintains an appropriate tone, neither too formal nor too conversational;

___ employs effective visuals—tables, graphs, charts, and the like—where necessary to clarify the text;

___ contains no typos or mechanical errors in spelling, capitalization, punctuation, or grammar.

■ EXERCISE 5.2

Write a report to the local police department regarding the rush-hour traffic patterns at a major intersection near campus. Observe for one hour during either the morning or evening rush period on one typical weekday. Record the number and kinds of vehicles (car, truck, bus, motorcycle) and the directions in which they were traveling, along with an estimate of pedestrian traffic. Also record, of course, any accidents that occur. Evaluate the layout of the intersection (including lights, signs, and so forth) in terms of safety, and suggest improvements. Use the booklet format and include visuals.

■ EXERCISE 5.3

Write a report to your communications instructor, outlining your progress in class. List attendance, grades, and any other pertinent information, including an objective assessment of your performance so far and the final grade you anticipate receiving. Use the memo format and include visuals.

■ EXERCISE 5.4

Write a report to the academic dean, urging that a particular college policy be modified. Be specific about the reasons for your proposal. Justify the change and provide concrete suggestions about possible alternative policies. Use the memo format and include visuals if appropriate.

■ EXERCISE 5.5

Write a report to your instructor, discussing any recent vacation trip you have taken. Summarize your principal activities during the trip, and provide an evaluation of how successful the vacation was. Use the letter format and include visuals.

■ EXERCISE 5.6

Write a report to a classmate, outlining the performance of your favorite sports team over the past three years. Using statistical data, be as factual and detailed as your knowledge of the sport will permit. Attempt to explain the reasons for the team's relative success or lack of it. Use the booklet format and include visuals.

■ EXERCISE 5.7

Write a report to the student services director or the physical plant director at your college, evaluating a major campus building with respect to accessibility to the physically challenged. Discuss the presence or absence of special signs, doors, ramps, elevators, restroom facilities, and the like. Suggest additional accommodations that should be provided if such needs exist. Use the booklet format and include visuals.

☑ Checklist   Evaluating a Booklet Report

A good booklet report

___ is accompanied by a cover memo or letter;

___ includes a title page that contains the following:
- ☐ Title of the report
- ☐ Name(s) of author(s)
- ☐ Name of company or organization
- ☐ Name(s) of person(s) receiving the report
- ☐ Date

___ is organized into separate, labeled sections, covering the subject fully in an orderly way;

___ includes only appropriate content;

___ uses clear, simple language;

___ maintains an appropriate tone, neither too formal nor too conversational;

___ employs effective visuals—tables, graphs, charts, and the like—where necessary to clarify the text;

___ contains no typos or mechanical errors in spelling, capitalization, punctuation, or grammar.

■ EXERCISE 5.8

Team up with a classmate of the opposite sex, and write a report to the physical plant director analyzing the differences, if any, between the men's and women's restroom facilities in the main building on your campus. Suggest any changes or improvements you think might be necessary. Use the booklet format and include visuals.

■ EXERCISE 5.9

Have you ever been the victim of or witness to a minor crime on campus? Write a report to the college security director, relating the details of that experience and offering suggestions about how to minimize the likelihood of similar occurrences in the future. Use the letter format and include visuals if appropriate.

■ EXERCISE 5.10

Write a report to your classmates in which you evaluate three nearby restaurants featuring similar cuisine (for example, seafood, Chinese, or Italian) or three nearby stores that sell essentially the same product (for example, athletic shoes, books and music, or clothing). Discuss such issues as selection, quality, price, and service. Use the booklet format and include visuals.

6

Summaries

Learning Objective   When you complete this chapter, you'll be able to write clear, concise, and complete summaries that convey the content and emphasis of the original sources.

In the broadest sense, *all* writing is a form of summary. Whenever we put words on paper or computer screen, we condense ideas and information to make them coherent to the reader. Ordinarily, however, the term *summary* refers to a brief statement of the essential content of something heard, seen, or read. For any kind of summary, the writer reduces a body of material to its bare essentials. Creating a summary is therefore an exercise in *compression,* requiring logical organization, clear and concrete terminology, and sensitivity to the reader's needs. By that definition, a summary is the same as any other kind of workplace communication. Summary writing, however, demands an especially keen sense of not only what to include but also of what to *leave out.* The goal is to highlight the key points and not burden the reader with unnecessary details. In the workplace context, the most common summary application is in the abstracts and executive summaries that accompany long reports. This chapter explores the main principles governing the writing of summaries, a valuable skill in many work settings.

Types of Summaries: Descriptive, Informative, and Evaluative

In general, summaries can be classified into three categories: descriptive, informative, and evaluative.

A **descriptive summary** states what the original document is about but does not convey any of the document's specific information. It is much like a table of contents in paragraph form. Its main purpose is to help a reader determine whether the document summarized is of any potential use in a given situation. For example, a pamphlet providing descriptive summaries of federal publications on workplace safety may be quite helpful to a personnel director wishing to educate employees about a particular job-related hazard. Similarly, a purchasing agent might consult descriptive summaries to determine the potential relevance of outside studies on needed equipment or supplies. A descriptive summary might look something like this:

> This report discusses a series of tests conducted on industrial-strength coil springs at the TopTech Laboratories in Northton, Minnesota, in January 2008. Three kinds of springs were evaluated for flexibility, durability, and heat resistance to determine their relative suitability for several specific manufacturing applications at Northton Industries.

After reading this summary someone seeking to become better informed about the broad topic of coil springs might decide to read the report.

An **informative summary,** on the other hand, goes considerably further and presents the document's content, although in greatly compressed form. A good informative summary that includes the document's conclusions and recommendations (if any) can actually enable a busy reader to *skip* the original altogether. Here is an informative version of the previous descriptive summary:

> This report discusses a series of tests conducted on industrial-strength coil springs at the TopTech Laboratories in Northton, Minnesota, in January 2008. Three kinds of springs—all manufactured by the Mathers Spring Co. of Marietta, Ohio—were tested: serial numbers 423, 424, and 425. The springs were evaluated for flexibility, durability, and heat resistance to determine their relative suitability for several specific manufacturing applications at Northton Industries. In 15 tests using a Flexor Meter, #423 was found to be the most flexible, followed by #425 and #424, respectively. In 15 tests using a Duro Meter, #425 proved the most durable, followed by #423 and #424, respectively. In 15 tests using a Thermal Chamber, #423 was the most heat resistant, followed by #424 and #425, respectively. Although #423 compiled the best overall performance rating, #425 is the preferred choice because the applications in question require considerable durability and involve relatively few high-temperature operations.

The **evaluative summary** is even more fully developed and includes the writer's personal assessment of the original document. The following is an evaluative version of the same summary. Notice that the writer inserts subjective value judgments throughout.

> This rather poorly written and finally unreliable report discusses a series of flawed experiments conducted on industrial-strength coil springs at the TopTech Laboratories in Northton, Minnesota, in January 2008. Three kinds of springs—all manufactured by the Mathers Spring Co. of Marietta, Ohio—were tested: serial numbers 423, 424, and 425. The springs were evaluated for flexibility, durability, and heat resistance to determine their relative suitability for several specific manufacturing applications at Northton Industries. In 15 tests using the notoriously unreliable Flexor Meter, #423 was rated the most flexible, followed by #425 and #424, respectively. In 15 tests using the equally outdated Duro Meter, #425 scored highest, followed by #423 and #424, respectively. In 15 tests using a state-of-the-art Thermal Chamber, #423 was found to be the most heat resistant, followed by #424 and #425, respectively. Although #423 compiled

the best overall performance rating, the report recommends #425 on the grounds that the specific applications in question require considerable durability and involve relatively few high-temperature operations. However, these conclusions are questionable at best. TopTech Laboratories has since shut down after revelations of improper procedures. Two of the three test sequences involved obsolete instruments, and #425 proved markedly inferior to #423 and #424 in the only test sequence that can be considered reliable.

Of the three categories, the informative summary is by far the most common. As in a *Reader's Digest* condensed version of a longer original article, the purpose of an informative summary is to convey the main ideas of the original in shorter form. To make an informative summary concrete and to-the-point rather than vague and rambling, be sure to include hard data—such as names, dates, and statistics—as well as the original document's conclusions and recommendations, if any. Sometimes including a good, well-focused quotation from the original can also be very helpful to the reader. Avoid lengthy examples and sidetracks, however, because a summary must always be *brief*—usually no more than a quarter of the original document's length.

In addition, a summary should retain the *emphasis* of the original. For example, a relatively minor point in the source should not take on disproportionate significance in the summary (and perhaps should be omitted altogether). However, crucial information in the original should be equally prominent in the summary, and all information in the summary should spring directly from something in the source. Unless the summary's purpose is to evaluate, no new or additional information should appear, nor should personal opinion or comments be included.

For clarity, all workplace writing should be worded in the simplest possible terms. This is especially important in a summary, which is meant to stand alone. If the reader must go back to the original to understand, the summary is a failure. Therefore, the summary should be coherently organized and written in complete sentences with unmistakably clear meaning. As mentioned before, active verbs are best. They are especially helpful in a summary, because they enable you to express ideas in fewer words than passive constructions do.

Depending on its nature, a summary that accompanies a long report is called an abstract or executive summary. If the summary is intended simply to provide a general overview of the report, it appears near the beginning of the report and is called an abstract (for an example of an abstract, see Figure 12.3). If the summary is intended to assist management in making decisions without having to read the report it precedes, it is called an executive summary.

Summarizing Print Sources

To summarize information that already exists in a written document, follow these simple steps:

1. Read the entire document straight through to get a general sense of its content. Pay particular attention to the introduction and the conclusion.
2. Watch for context clues (title, subheadings, visuals, boldface print, etc.) to ensure that you have an accurate understanding of the document.
3. Go back and underline or highlight the most important sentences in each paragraph. Write down all those sentences.
4. Now edit the sentences you selected, compressing, combining, and streamlining. When producing a summary of something you've written yourself, it's permissable to *abridge* the material, retaining some of the original wording. This is strictly prohibited, however, when summarizing someone else's work. Instead, you must rephrase the content in your own words. Otherwise, you're guilty of *plagiarism*—a serious offense for which you can incur severe penalties. This issue is discussed at greater length in Chapter 12.
5. Reread your summary to check that it flows smoothly. Insert transitions—such as *therefore*, *however*, and *nevertheless*—where necessary to eliminate any abrupt jump from one idea to another.
6. Include concrete facts such as names, dates, statistics, conclusions, and recommendations. This is especially important in a summary, which is typically written as one long paragraph incorporating many ideas.
7. Correct all typos and mechanical errors in spelling, capitalization, punctuation, and grammar.

Figures 6.1 through 6.5 depict the major steps in the creation of an effective summary from an existing text, in this case a two-page magazine article about the evolution of the baseball pitching machine.

Summarizing Nonprint Sources

To summarize a speech, briefing, broadcast, or other oral presentation for which no transcript exists, you must rely on your own notes. Therefore, you should develop some sort of personal system of shortcuts, incorporating abbreviations, symbols, and other notations, to enable you to take

THE FIRST PITCHING MACHINE

What kind of device can throw a baseball? A cannon, of course.

BY STEPHEN ESCHENBACH

IF YOU WANTED TO BUILD A BASEBALL PITCHING MACHINE and had never seen one, how would you do it? By analogy, you would probably use some sort of mechanical arm. If that didn't work, you might try a sharp impact with a piston, or perhaps some sort of slingshot. But when Charles Hinton, a mathematics instructor at Princeton University in the mid-1890s, saw his school's pitchers getting sore arms from throwing too much batting practice, he came up with a more imaginative solution.

First Hinton tried a catapult, which, as he wrote in 1897, "failed altogether" in point of accuracy of aim" and was incapable of throwing a curve. Then "it occurred to me that practically whenever men wished to impel a ball with velocity and precision, they drove it out of a tube with powder." With this realization, he devised a machine that was even scarier to face than Pedro Martinez is today.

Hinton assembled a breechloading smoothbore cannon whose breech could be expanded or contracted, like a telescope, to regulate the speed of the pitch. To operate it, the user pulled the trigger on a rifle loaded with blanks. Hot gases from the rifle passed through a thin tube into the cannon, out of which they propelled the ball. (Hinton chose this two-stage method instead of creating an explosion within the pitching gun's breech because "the powder impinging directly on the ball tended to destroy it" and "the most absolute accuracy in loading and uniformity in wadding" were necessary to get a useful pitch.) A spring-operated safety valve prevented the gases from creating too high a pressure. One version of the gun could be fired from the shoulder; another was mounted on a platform.

Hinton's prototype pitching cannon threw "a good strong ball of no great divergence up and down." The next step was to teach it to throw curveballs. A lot of trial and error went into this. First he tried placing small studs on one side of the barrel to create a sort of crude asymmetrical rifling that would, he hoped, provide the desired spin. Instead of curves, this resulted in straight but wild pitches.

Then he tried winding a ribbon around the ball, with the ribbon meant to impart spin as the ball unwound from it. The ribbon did create spin, but it took away so much velocity that the ball wouldn't reach home plate. Finally Hinton asked himself: How does a pitcher throw a curve? With his fingers, of course. So he "resolved to copy the pitcher."

He accomplished this by attaching a pair of rubber-coated iron blades that projected forward from the cannon's muzzle. Bending them produced more of a curve, though the results must have been inconsistent. Every pitcher knows that the movement you get on a pitch depends on where along the seam you grip the ball, and this would have been very hard to control precisely using a cannon.

Princeton's baseball team used the gun in batting practice but immediately ran into a problem: People don't like to get shot at, even with a baseball. Hinton expected that his gun would be popular because of "the deeply implanted love of shooting which exists in every boy," but there was no corresponding love of receiving fire. He responded by letting the batter control the gun himself, using a button he could depress with his foot.

Hinton's mechanical pitcher had its first public demonstration on December 15, 1896, in Princeton's gymnasium. In the spring of 1897, when the Boston Beaneaters (forerunners of the Braves) came to Princeton to play an exhibition game against the varsity, Boston's manager, Frank Selee, was quoted as endorsing the machine ("when perfected, the gun can be used to advantage early in the season, before the pitchers' arms are strong"). He did not, however, let his players bat against it.

On June 10, before a crowd that included Mrs. Grover Cleveland, the machine pitched for both sides in a three-inning intramural game between Ivy Club and Tiger Inn, two Princeton eating clubs. It struck out eight batters, walked one, and allowed four hits. According to an account of the game, "There is but one serious defect in the operation of the machine and that is the long time required for reloading. The frequent delays did not allow a full nine-inning game to be played."

The Princeton team continued to use the pitching gun, and over the next few years it was written up in *Scientific American* and other publications. The high point came on August 13, 1900, in Memphis, Tennessee. Before a crowd of more than

A button fired the rifle, whose gases shot a ball from the cannon.

FIGURE 6.1   **Article with Most Important Sentences Underlined**

In the shoulder version, rifle gases passed through a tube coiled around the barrel.

1,000, it pitched to both sides in a Southern Association game between the hometown Chickasaws and the Nashville Volunteers. The gun struck out the first two batters and gave up no runs in two innings, with only one ball hit out of the infield.

All to no avail. In 1907, when Hinton died at the age of 54, an admirer recalled that the gun "was subsequently discarded on account of the fear it inspired in the batter." *Popular Mechanics* later wrote that "the average batter would step on [the foot control] and then jump back about 4 ft., letting the ball go by." The magazine also noted that the hot rifle gases baked baseballs until they were "as hard as bricks."

Hinton was the son of James Hinton, an English surgeon and philosopher whose works were a major influence on the psychologist Havelock Ellis. Charles was a mathematical prodigy who graduated from Oxford and in 1880, while teaching at Cheltenham Ladies' College, published the first major work on the fourth dimension. Charles Dodgson, alias Lewis Carroll, had a copy of this book in his library. In numerous works exploring the fourth dimension, Hinton coined the word *tesseract*, meaning the four-dimensional counterpart of a cube, and he invented the representation of an unfolded tesseract that later appeared in Salvador Dali's painting *Christus Hypercubus*. He speculated that the fourth dimension might explain God, ghosts, and the afterlife, and his works remain popular today among devotees of the paranormal.

He also wrote a number of "scientific romances," an early form of science fiction. (To show his topological versatility, some of them were set in a two-dimensional world called Astria.) These, too, retain a following. Of one 1886 Hinton story, Professor Bruce Clarke of Texas Tech writes: "The self-exegesis of 'The Persian King' ends by conflating Hegelian sublation with the Schopenhauerian transumption of the material universe by an absolute will. . . . [and] outlines a dialectical approach to creative selfhood that anticipates modernist aesthetic manifestoes. . . ."

Along the way Hinton married a daughter of the logician George Boole. Unfortunately, having failed to grasp the concept of an either/or proposition, he was convicted of bigamy and fled England for Japan in 1886 after serving a brief prison term. In 1893 he arrived at Princeton, from which he was dismissed shortly after introducing the mechanical pitcher. He went on to jobs at the University of Minnesota, the U.S. Naval Observatory, and, starting in 1902, the U.S. Patent Office. He was employed at the Patent Office as an examiner when he died suddenly while delivering a banquet toast to "female philosophers."

Despite the failure of Hinton's mechanical pitcher, inventors continued to pursue the idea. In 1908 a patent was issued on a "mechanical ball-thrower" and a similar device was described in *Baseball* magazine. Both machines used air-powered guns; neither proved practical. Later decades saw unsuccessful attempts to create pitching machines using springs and even a trip hammer. In 1938 a pitching machine developed by the St. Louis banker Byron Moser, which used what amounted to a giant rubber band, was demonstrated before a Cardinals game.

Pitching machines that relied on mechanical arms started appearing during World War II. The first commercially successful mass-produced machine was the Iron Mike, whose prototype was built by Paul Giovagnoli in 1952. He ran a golf driving range near Topeka, Kansas, and wanted to add a batting cage, and when he could not find a satisfactory pitching machine, he built his own. Giovagnoli continued to improve his design and sold it to a manufacturer before eventually opening his own company. It took until the late 1960s for a pitching machine to once again throw curveballs, with the Curvemaster, invented by J. C. Kester.

Today buyers can choose from pitching machines that use wheels, mechanical arms, or compressed air. Some simulate the underhand delivery of a softball pitcher. An advanced machine called Abner can throw any kind of pitch, even a knuckleball, at any speed. Reality is simulated with a video projection of a pitcher winding up, and the ball is released through a flap where the pitcher's hand would be—a high-tech method of avoiding Hinton's problem with gun-shy batters. ★

STEPHEN ESCHENBACH *is a writer in Millburn, New Jersey.*

FIGURE 6.2　**Second Page of Article with Most Important Sentences Underlined**

. . . when Charles Hinton, a mathematics instructor at Princeton University in the mid-1980s, saw his school's pitchers getting sore arms from throwing too much batting practice, he came up with a more imaginative solution.

First Hinton tried a catapult, which, as he wrote in 1837, "failed altogether . . ."

. . . he devised a machine . . .

Hinton devised a breechloading smoothbore cannon. . . .

Hinton's prototype pitching cannon threw "a good strong ball of no great divergence up and down." The next step was to teach it to throw curveballs.

He accomplished this by attaching a pair of rubber-coated iron blades that projected forward from the cannon's muzzle.

Princeton's baseball team used the gun in batting practice but . . . people don't like to get shot at, even with a baseball.

He responded by letting the batter control the gun himself, using a button he could depress with his foot.

Hinton's mechanical pitcher had its first public demonstration on December 15, 1896, in Princeton's gymnasium. In the spring of 1897, when the Boston Beaneaters (forerunners of the Braves) came to Princeton to play an exhibition game against the varsity, Boston's manager, Frank Selee, was quoted as endorsing the machine . . .

On June 10, before a crowd that included Mrs. Grover Cleveland, the machine pitched for both sides in a three-inning intramural game. . . .

The high point came on August 13, 1900, in Memphis, Tennessee. Before a crowd of more than 1,000, it pitched to both sides in a Southern Association game. . . .

In 1907, when Hinton died at the age of 54, an admirer recalled that the gun "was subsequently discarded on account of the fear it inspired in the batter."

Hinton was the son of James Hinton, an English surgeon and philosopher whose works were a major influence on the psychologist Havelock Ellis.

FIGURE 6.3   **Compilation of Article's Most Important Sentences**

In numerous works exploring the fourth dimension, Hinton coined the word *tesseract*. . . .

. . . his works remain popular today among devotees of the paranormal.

He also wrote a number of "scientific romances," an early form of science fiction.

In 1893 he arrived at Princeton, from which he was dismissed shortly after introducing the mechanical pitcher. He went on to jobs at the University of Minnesota, the U.S. Naval Observatory, and, starting in 1902, the U.S. Patent Office.

Despite the failure of Hinton's mechanical pitcher, inventors continued to pursue the idea.

In 1908 a patent was issued on a "mechanical ball-thrower" and a similar device was described in *Baseball* magazine.

Both machines used air-powered guns . . . .

Later decades saw unsuccessful attempts to create pitching machines using springs and even a trip hammer.

In 1938 a pitching machine developed by the St. Louis banker Byron Moser, which used what amounted to a giant rubber band, was demonstrated. . . .

Pitching machines that relied on mechanical arms started appearing during World War II.

The first commercially successful mass-produced machine was the Iron Mike, whose prototype was built by Paul Giovagnoli in 1952.

It took until the late 1960s for a pitching machine to once again throw curve-balls, with the Curvemaster, invented by J. C. Kester.

Today buyers can choose from pitching machines that use wheels, mechanical arms, or compressed air.

Reality is simulated with a video projection of a pitcher. . . .

FIGURE 6.4   **Compilation of Article's Most Important Sentences**

In the 1890s, Princeton math instructor Charles Hinton decided to prevent sore arms among the baseball team's pitchers by inventing a machine to throw batting practice.

After experimenting with a catapult, he tried a small cannon that threw "a good strong ball."

But it couldn't throw curves.

So Hinton attached rubber-coated blades to the muzzle.

The team used the gun for batting practice, but players feared it.

So Hinton supplied a remote control feature that enabled batters to release the pitch themselves by using a foot button.

After a public demonstration in December 1896, the machine was used in an exhibition game between the professional Boston Beaneaters and the Princeton varsity the following spring.

Later that season it pitched for both sides in an intramural game, and in August it pitched in a pro game in Nashville between Southern Association teams.

But batters still feared the gun and it was shelved after Hinton died in 1907.

Hinton's father had been an influential English doctor and philosopher, and Hinton himself published works theorizing about the fourth dimension.

His writings are still read today, particularly his science fiction.

After being dismissed from Princeton, Hinton worked at the University of Minnesota, the U.S. Naval Observatory, and the U.S. Patent Office.

Despite Hinton's problems with the pitching machine, it continued to evolve.

Air gun machines appeared in the early 1900s.

Later models used springs and other devices, including a trip hammer and even a large rubber band.

Mechanical arm machines appeared during the early 1940s, culminating in Paul Giovagnoli's Iron Mike, introduced in 1952.

But it wasn't until the 1960s that a machine would again throw curves.

This was J. C. Kester's Curvemaster.

Today's greatly improved machines use a variety of methods involving wheels, mechanical arms, and compressed air.

To heighten the sense of realism, some feature video of a pitcher.

FIGURE 6.5   **Article's Most Important Sentences, Edited and Revised**

County Community College

MEMORANDUM

DATE: March 24, 2008

TO: Professor Mary Ann Evans, Ph.D.
            English Department

FROM: George Eliot, Student

SUBJECT: Summary

In fulfillment of the "summary" assignment in English 110, Workplace Communications, here is a memo report. I have summarized a magazine article, "The First Pitching Machine," by Stephen Eschenbach. It was published in the Fall 2004 issue of *Invention and Technology* on pages 63 and 64. The article is attached.

The First Pitching Machine

In the 1890s, Princeton math instructor Charles Hinton decided to prevent sore arms among the baseball team's pitchers by inventing a machine to throw batting practice. After experimenting with a catapult, he tried a small cannon that threw "a good strong ball." But it couldn't throw curves. So Hinton attached rubber-coated blades to the muzzle. The team used the gun for batting practice, but players feared it. So Hinton supplied a remote control feature that enabled batters to release the pitch themselves by using a foot button. After a public demonstration in December 1896, the machine was used in an exhibition game between the professional Boston Beaneaters and the Princeton varsity the following spring. Later that season it pitched for both sides in an intramural game, and in August it pitched in a pro game in Nashville between Southern Association teams. But batters still feared the gun and it was shelved after Hinton died in 1907. Hinton's father had been an influential English doctor and philosopher, and Hinton himself published works theorizing about the fourth dimension. His writings are still read today, particularly his science fiction. After being dismissed from Princeton, Hinton worked at the University of Minnesota, the U.S. Naval Observatory, and the U.S. Patent Office. Despite Hinton's problems with the pitching machine, it continued to evolve. Air gun machines appeared in the early 1900s. Later models used springs and other devices, including a trip hammer and even a large rubber band. Mechanical arm machines appeared during the early 1940s, culminating in Paul Giovagnoli's Iron Mike, introduced in 1952. But it wasn't until the 1960s that a machine would again throw curves. This was J. C. Kester's Curvemaster. Today's greatly improved machines use a variety of methods involving wheels, mechanical arms, and compressed air. To heighten the sense of realism, some feature video of a pitcher.

FIGURE 6.6 **Summary (Memo Report Format)**

Notation	Meaning	Explanation
=	Is	Symbol instead of word
#	Number	Symbol instead of word
&	And	Symbol instead of word
∴	Therefore	Symbol instead of word
2	To, too, two	Numeral instead of word
4	For, four	Numeral instead of word
B	Be, bee	Letter instead of word
C	See, sea	Letter instead of word
U	You	Letter instead of word
Y	Why	Letter instead of word
R	Are	Letter instead of word
R̸	Are not	Slash to express negation
w.	With	Abbreviation
w̸.	Without	Slash to express negation
bcs	Because	Elimination of vowels
2B	To be	Blend of numeral and letter
B4	Before	Blend of letter and numeral
rathan	Rather than	Blend of two words
rite	Right	Phonetic spelling
turn handle	Turn the handle	Elimination of obvious

FIGURE 6.7   **Note-Taking Shortcuts**

notes quickly without missing anything important. Figure 6.7 lists 20 such shortcuts. You will likely develop others of your own. This strategy is no help, however, if you have to *think* about it. To serve its purpose, your shortcuts have to become instinctive. Furthermore, you must be able to translate your shortcuts back into regular English as you review your notes. Like anything, this process becomes easier with practice.

To facilitate summarizing from nonprint sources, you can use a hand-held microcassette recorder or download the material to your computer via digital recorder. This will allow you to listen more attentively afterward, at your own pace, under more conducive conditions. But this is a good strategy only if there's no rush or if exact quotation is crucial. And even if recording, it's still important to take good notes—both to maximize understanding through attentive listening and to guard against mechanical failure. Of course, your notes should always highlight the most important points so that you can review them later. But searching for those sections on the tape or in audio files can be very time-consuming

 **Checklist**   **Evaluating a Summary**

A good summary

—— is no more than 25 percent as long as the original;

—— accurately reports the main points of the original;

—— includes no minor or unnecessary details;

—— includes nothing extraneous to the original;

—— preserves the proportion and emphasis of the original;

—— is well organized, providing transitions to smooth the jumps between ideas;

—— maintains an objective tone;

—— uses clear, simple language;

—— contains no typos or mechanical errors in spelling, capitalization, punctuation, or grammar.

unless your notes provide orientation. Helpfully, the better cassette recorders are equipped with a counter similar to an automobile's mileage odometer. You can save yourself a lot of frustration by including counter numbers in your notes. If your notes indicate, for example, that Point A was discussed when the counter was at 075, Point B was discussed at 190, and Point C at 250, locating the desired sections of the tape will now be much easier. You can achieve an even higher level of efficiency by using a digital recorder. Even the least expensive ones are available with DSS Player Pro software, which helps you manage and locate recorded files. Higher-end models enable you to navigate through the menu to assign contact points and then easily find and make selections. Some even use voice activation to access specific texts.

 # Exercises

■ EXERCISE 6.1

Here are three summaries of the same article, Stephen Kelly's "Resurrection of a Garden" in the April 2007 issue of *Landscape Superintendent and Maintenance Professional,* a trade magazine aimed at institutional groundskeeping managers. Identify each of the three as descriptive, informative, or evaluative.

Summary A

The 1500-acre City Park in New Orleans was originally home to Native Americans but was acquired by the French after the city's founding in 1718 and became a park in 1854. Its attractions include the world's largest collection of mature oak trees, an art museum and sculpture garden, a 12-acre botanical garden, an arboretum, an amusement park, and many sporting facilities, including a 26,500-seat stadium and three golf courses. After Hurricane Katrina in 2005, however, 90% of the park was under water. Trees, grass, plants, buildings, and equipment were destroyed. Damages totaled $43 million, and all but 23 of 260 employees were laid off. Thanks to donors and thousands of volunteers, the botanical garden was reopened in March 2006 and by the end of the summer over $5.6 million had been raised. But park officials are fearful that state insurance coverage and FEMA support will be inadequate, mere "pennies on the dollar."

Summary B

In general this article seems quite optimistic and upbeat. Even its title reinforces that impression. And the opening paragraphs focus on the park's role as the site of many European-style pistol and saber duels, a grim but colorful feature of the park's history. Photo captions provide horticultural details that will interest the target readership, and much of the text celebrates the park's many outstanding features. But this congratulatory tone belies the facts. Of $43 million in damages caused by Hurricane Katrina in 2005, only $5.6 million in donations had been raised by the end of summer 2006, plus a mere $216,000 in FEMA reimbursements, despite an agency pledge to pay 90%. A park official has noted that "eligible expenses" is a term open to interpretation, and has expressed fears that state insurance payments "will be pennies on the dollar." Interestingly, the magazine's Table of Contents page includes a section of fine print identifying two New Orleans park officials as "editorial contributors" to the article. Their presence lends credibility to the technical details, but raises questions about the article's intentions. Given those individuals' vested interest in drawing attention to the dire challenges facing City Park, one would expect a more urgent tone.

Summary C

This illustrated three-page article summarizes the history and many attractions of City Park in New Orleans. It then details the park's devastation by Hurricane Katrina in August of 2005, and discusses current efforts to repair that damage and continue restoration projects. The article praises the generosity of philanthropists and other donors, and acknowledges the help of volunteer workers.

However, it does express doubts about the adequacy of promised financial assistance from state insurance coverage and FEMA reimbursement.

■ EXERCISE 6.2

Write a 100-word descriptive summary of a recent article from a reputable periodical or Web site in your field of study or employment. Submit the article along with the summary.

■ EXERCISE 6.3

Write a 250-word informative summary of the same article mentioned in Exercise 6.2. Submit the article along with the summary.

■ EXERCISE 6.4

Write a 300-word evaluative summary of the same article mentioned in Exercises 6.2 and 6.3. Submit the article along with the summary.

■ EXERCISE 6.5

Write a 200-word informative summary of the plot of a recent episode of your favorite television show.

■ EXERCISE 6.6

Write a 250-word informative abstract of a term paper you have completed in the past for another course. Submit the term paper along with the abstract.

■ EXERCISE 6.7

Write an informative summary of an article from a popular periodical (for example, *Newsweek, Rolling Stone,* or *Sports Illustrated*). Make the summary no more than 20 percent as long as the article, and submit the article along with the summary.

■ EXERCISE 6.8

Summarize a lecture given by the instructor of one of your other classes. Limit the summary to roughly 500 words.

■ **EXERCISE 6.9**

Write a 75-word informative summary of an article from your local newspaper. Select an article at least 300 words long. Submit the article along with your summary.

■ **EXERCISE 6.10**

Write a 50-word descriptive abstract of the sample report in Chapter 12.

7

Mechanism and Process/Procedure Descriptions

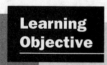 **Learning Objective** When you complete this chapter, you'll be able to write clear, accurate mechanism and process/procedure descriptions.

◼ **Mechanism Description**
   Checklist: Evaluating a Mechanism Description

Exercises

◼ **Process/Procedure Description**
   Checklist: Evaluating a Process/Procedure Description

Exercises

T he selective, well-organized presentation of significant details accompanied by visuals is an important form of workplace writing called description. An effective description enables a reader to accurately envision (and thereby better understand) an inanimate object, organism, substance, physical site, or activity. Obviously, the description's basic purpose is always to inform, but its specific uses are very broad. Like all workplace communications, the description is governed by its immediate purpose and the needs of the intended reader.

Depending on circumstances, a description may be quite short—like the one- or two-sentence caption accompanying a photograph of a house in a real estate agency's advertising pamphlet—or fully developed—like the highly detailed description a specialist would consult when preparing to service or repair the air-conditioning system in that same house. Accordingly, a description can stand alone or appear as part of a longer report or other document, such as a proposal, feasibility study, manual, or brochure.

This chapter focuses on the most common workplace applications: descriptions of mechanisms, and of processes and procedures.

Mechanism Description

Mechanism refers to a tool, machine, or other mechanical device—usually with moving parts—designed to perform a specific kind of work. Naturally, your approach to writing a mechanism description (sometimes called a *device* description) will be influenced by your reader's needs. Your reader may need the description to identify, explain, advertise, display, package, ship, purchase, assemble, install, use, or repair the mechanism. It's also possible that your reader's technical understanding is less highly developed than your own. You must therefore gear your description accordingly, taking all the reader's circumstances into account.

Your writing will also be influenced by whether your description is general or specific in nature. As the term suggests, a general description is accurate for every variation of the mechanism, regardless of manufacturer, model, special features, or other variables. A general description of a camera, for example, would apply to all cameras—digitals, disposables, point-and-shoots, Polaroids, 35 mm, and others—by concentrating on the features common to all. A specific description, on the other hand, deals with one particular example of a mechanism—the Minolta Freedom Zoom 125 camera, for instance—and emphasizes its particular and unique features.

Whether general or specific, nearly all mechanism descriptions include the following features:

- Brief introduction defining the mechanism and explaining its purpose

- Precise description of the mechanism's appearance

- List of the mechanism's major parts

- Explanation of how the mechanism works

- One or more visuals that clearly depict the mechanism—photos and drawings, especially exploded and cutaway views, are best in this context (see Chapter 4)

- Conclusion, sometimes incorporating information about the mechanism's history, availability, manufacturer, cost, and so on

- List of outside sources of information, if any

Obviously, the most *descriptive* parts of the description are the second, third, and fourth items on the list, which constitute the bulk of the text and necessitate certain procedures. You must decide, for example, what order of coverage to use in describing the object:

- Top to bottom or bottom to top

- Left to right or right to left

- Inside to outside or outside to inside

- Most important features to least important features or least important features to most important features

You should use specific, concrete wording—including the correct name of each part—and avoid vague, subjective expressions that may result in misinterpretation. To a reader from a small town, for example, "a tall building" may mean any structure more than two or three stories high. To a reader from New York or Chicago, however, "a tall building" means something quite different. Write exactly what you mean: "a 50-story building" or "a 5-story building." Similarly, don't write "a big long skinny thing"; instead, write "a 17-inch carbide spindle." Sometimes a little research is necessary to determine the correct specifications and terms, but this information is certainly available in dictionaries, encyclopedias, owner's and operator's manuals, merchandise catalogs, specialized reference works, on-line sources such as *www.howstuffwoks.com*, and—for subject matter related to your major field—your textbooks. If you experience difficulty tracking down such information, any reference librarian can assist you.

Using the present tense and predominantly active verbs, explain completely how the mechanism looks. Mention all significant details: size, weight, shape, texture, and color. Identify what the mechanism is made of. Using familiar words and expressions such as *above, behind, to the left of, clockwise, counterclockwise,* and the like, convey a clear sense of where the various parts are located in relation to each other and how they interact. Evaluative comments can highlight the importance or significance of key details, as in these examples:

> The base of the machine is fitted with heavy-duty casters that, when unlocked, make it easy to move the machine from one location to another despite its great weight.

> The machine's simple design provides ready access to the motor, thus facilitating routine servicing and repairs.

> The housing's neutral color (standard on all models) enables it to blend in with the decor of most offices.

Use *analogy* and other forms of comparison to describe parts that are difficult to portray otherwise. Analogy is evident in terms that include capital letters and hyphens, like *A-frame, C-clamp,* and *T-square,* and terms that include descriptive words, like *wing nut, needle-nose pliers,* and *claw hammer.* A little inventiveness enables you to create fresh, original analogies to help the reader "see" what you're describing. But avoid vague, meaningless comparisons, such as "the design resembles a European flag," which may be essentially accurate but, like the "tall building" example mentioned earlier, can be interpreted in many different ways.

Likewise, avoid analogies that depend on knowledge or understanding the reader may not possess. This is especially relevant now that the workplace is becoming increasingly diverse with respect to employees' national origins. Not everyone, for example, will understand sports analogies, especially those based on lesser-known or exclusively American games. For example, the statement that a machine housing is "about as high and as wide as a lacrosse goal" would mean very little to a reader unfamiliar with that sport. Instead, use analogies that most people can relate to. Restrict yourself to comparisons involving the universally known and recognized. To evoke the image of a wire surrounded by a layer of insulation, for example, you could liken it to the lead in a wooden pencil.

Ideally, of course, a visual will supplement the text to prevent misunderstanding. In a mechanism description, the most useful visuals are photos and line drawings, especially cutaway and exploded views. As mentioned in Chapter 4, a familiar object such as a coin, a ruler, or even a human figure can be included in the picture to convey a sense of the mechanism's size, if that is not otherwise obvious. In a sense, this strategy is akin to analogy, which seeks to clarify by comparing the unknown to the known.

On the following pages are two mechanism descriptions for your consideration, commonplace examples that demonstrate basic formats, approaches, and strategies that can be adapted to actual workplace applications. Figures 7.1–7.3 constitute a general description of a conventional flush toilet, and Figures 7.4–7.6 a specific description of an Ajax Super® ballpoint pen.

☑ Checklist　**Evaluating a Mechanism Description**

A good mechanism description

—— opens with a brief introduction that defines the mechanism and explains its function;

—— fully describes the mechanism's component parts and how they interrelate;

—— is clear, accurate, and sufficiently detailed to satisfy the needs of the intended audience;

—— is organized into separate, labeled sections, covering the subject fully in an orderly way;

—— includes helpful comparisons and analogies to clarify difficult concepts;

—— uses the present tense and an objective tone throughout;

—— uses clear, simple language;

—— concludes with a brief summary;

—— includes effective visuals (photographs and line drawings—exploded and/or cutaway views) to clarify the text;

—— contains no typos or mechanical errors in spelling, capitalization, punctuation, or grammar.

A Conventional Flush Toilet

Introduction

A flush toilet is a mechanical device for the sanitary disposal of bathroom waste matter.

Appearance

Typically made of white porcelain, the toilet consists of two basic components: an oval, water-filled bowl with a hinged plastic seat and cover; and a rectangular water tank positioned directly behind the bowl and fitted with a metal or porcelain flush/trip handle on the upper-left side of its front surface.

The rim of the bowl is approximately 15" from the floor. The bowl is approximately 15" across at its widest point. The tank is approximately 20" wide, 14" high, and 8" deep. The tanks of older models held approximately 3.5 gallons of water, while current models hold 1.5 gallons.

The seat and cover on newer models are easily removable to facilitate cleaning. The tank lid is also removable, to allow adjustment and repair of the mechanical parts housed inside.

Major Parts

Virtually all the major parts are inside the tank:

- Lift wires
- Guide arm
- Tank ball
- Valve seat
- Float ball

- Float arm
- Ball-cock assembly
- Inlet tube
- Filler tube
- Overflow tube

FIGURE 7.1   **General Mechanism Description, Page 1**

2

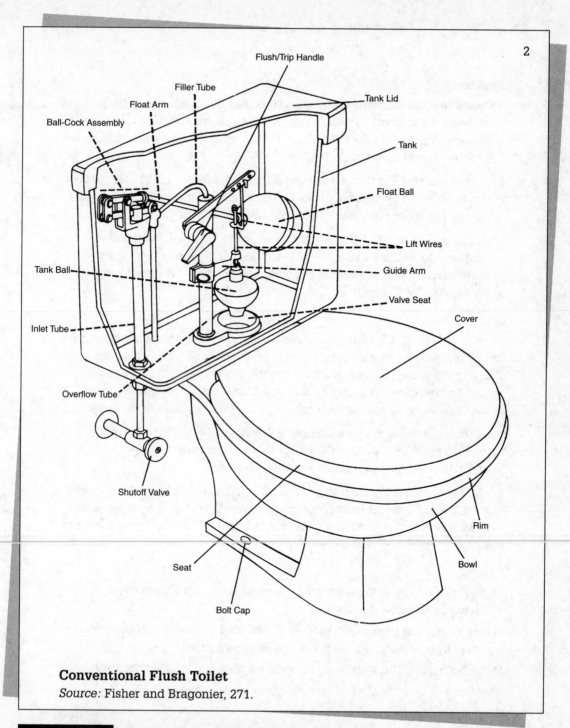

Flush/Trip Handle

Filler Tube

Float Arm

Ball-Cock Assembly

Tank Lid

Tank

Float Ball

Lift Wires

Tank Ball

Guide Arm

Valve Seat

Inlet Tube

Cover

Overflow Tube

Rim

Shutoff Valve

Bowl

Seat

Bolt Cap

Conventional Flush Toilet

Source: Fisher and Bragonier, 271.

FIGURE 7.2 **General Mechanism Description, Page 2**

3

Operation

1. Depressing the flush/trip handle lifts the tank ball from the valve seat, allowing water from the tank to empty into the bowl and carry away waste through a pipe in the floor. When the tank is nearly empty, the ball falls back into the seat and stops the flow.

2. As the water level in the tank falls, so does the float ball. This causes the float arm to open a valve in the ball-cock assembly, letting new water into the inlet tube and allowing both the tank and the bowl to refill through the filler tube.

3. As the water level in the tank rises, so does the float ball. Eventually the float arm closes the valve in the ball-cock assembly, shutting off the water until the next flush. In the event of malfunction, excess water escapes through the overflow tube.

Conclusion

For more than 400 years people have disposed of waste matter efficiently and hygienically by means of the flush toilet. Sir John Harrington, a godson of Queen Elizabeth I of England, invented the flush toilet in 1589. A valve released a flow of water from a cistern tank into a flush pipe. But the valve tended to leak, creating a nearly continuous trickle of water into the bowl.

Chelsea plumber Thomas Crapper's Valveless Water-Waste Preventer, introduced at the Health Exhibition of 1884, solved this problem by incorporating the float-ball principle in use ever since.

Today the leading manufacturers of flush toilets are Kohler and American Standard. A basic model retails for approximately $150, but special features such as brass hardware, elongated bowls, lined tanks, and designer colors can boost the price to $1,000 or more.

Sources

Brain, Marshell. "How Toilets Work." *HowStuffWorks,* 21 May 2007, *www.howstuffworks.com/.*

Fisher, David, and Reginald Bragonier, Jr. *What's What: A Visual Glossary of the Physical World.* Maplewood, NJ: Hammond, 1981.

Macaulay, David. *The Way Things Work.* Boston: Houghton Mifflin, 1988.

Reyburn, Wallace. *Flushed with Pride.* London: MacDonald, 1969.

FIGURE 7.3   **General Mechanism Description, Page 3**

An Ajax Super® Ballpoint Pen

Introduction

A ballpoint pen is a common writing implement used in homes, schools, and offices—indeed, in virtually every setting where writing is done—all over the developed world.

Appearance

Although an inch or two shorter, the ballpoint pen looks much like a pencil. Some disposable ballpoint pens are of unified construction, but most consist of a tapered barrel and a cap, which—fitted together—give the pen its elongated shape and allow it to be disassembled for the purpose of replacing the tubular ink reservoir inside. Most ballpoint pens have a tension clip mounted on the cap to enable the pen to be secured in the owner's shirt pocket when not in use. (The clip also prevents the pen from rolling off inclined surfaces.) In addition, there is a small push button that protrudes from the top of the cap, where the eraser would be on a pencil. This activates the inner workings, enabling the tiny, socket-mounted, rolling ballpoint writing tip at the end of the reservoir to be extended or retracted.

The visible parts of the pen can be made entirely of metal, although many pens are both metal and plastic (metal cap, clip, and button; plastic barrel). Typically, however, it is made mostly of plastic. Metal surfaces can be shiny or textured. Plastic parts are manufactured in a wide range of colors, and some ballpoint pens are two-tone (one color for the cap, another for the barrel).

The Ajax Super model described here is exactly 5" long, with a 3/8" diameter at its widest point, where the cap and barrel join. Both cap and barrel are made of bright red styrene plastic. The tension clip and the push button are made of chromed metal.

Major Parts

Exterior parts:
- Push button
- Cap
- Tension clip
- Barrel

Interior parts:
- Plunger mechanism
- Cam recess
- Cam ball
- Ink reservoir
- Spring
- Ball point

FIGURE 7.4   **Specific Mechanism Description, Page 1**

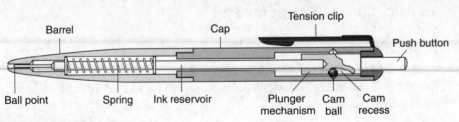

Ajax Super® Ballpoint Pen
Source: How Things Work, 313.

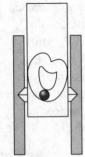

Initial position: ball in
bottom holding point

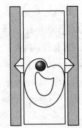

Button pressed: ball
in recess

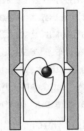

Position of ball determines
position of reservoir

Operating Principle
Source: How Things Work, 313.

Operation

1. Depressing the push button causes the interior plunger mechanism to
   activate, thereby forcing the ink reservoir downward, locking it in place,
   and causing the ball point to extend through the opening at the tapered
   end of the barrel. Plunger mechanisms vary from pen to pen, with some
   more complicated than others.

FIGURE 7.5   **Specific Mechanism Description, Page 2**

3

2. The Ajax Super boasts a rather simple mechanism. When the push button is depressed, a tiny ball rotates in a heart-shaped cam recess in the plunger. After the push button is depressed, the pressure of the spring forces this ball into the topmost holding point within the recess and prevents its return, thus locking the reservoir and the ball point in the extended position.

3. As the ball point rolls across the writing surface, ink is drawn from the reservoir and onto the ball, which then deposits the ink.

4. When the push button is again depressed, the mechanism is disengaged, and the spring causes the cam ball to return to its original holding point within the recess, allowing the reservoir and its ball point to retract into the barrel. The now stationary ball point seals the reservoir, preventing unwanted discharge of ink while the pen is not in use.

Conclusion

The ballpoint pen has evolved greatly since its introduction in the 1940s. Early models were notoriously messy and unreliable, with leakage a constant problem. Indeed, the ballpoint pen was initially banned in many public schools. Since then, however, manufacturers such as Parker, Papermate, Cross, Bic, and others have perfected the device, which is now the most popular handheld writing instrument, having almost completely supplanted the traditional fountain pen. Many varieties of ballpoint pens are available, with prices ranging from less than a dollar for unmechanized, disposable plastic models to literally hundreds or even thousands of dollars for high-prestige, brand-name instruments made of gold or silver.

Sources

Fisher, David, and Reginald Bragonier, Jr. *What's What: A Visual Glossary of the Physical World.* Maplewood, NJ: Hammond, 1981.
How Things Work: The Universal Encyclopedia of Machines. London: Paladin, 1972.
Macaulay, David. *The Way Things Work.* Boston: Houghton Mifflin, 1988.
Russell-Ausley, Melissa. "How Ballpoint Pens Work." *HowStuffWorks,* 21 May 2007, *www.howstufffworks.com/.*

FIGURE 7.6 **Specific Mechanism Description, Page 3**

Exercises

■ **EXERCISE 7.1**

As discussed in the text and mentioned on the checklist, a mechanism description should open with a brief introduction that defines the mechanism and explains its function. To acquire some practice with this task, write introductions for three of the following metering devices:

- Ammeter
- Barometer
- Odometer
- Psychrometer
- Spectrophotometer

■ **EXERCISE 7.2**

Write a general mechanism description of a common device used in your field of study or employment—for example, a welding torch, compass, or stethoscope.

■ **EXERCISE 7.3**

Write a specific mechanism description of a common kitchen appliance—for example, a toaster, blender, or coffeemaker.

■ **EXERCISE 7.4**

Write a specific mechanism description of a piece of sporting equipment—for example, a ski boot, baseball or softball glove, or golf club.

■ **EXERCISE 7.5**

Write a general mechanism description of a tool or other piece of equipment commonly used in automobile repair—for example, a creeper, ratchet wrench, or bumper jack.

■ **EXERCISE 7.6**

Write a specific mechanism description of a Swiss Army knife.

■ EXERCISE 7.7

Write a general mechanism description of a common piece of office equipment—for example, a stapler, locking file cabinet, or telephone answering machine.

■ EXERCISE 7.8

Consult some textbooks, periodicals, and Web sites devoted to your field of study or employment and find ten examples of the creative use of analogy. Write a memo report to your instructor, discussing your findings.

■ EXERCISE 7.9

Consult some textbooks, periodicals, and Web sites devoted to your field of study or employment and find five examples of effective visuals that successfully clarify the appearance or workings of mechanisms. Write a booklet report to your instructor, in which you discuss your findings. Be sure to include copies of the visuals.

■ EXERCISE 7.10

As an exercise in precise writing, create a detailed description of the following illustration. When you think your description is as clear as possible, give it to a friend, relative, or co-worker who has not seen the illustration and ask the person to read the description and reproduce the illustration. If the resulting drawing is not an exact replication of the original, it's probably because your description was not 100 percent clear. Discuss the results with your "artist" to determine exactly what was misleading.

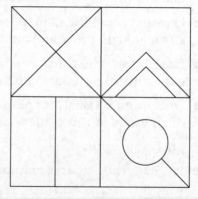

Process/Procedure Description

A process description is similar to a mechanism description. As the term suggests, however, a process description focuses not on an object but on an unvarying series of events producing a predictable outcome. Sometimes referred to as process *analysis*, it enables the reader to understand—but not necessarily to create—a particular process. Indeed, processes are strictly defined as natural phenomena governed by physical laws and are therefore beyond the scope of deliberate human involvement. Photosynthesis is one example of a process, as is continental drift or gene mutation. A more flexible definition of process would include human-controlled activities, such as data processing.

A predetermined series of events that occurs under human control is most typically referred to as a procedure. A manufacturing operation such as injection molding, for example, is a procedure, as is balancing a checkbook or measuring a pulse rate. Therefore, if a process description most commonly answers the question of how and why X *happens,* a procedure description always answers the question of how and why X is *done.* This is a useful distinction.

A procedure description differs sharply from instructions (covered in Chapter 8) because it enables the reader to understand the procedure but not necessarily to perform it. The purpose of a procedure description, like that of a process description, is simply to inform. Indeed, both kinds of descriptions are treated together here because they are so similar. In addition to their common purpose, they are also structured the same. Furthermore, both resemble a mechanism description: both can be presented in a variety of contexts and usually include the following features, which are similar to those of a mechanism description:

- Brief introduction explaining the nature, purpose, and importance of the process or procedure

- Explanation of the natural forces involved, and explanations of any materials, tools, and other equipment that might be needed

- Stage-by-stage explanation of how the process or procedure occurs, with all necessary details; transitions are helpful here

- One or more visuals for purposes of clarification; flowcharts are often useful in this context (see Chapter 4)

- Brief conclusion

- List of outside sources of information, if any

As in other kinds of workplace writing, use *parallel structure* when phrasing the stage-by-stage explanation. Do not say, for example,

1. Customer drops off the clothing.
2. Clothing is sorted and marked.
3. Clothes you want washed go to washing machines, and clothes to be dry-cleaned go to dry-cleaning machines.

Instead, be consistent by phrasing the description as follows:

1. Clothing is dropped off.
2. Clothing is sorted and marked.
3. Clothing to be washed is sent to washing machines, and clothing to be dry-cleaned is sent to dry-cleaning machines.

The revision is better because the emphasis is now on the same word ("clothing") in each of the three stages, and the verbs are now all passive. Since the focus in this kind of description is on the process or procedure itself rather than on a human agent, this is one of the few situations in which passive verbs rather than commands or other active constructions are preferable. Indeed, when there is no human agent—as in a sentence like "steam is created as water evaporates"—passive voice is the most natural way to express the idea.

As with mechanism descriptions, the level of detail and technicality in process/procedure descriptions will depend on the needs and background of the audience. If a process description is especially detailed, it may even include sections of mechanism description within it. In any case, the sequential, cause-and-effect, action-and-reaction nature of the information must be conveyed clearly to ensure the reader's understanding. Do not simply say, for example:

1. X happens.
2. Y happens.
3. Z happens.

Instead, use transitions to reveal the relationships among the stages of the process or procedure, like this:

1. X happens.
2. Meanwhile, Y happens.
3. As a result, Z happens.

Just as you might when writing a mechanism description, you can use analogies and familiar comparisons to convey difficult concepts involved in the process or procedure you're describing. Visuals can also be quite helpful. In general, the most appropriate kind of visual to accompany a process/procedure description is the flowchart, which by nature is intended to illustrate activity through a series of stages (see Figure 4.8). Sometimes, though, a more pictorial touch is helpful, as in the process description in Figure 7.8. Conversely, a simple step-by-step narrative can be sufficiently clear by itself, as demonstrated by the procedure description in Figure 7.10.

Evaluating a Process/Procedure Description

A good process/procedure description

____ opens with a brief introduction that identifies the process or procedure and explains its function;

____ fully describes the process or procedure, providing all details as to when, where, why, and how it occurs;

____ is clear, accurate, and sufficiently detailed to satisfy the needs of the intended audience;

____ is organized into separate, labeled sections, covering the subject fully in an orderly way;

____ includes helpful comparisons and analogies to clarify difficult concepts;

____ uses the present tense and an objective tone throughout;

____ uses clear, simple language;

____ concludes with a brief summary;

____ includes effective visuals (flowcharts and organizational charts, for example) to clarify the text;

____ contains no typos or mechanical errors in spelling, capitalization, punctuation, or grammar.

Erosion and Sedimentation

Introduction

Broadly defined, erosion and sedimentation constitute the two-step process whereby natural forces carry away soil, rock, and other surface materials and transport them to new locations on the earth's surface.

This process causes a gradual and ongoing reconfiguration of the earth's topography. Over the centuries it has created riverbeds, waterfalls, rapids, and other features.

Natural Forces

The main natural forces involved in erosion and sedimentation are water, ice, and wind.

Process

WATER—According to Professor W. H. Matthews III of Lamar University, "streams cause more erosion than all other geological agents combined." The forceful scouring action of rushing water in rivers and estuaries, abetted by abrasive sediment churned up from beneath the surface and carried along, erodes the banks, creates more sediment, and eventually widens the channel. This process is accelerated during flooding, which increases the volume and therefore the velocity of the stream flow. In coastal regions, seawater creates much the same effect. Ocean waves—aided by gravity, wind, and rain—slowly break down bedrock and reshape shoreline cliffs. Just as freshwater carries abrasive sediment that enhances the water's erosive capability, seawater contains grit created by subaqueous erosion resulting from turbulent currents.

FIGURE 7.7   **Process Description, Page 1**

2

U.S. NATIONAL PARK SERVICE

Landscape Arch in Utah, 291 feet (88 meters) long, was chiseled from bedrock by wind-driven sand.

Source: Encyclopedia Americana, 556.

ICE—As water freezes, it expands with great force, breaking apart rocks whose crevices it occupies. Glaciers too have played a major role in erosion. As a glacier moves slowly along, it abrades the earth's surface, partly because of debris quarried from the bedrock by the glacier and embedded in the ice along its base. North America's Great Lakes, in fact, were formed by such glacial activity.

WIND—Wind is a factor primarily in arid, sandy regions where the ground is unprotected by vegetation or other cover. In such areas whole landscapes of hills and valleys can result, as on the planet Mars and in several locations on Earth.

FIGURE 7.8   **Process Description, Page 2**

3

Conclusion

The process of erosion and sedimentation is positive because in addition to creating some spectacular geophysical phenomena (see illustration) it contributes to the formation of new soil and causes rich deposits on valley floors and at the mouths of rivers. Its harmful effects include the depletion of existing topsoil and fertilizer, and the clogging of drainpipes and reservoirs. Although significant, the process is but one of several related influences on the earth's topography. Others include tectonic activity and surface earth movement (landslides, for example). In recent years more attention has been paid to the role of human ecology, particularly the consequences of such practices as quarrying, strip mining, and large-scale deforestation.

Sources

"Erosion." *New Encyclopædia Britannica: Micropædia,* 2002 ed.

"Erosion." *Wikipedia,* 21 May 2007, *en.wikipedia.org/wiki/Erosion.*

Garner, H. F. "Erosion and Sedimentation." *Academic American Encyclopedia,* 1993 ed.

Laflen, John M. "Erosion." *World Book Encyclopedia,* 2000 ed.

Matthews, William H. "Erosion." *Encyclopedia Americana,* 1998 ed.

"Sedimentation." *Wikipedia,* 21 May 2007, *www.wikipedia.org/.*

FIGURE 7.9   **Process Description, Page 3**

Problem Resolution at the Conover Corporation

Introduction

   The Conover Corporation is committed to maintaining a climate of open, honest communication between employees and their immediate supervisors for the purpose of resolving problems that may undermine morale and thus hinder the achievement of corporate goals. To ensure that problems are resolved promptly and fairly, a procedure has been established, subject to periodic review.

Procedure

1. In the event of a job-related problem, the employee requests a brief conference with the immediate supervisor, to agree on a mutually acceptable time, date, and place to meet for discussion.

2. The employee and the supervisor meet. If possible, the supervisor resolves the problem. If additional information, assistance, or time is required, the supervisor arranges a second meeting with the employee, again by mutual agreement.

3. If dissatisfied with the outcome, the employee asks that the matter be referred to the next higher level of supervision. The supervisor tries to arrange this meeting within two working days of the employee's request and summarizes in a memo report the nature of the problem and the initial response given to the employee. Prior to this meeting, copies of the report are given to the employee, the next higher level of supervision, and the Human Resources Department. At the meeting, the employee may explain the problem informally (in conversation, which will result in an oral response) or formally (in the form of a memo report, which will result in a written response).

4. If still dissatisfied, the employee may ask that the matter be referred to the next higher level of management; if necessary, the procedure is repeated until it reaches the point at which a representative of the Human Resources Department joins in the review and the matter is finally resolved.

Conclusion

   Employees are encouraged to use this procedure without fear of reprisal or penalty. Records of problem review procedures are not entered into employees' personnel files, nor are they a factor in performance reviews. Such records are maintained in a separate file in the Human Resources Department, for reference only, to ensure consistency in the handling of other such situations.

FIGURE 7.10   **Procedure Description**

Exercises

■ **EXERCISE 7.11**

Identify each of the following as either a process or a procedure:

- Alphabetizing and filing
- Corrosion
- Intubation
- Solving a quadratic equation
- Vaporization

■ **EXERCISE 7.12**

As discussed in the text and mentioned on the checklist, a process/procedure description should open with a brief introduction that defines the process or procedure and explains its function. Write such introductions for three of the items in Exercise 7.11.

■ **EXERCISE 7.13**

Write a description of a process related to your field of study or employment—for example, pulmonary arrest, cell regeneration, or food spoilage.

■ **EXERCISE 7.14**

Write a description of a procedure related to your field of study or employment—for example, interviewing, stock rotation, or safety check.

■ **EXERCISE 7.15**

Write a description of a procedure that occurs in the world of sports—for example, the annual National Basketball Association (NBA) draft, the way in which points are awarded in diving competitions, or the way the starting line is organized at the Boston or New York Marathon.

■ **EXERCISE 7.16**

Write a process description of how cigarette smoking affects the lungs.

■ **EXERCISE 7.17**

Write a process description of how body rot forms on a motor vehicle.

■ **EXERCISE 7.18**

Write a procedure description of how a dealer determines the market value of a collectible—for example, baseball cards, coins, comic books, figurines, or postage stamps.

■ **EXERCISE 7.19**

Write a process description of how spontaneous combustion occurs.

■ **EXERCISE 7.20**

Consult some textbooks, periodicals, and Web sites devoted to your field of study or employment and find five examples of effective visuals that successfully clarify processes or procedures. Write a booklet report to your instructor in which you discuss your findings. Be sure to include copies of the visuals.

8

Instructions

Instructions
Checklist: Evaluating Instructions

Avoiding Liability

Exercises

nstructions serve a wide variety of functions. You might write instructions for co-workers to enable them to install, operate, maintain, or repair a piece of equipment, or to follow established policies such as those explained in employee handbooks. You might also write instructions for customers or clients to enable them to assemble, use, or maintain a product (as in owner's manuals, for example) or to follow mandated guidelines. As in procedure description writing, the broad purpose of instructions is to inform. The more specific purpose, however, is to enable the reader to *perform* a particular procedure rather than simply understand it.

Clearly, instructions must be closely geared to the needs of the intended reader. The level of specificity will vary greatly, depending on the procedure's complexity and context and the reader's level of expertise or preparation. Computer documentation intended for a professional programmer, for example, is very different from documentation written for someone with little experience in such matters. Obviously, audience analysis is crucial to writing effective instructions.

Instructions

Just as there are general and specific mechanism descriptions, there are also general and specific instructions. The differences are essentially the same for both types of workplace writing. General instructions explain how to perform a generic procedure—trimming a hedge, for example—and can be adapted to individual situations. Specific instructions explain how to perform a procedure under conditions involving particular equipment, surroundings, or other such variables—operating a 22-inch Craftsman Bushwacker electric hedge trimmer, for instance.

Like other kinds of workplace writing, instructions appear in diverse contexts, from brief notes, such as the reminder to "Close cover before striking" that appears on many matchbooks, to lengthy manuals and handbooks. Regardless of context, however, most instruction writing follows a basic format resembling that of a recipe in a cookbook. This format includes the following features:

- Brief introduction explaining the purpose and importance of the procedure

  Note: An estimate of how much time is required to complete the procedure may be included as well as any unusual circumstances that the reader must keep in mind *throughout the procedure,* such as safety considerations.

- Lists of materials, equipment, tools, and skills required, enabling the reader to perform the procedure uninterrupted
- Actual instructions: a numbered, step-by-step, detailed explanation of how to perform the procedure
- In most cases, one or more visuals for clarification
- Brief conclusion
- List of outside sources of information, if any

Although they *look* very easy, instructions are actually among the most difficult kinds of writing to compose. The slightest error or lapse in clarity can badly mislead—or even endanger—the reader. Instructions should always be read in their entirety before the reader attempts the task. Many readers, however, read the instructions a bit at a time, "on the fly," while already performing the procedure. This puts an even greater burden on the writer to achieve standards of absolute precision and clarity.

The best approach is to use short, simple commands that start with verbs and are arranged in a numbered list. This enables the reader to follow the directions without confusion and also fosters consistent, action-focused wording, as in this example:

1. Push the red "On" button.
2. Insert the green plug into the left outlet.
3. Push the blue "Direction" lever to the right.

Notice that instructions are not expressed in "recipe shorthand." Small words such as *a, an,* and *the,* which would be omitted in a recipe, are included in instructions.

Although it's usually best to limit each command to one action, sometimes closely related steps can be combined to prevent the list from becoming unwieldy. Consider the following example:

1. Hold the bottle in your left hand.
2. Twist off the cap with your right hand.

These steps should probably be combined as follows:

1. Holding the bottle in your left hand, twist off the cap with your right hand.

When the procedure is very complicated, requiring a long list, a good strategy is to use subdivisions under major headings, like this:

1. Prepare the solution:
   a. Pour two drops of the red liquid into the vial.
   b. Pour one drop of the blue liquid into the vial.
   c. Pour three drops of the green liquid into the vial.
   d. Cap the vial.
   e. Shake the vial vigorously for 10 seconds.
2. Pour the solution into a beaker.
3. Heat the beaker until bubbles form on the surface of the solution.

If two actions *must* be performed simultaneously, however, present them together. For example, do not write something like this:

1. Push the blue lever forward.
2. Before releasing the blue lever, push the red button twice.
3. Release the blue lever.

Instead, write this:

1. While holding the blue lever in the forward position, push the red button twice.
2. Release the blue lever.

Frequently, the conclusion to a set of instructions takes the form of a troubleshooting section, in which possible causes of difficulty are identified along with remedies. This example is from a bank's instructions on how to balance a checkbook:

> Subtract Line 4 from Line 3. This should be your present register balance. If not, the most common mistakes are either an error in arithmetic or a service charge not listed in your register. If you need further assistance, please bring this statement to your banking office.

Sometimes the troubleshooting guide will be in the form of a three-column "fault table" like the one in Figure 8.1, which appeared in an automobile owner's manual.

Another helpful feature of good instructions is the use of effective visuals. Photographs, line drawings (especially cutaway and exploded views), and flowcharts can clarify concepts that might otherwise be difficult to understand. As explained in Chapter 4, however, you must choose the right type of visual for each situation, and this is certainly true with respect to writing instructions. Different kinds of instructions are best illustrated by different kinds of visuals. A precise operation

Symptom	Probable Cause	Solution
Starter motor won't work	1. Loose connections 2. Weak battery 3. Worn-out motor	1. Tighten connections 2. Charge battery 3. Replace motor
Starter motor works, but engine won't start	1. Wrong starting procedure 2. Flooded engine 3. No fuel 4. Blown fuse 5. Ignition defect, fuel-line blockage	1. Correct procedure 2. Wait awhile 3. Refuel 4. Replace fuse 5. Contact dealer
Rough idle, stalling	1. Ignition defect, fuel-line blockage	1. Contact dealer

FIGURE 8.1   **Fault Table**

involving the manipulation of small parts, for example, may best be rendered by a close-up photograph or line drawing of someone's hands performing the operation. Instructions emphasizing the correct sequence for the steps in a less delicate task, on the other hand, may best be illustrated by a conventional flowchart.

Increasingly, instructions designed to accompany products feature visuals alone or with minimal text. The principal reason for this development is that manufacturers wish to target the broadest possible market by accommodating consumers from various countries and cultures. This trend is likely to grow as we move ever closer to a global economy.

A good way to determine the effectiveness of a set of instructions you have created—whether with text and visuals or with visuals alone—is to field-test them by observing while someone unfamiliar with the procedure attempts to perform it using your directions. For the test to be valid, however, you must resist the temptation to provide verbal assistance if the person expresses uncertainty. This will enable you to detect any unclear sections within the instructions and to determine the cause of the confusion. Another effective test is to ask someone who *is* familiar with the procedure to critique your instructions. Even better, subject your instructions to both forms of evaluation.

Figures 8.3–8.6 and 8.7 illustrate the two main types of instructions: general and specific. Figures 8.3–8.6 explain how to perform a very common procedure: changing a flat tire. Figure 8.7 is the first part of insructions showing how to assemble a specific product: a Weber® barbecue grill. Note that although the Weber instructions rely almost exclusively on visuals, the reader is referred to the hazard alerts explained in the accompanying owner's guide.

Avoiding Liability

Remember that what may seem obvious to you is not necessarily apparent to the reader. Include all information, and provide the reason for each step if the reason is important to enhance performance or prevent error. Sometimes this is best done as a note, as in this example:

- Note: Lubricate the axle now, because it will be much more difficult to reach after the housing is in place.

Often, as in the preceding example, the reason for doing something a certain way is simply to avoid inconvenience. But if a serious hazard exists, you must alert the reader by using LARGE PRINT, <u>underlining</u>, **boldface,** or some other attention-getter, *before* the danger point is reached. By law, any such alert must identify the hazard, specify the consequences of ignoring it, and explain how to avoid it. There are three levels of hazard alerts:

- **Caution:** Alerts the reader to the risk of equipment failure or damage, as in this example:

  CAUTION: The cutter blades are not designed to cut metal. To prevent damage to the blades, never put tools or other metal objects on the conveyor belt.

- **Warning:** Alerts the reader to the possibility of serious injury, as in this example:

  WARNING: The drill press bit can shred your fingers. To avoid injury, keep your hands far away from the bit.

■ **Danger:** Alerts the reader to the probability of serious injury or death, as in this example:

> DANGER: This machine is powered by high-voltage electricity. To avoid death by electrocution, turn the power off before removing the cover plate.

Hazard alerts are commonly accompanied by attention-getting icons like the one in Figure 8.2, which represents the danger of electrical shock. These are often displayed in red for added impact.

Hazard alerts are now more important than ever, not only to avoid malfunction and physical danger, but also to minimize legal liability in case of a mishap. The number of product liability lawsuits has skyrocketed in recent years, with the majority of suits alleging not that the products themselves are defective but that manufacturers have failed to provide sufficient warnings about dangers inherent to their use. As a result, even obvious precautions must be spelled out in very explicit terms. McDonald's coffee cups, for example, now include a warning that the beverage is hot. This is in response to losing $2.7 million in a lawsuit brought by a customer who had been scalded by a spill.

FIGURE 8.2   **Hazard Icon**

Another recent example is the superhero costume that actually carried the following message on its packaging:

> FOR PLAY ONLY: Mask and chest plates are not protective; cape does not enable user to fly.

These are, of course, extreme cases. But they underscore the importance of providing ample warning in your instructions about any potential hazard. Similarly, if malfunction can occur at any point, you should explain corrective measures, as in these examples:

> If the belt slips off the drive wheel, disengage the clutch.

> If any of the solution splashes into the eyes or onto exposed skin, wash immediately with cold water.

> If the motor begins to whine, immediately turn off the power.

✓ Checklist   Evaluating Instructions

A good set of instructions

___ opens with a brief introduction that identifies the procedure and explains its function;

___ lists the materials, equipment, tools, and skills required to perform the procedure;

___ provides a well-organized, step-by-step explanation of how to perform the procedure;

___ provides any appropriate warnings, cautions, or notes to enable the reader to perform the procedure without unnecessary risk;

___ is clear, accurate, and sufficiently detailed to enable the reader to perform the procedure without unnecessary difficulty;

___ employs helpful comparisons and analogies to clarify difficult concepts;

___ uses clear, simple "commands";

___ concludes with a brief summary;

___ employs effective visuals (photographs and line drawings— exploded and/or cutaway views) to clarify the text;

___ contains no typos or mechanical errors in spelling, capitalization, punctuation, or grammar.

How to Change a Flat Tire

Introduction

Nearly every motorist experiences a flat tire sooner or later. Therefore, you should know what to do in such a situation. Changing a flat is fairly simple, but the correct procedure must be followed to prevent injury or vehicle damage.

Tools and Equipment

To change a tire you will need the following:

- Flares (6–10)
- Flashlight (if at night)
- Spare tire, mounted
- Tire pressure gauge
- Wheel blocks (2)
- Jack handle

- Screwdriver
- Penetrating oil
- Lug wrench
- Wide board
- Automobile jack
- Rubber mallet

Procedure

As soon as you realize you are developing a flat, leave the road and drive your vehicle onto the shoulder. Park as far from the road and on as flat and level a surface as possible. Turn off the engine and activate the hazard warning flashers. Put the transmission in park. (Put a manual transmission in reverse.) Set the parking brake. Ask all passengers to get out of the vehicle and to stand well away from traffic and clear of the vehicle. Raise the hood to warn other motorists and to signal that you may need help. Now you are ready to assess the situation.

WARNING: DO NOT ATTEMPT TO CHANGE A TIRE IF YOUR VEHICLE IS ON AN INCLINE OR SLOPE, OR IF ONCOMING TRAFFIC IS DANGEROUSLY CLOSE TO YOUR VEHICLE. UNDER THESE CONDITIONS, WAIT FOR PROFESSIONAL ASSISTANCE.

1. If conditions are acceptable, open the trunk and set up flares behind and in front of the vehicle to alert other motorists.

FIGURE 8.3   **General Instructions, Page 1**

2

2. Remove the spare and other equipment from the trunk.

3. Using the jack handle, pry off the hubcap. If the jack handle is not satisfactory for this, use the screwdriver.

4. Using the lug wrench, loosen (but do not remove) the lug nuts. Nearly all lug nuts are loosened by turning counterclockwise. (If the nuts have lefthand threads and are therefore loosened clockwise, there will be an "L" on the lug bolt.) If the nuts are too tight, apply the penetrating oil, wait a few minutes, and try again.

5. Assemble and position the jack. Because there are several kinds, you must consult your owner's manual for proper assembly and use. If the ground is soft, put the wide board under the jack base to stabilize it.

6. Put the wheel blocks in front of and behind the tire diagonally opposite the one you are changing to minimize the risk of the vehicle rolling off the jack (see Figure 1).

7. Raise the vehicle until the flat tire is just clear of the ground. ALWAYS REMOVE THE JACK HANDLE WHEN NOT IN USE.

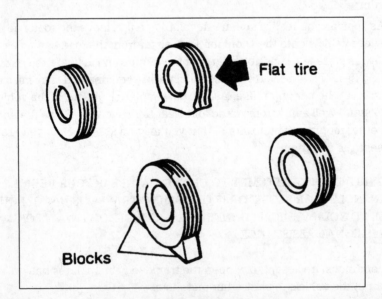

Figure 1   Position of Wheel Blocks

FIGURE 8.4   **General Instructions, Page 2**

3

8. Remove the lug nuts by hand. NEVER USE THE LUG WRENCH WHILE THE VEHICLE IS JACKED UP. If the lug nuts will not come off by hand, lower the car, further loosen them with the wrench, jack the car back up, and then remove them by hand. (Like removing the jack handle, this will minimize the risk of accidentally dislodging the jack—a dangerous error!) Put the lug nuts into the hubcap for safekeeping.

9. Remove the flat.

10. Roll the spare into position and put it on the wheel by aligning the holes in the spare's rim with the lug bolts on the wheel. You may have to jack the vehicle up a bit more to accomplish this because the properly inflated spare will have a larger diameter than the flat tire had.

11. Holding the spare firmly against the wheel with one hand, use your other hand to replace the lug nuts as tightly as possible. Again, DO NOT USE THE WRENCH.

12. Lower the vehicle. Now you may use the wrench to fully tighten the nuts. To ensure that the stress is distributed evenly, tighten the nuts in the proper sequence, as shown in Figure 2.

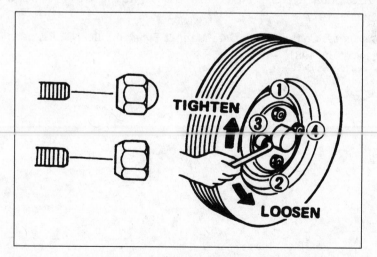

Figure 2   Lug Nut Sequence

FIGURE 8.5   **General Instructions, Page 3**

4

13. Replace the hubcap, checking that the tire valve is correctly positioned, protruding through the hole in the hubcap. You may need to tap the hubcap into place with the rubber mallet.

14. Put the flat, jack, and other tools into the trunk.

Conclusion

Most motorists who follow the procedure correctly are able to change a flat tire successfully. The only difficult part of the task is the removal of the lug nuts, which does require some physical strength. As explained earlier, however, penetrating oil will help, as will a long-handled lug wrench, which provides greater leverage. A common practice is to use your foot to push down on the wrench handle.

Sources

Nissan Pulsar NX Owner's Manual. Tokyo, Japan: Nissan Motor Co., Ltd., 1988.

Pettis, A. M. *Monarch Illustrated Guide to Car Care.* New York: Simon & Schuster, 1977.

Reader's Digest Complete Car Care Manual. Pleasantville, NY: Reader's Digest Association, 1981.

FIGURE 8.6   **General Instructions, Page 4**

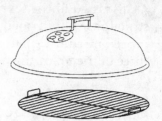 **weber. BAR-B-KETTLE™** GRILL

**18½ in.
(47 cm.)**

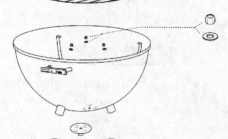

**22½ in.
(57 cm.)**

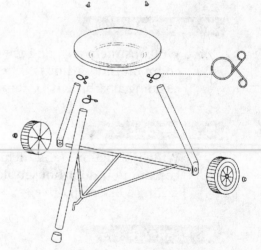

Read important DANGERS, WARNINGS and CAUTIONS in Owner's Guide before operating this barbecue.

30786 11/93

FIGURE 8.7 **Specific Instructions, Page 1**

Exercises

■ EXERCISE 8.1

As discussed in the text and mentioned on the checklist, written instructions should open with a brief introduction that identifies the procedure and explains its purpose. Write such introductions for three of the following procedures:

- Balancing a checkbook
- Creating a play list on an MP3 player
- Measuring a person's blood pressure
- Programming a digital wristwatch
- Hemming a pair of pants

■ EXERCISE 8.2

Write instructions (and include visuals) explaining how to perform a common procedure related to your field of study or employment—for example, welding a lap joint, administering a bed bath, or restraining a potentially troublesome person.

■ EXERCISE 8.3

Write instructions (and include visuals) explaining how to perform a common indoor household chore—for example, washing laundry, cleaning a bathroom, or repairing a leaky faucet.

■ EXERCISE 8.4

Write instructions (and include visuals) explaining how to perform a common outdoor household chore—for example, mowing a lawn, sealing a blacktop driveway, or installing a rain gutter.

■ EXERCISE 8.5

Write instructions (and include visuals) explaining how to perform a common sports-related procedure—for example, waxing a pair of skis, suiting up for an ice hockey game, or performing stretching exercises.

■ **EXERCISE 8.6**

Write instructions (and include visuals) explaining how to perform a common procedure related to automobile maintenance and repair—for example, changing the engine oil and filter, using jumper cables, or washing and cleaning a vehicle.

■ **EXERCISE 8.7**

Write instructions (and include a map) explaining how to travel from your home to your college.

■ **EXERCISE 8.8**

Write instructions (and include visuals) explaining how to perform one of these procedures:

- Cooking a favorite meal
- Laying track on a model railroad
- Building a dog house
- Changing a baby's diaper
- Waterproofing a pair of work boots

■ **EXERCISE 8.9**

Consult the owner's manual accompanying a household appliance or other product you have purchased, and examine the visuals provided to facilitate assembly or proper use. How helpful are they? Write a memo report to your instructor in which you discuss your findings. Be sure to include copies of the visuals.

■ **EXERCISE 8.10**

Consult textbooks, periodicals, and Web sites devoted to your field of study or employment, and find five examples of visuals designed to accompany instructions. How helpful are they? Write a booklet report to your instructor in which you discuss your findings. Be sure to include copies of the visuals.

9

Job Application Process: Letter, Résumé, Interview, and Follow-Up

Learning Objective

When you complete this chapter, you'll be able to write an effective job application letter and résumé, and to interview and follow up successfully.

■ **Application Letter**

■ **Résumé**
Traditional Résumé
Scannable Résumé

■ **Interview**

■ **Follow-Up**
Checklist: Evaluating an Application Letter, Résumé, and Follow-Up

■ **Exercises**

The employment outlook today is quite challenging, with many qualified applicants vying for every available position, and all indicators suggest that the competition will continue to get tougher. Therefore, it's now more important than ever to fully understand the process of applying for a job. Essentially, it involves four components: an effective application letter, an impressive résumé, a strong interview, and a timely follow-up.

Some job announcements provide only a phone number or an address, with no mention of a written response. In such cases you will likely complete a standard questionnaire like the one shown in Figures 9.1 and 9.2, instead of submitting a letter and résumé. Generally, however, these are not the most desirable positions. The better openings, those that pay more and offer greater opportunity for advancement, typically require you to respond in writing, either by mail, by fax, or on-line. This enables employers to be more selective, by automatically eliminating applicants unable to compose a letter and résumé or too unmotivated to do so.

It's important to understand that employers require a written response partly to secure a representative sample of your *best work*. Therefore, the physical appearance of your job application correspondence is crucially important. You may be well qualified, but if your letter and résumé are sloppy, crumpled, handwritten, poorly formatted, or marred by mechanical errors, they will probably be discarded unread. Unless your keyboarding skills and sense of page design are well developed, you might consider hiring a professional typist to prepare your documents. If your résumé is saved in an electronic file, it can be easily customized to match each position for which you apply and, if you're applying on-line, can be sent as an e-mail attachment. But you cannot expect software, or a typist, to work from scratch. You must understand the basic principles governing the preparation of job application correspondence. This chapter provides you with that knowledge, along with information about how to interview and follow up successfully.

Application Letter

Prepared in a conventional format and three-part structure, a job application letter is no different from any other business letter (see Chapter 3). It should be neatly typed on 8½-by-11-inch white paper and should be framed by ample (1- to 1½-inch) margins. In nearly every case the letter should be no longer than one page. The writer's address, the date, the reader's name and address, the salutation, and the complimentary close are handled just as they would be in any other letter, except that all punctuation should be included. Most employment counselors agree that open punctuation and/or an "all caps" inside address should be avoided in an application letter because some personnel directors dislike these practices.

Ideally, the job posting will provide the name and title of the person to contact, as in the following example:

> **ELECTRICIAN:** Permanent, full time. Associate's degree, experience preferred. Good salary, benefits. Cover letter and résumé to: Maria Castro, Director of Human Resources, The Senior Citizens' Homestead, 666 Grand Boulevard, Belford, CT 06100. Equal opp'ty employer.

Sometimes, however, the ad doesn't mention an individual's name but provides only a title—Personnel Manager, for example—or simply the company's name. In such cases you should call the employer and explain that you are interested in applying for the job and would like to know the name and title of the contact person. Be sure to get the correct spelling and, unless the name plainly reveals gender, determine whether the individual is a man or a woman. This ensures that your letter will be among the only personalized ones received, thereby creating a more positive first impression. For various reasons, some ads reveal almost nothing—not even the name of the company—and simply provide a box number at the newspaper or the post office, like this:

> **ACCOUNTING ASSISTANT:** Computer skills and one year hands-on experience with A/R & A/P required. Reply to Box 23, The Bayonne Times, 500 Broadway, Bayonne, NJ 07002.

In such an instance set up the inside address in your letter as follows:

> Box 23
> The Bayonne Times
> 500 Broadway
> Bayonne NJ 07002

When there is no way to identify whom you are addressing, use "Dear Employer" as your salutation. This is a bit more original than such unimaginative greetings as the impersonal "To Whom It May Concern," the gender-biased "Dear Sir," or the old-fashioned "Dear Sir or Madam."

Again, your letter will stand out from the others received, suggesting you are more resourceful than the other applicants.

Incidentally, newspaper classified sections are always larger on Sunday than on weekdays, because of Sunday's larger readership. Also, most papers are now online, so you can easily review job postings from all over the country. This is very convenient if you're interested in relocating to a particular place. Here are Web sites of 20 major American papers:

Atlanta Journal-Constitution	www.ajc.com/
Baltimore Sun	www.baltimoresun.com/
Boston Globe	www.boston.com/
Chicago Tribune	www.chicagotribune.com/
Cleveland Plain Dealer	www.cleveland.com/
Denver Post	www.denverpost.com/
Detroit News	www.detnews.com/
Hartford Courant	www.courant.com/
Houston Chronicle	www.chron.com/
Kansas City Star	www.kansascity.com/
Los Angeles Times	www.latimes.com/
Miami Herald	www.miamiherald.com/
New York Times	www.nytimes.com/
Pittsburgh Post-Gazette	www.post-gazette.com/
Sacramento Bee	www.sacbee.com/
San Francisco Chronicle	www.sfgate.com/
Toledo Blade	www.toledoblade.com/
USA Today	www.usatoday.com/
Wall Street Journal	www.online.wsj.com/public/us
Washington Post	www.washingtonpost.com/

For links to other American newspapers—and those in other countries as well—go to *www.thebigproject.co.uk/USNewspapers/index.htm*.

In your opening paragraph, directly state your purpose: that you are applying for the job. Strangely, many applicants fail to do this. Wordy and ultimately pointless statements—for example, "I read with great interest your classified advertisement in the Tuesday edition of my hometown newspaper, the *Daily Gazette*"—invite the reader to respond, "So? Do you *want* the job, or what?" Instead, compose a one-sentence opening that comes right to the point: "As an experienced sales professional, I am applying for the retail position advertised in the *Daily Gazette*." This approach suggests that you're a confident, focused individual—and therefore a desirable applicant.

SUPER DUPER GROCERY SHOPPE

APPLICATION FOR EMPLOYMENT   DATE: _____

PERSONAL

NAME	
ADDRESS	
CITY STATE ZIP	
PHONE SOC. SEC. #	
HOW LONG AT THIS ADDRESS? _____	

DESIRED EMPLOYMENT LOCATION:

_____

POSITION APPLIED FOR: FULL OR PART TIME

DAYS AVAILABLE: S M T W T F S

HOURS AVAILABLE: _____

DATE AVAILABLE TO START: _____

ARE YOU OVER 18 YEARS OF AGE?   YES NO

IF NOT, DO YOU HAVE THE PROPER WORK PERMIT?   YES NO

HAVE YOU EVER BEEN EMPLOYED BY US BEFORE? YES NO

IF SO, UNDER WHAT NAME, WHAT LOCATION & WHEN?

_____

STATE YOUR MILITARY SERVICE EXPERIENCE _____

DO YOU POSSESS A VALID DRIVER'S LICENSE?   YES ____ NO ____

IF YES, CLASS _____   STATE _____   EXP. DATE _____

ARE YOU PREVENTED FROM LAWFULLY BECOMING EMPLOYED IN THIS COUNTRY BECAUSE OF VISA OR
IMMIGRATION STATUS? (PROOF OF CITIZENSHIP OR IMMIGRATION STATUS WILL BE REQUIRED UPON
EMPLOYMENT.)   YES ____ NO ____

IF YES, PLEASE EXPLAIN _____

HAVE YOU EVER BEEN CONVICTED OF A CRIME, JOB RELATED OR OTHER?   YES ____ NO ____

IF YES, PLEASE EXPLAIN _____

_____

NONE OF THE ABOVE CIRCUMSTANCES REPRESENTS AN AUTOMATIC BAR TO EMPLOYMENT. EACH CASE IS
CONSIDERED AND EVALUATED ON INDIVIDUAL MERITS IN RELATION TO THE DUTIES AND RESPONSIBILITIES OF
THE POSITION(S) FOR WHICH YOU ARE APPLYING.

EDUCATION

SCHOOL	NAME & LOCATION OF SCHOOL	COURSE OF STUDY	NO. OF YEARS COMPLETED	DID YOU GRADUATE?	DEGREE OR DIPLOMA
HIGH SCHOOL					
COLLEGE					
BUSINESS/ TRADE/ TECHNICAL					

FIGURE 9.1   **Job Application Questionnaire, Page 1**

LIST YOUR LAST 3 EMPLOYERS, STARTING WITH YOUR PRESENT ONE

EMPLOYMENT HISTORY		
LENGTH OF EMPLOYMENT	NAME OF EMPLOYER	
FROM TO	ADDRESS OF EMPLOYER	
ENDING SALARY	NAME OF SUPERVISOR	PHONE
DUTIES		
REASON FOR LEAVING		
LENGTH OF EMPLOYMENT	NAME OF EMPLOYER	
FROM TO	ADDRESS OF EMPLOYER	
ENDING SALARY	NAME OF SUPERVISOR	PHONE
DUTIES		
REASON FOR LEAVING		
LENGTH OF EMPLOYMENT	NAME OF EMPLOYER	
FROM TO	ADDRESS OF EMPLOYER	
ENDING SALARY	NAME OF SUPERVISOR	PHONE
DUTIES		
REASON FOR LEAVING		

REFERENCES

MAY WE CONTACT YOUR PRESENT EMPLOYER?   YES ____   NO ____

LIST BELOW 3 PEOPLE OTHER THAN RELATIVES AND PAST EMPLOYERS WHOM YOU HAVE KNOWN FOR AT LEAST 1 YEAR

NAME _____ ADDRESS _____ PHONE _____
AFFILIATION _____

NAME _____ ADDRESS _____ PHONE _____
AFFILIATION _____

NAME _____ ADDRESS _____ PHONE _____
AFFILIATION _____

Applicant's Statement

I certify that answers given herein are true and complete to the best of my knowledge.

I authorize investigation of all statements contained in this application for employment as may be necessary in arriving at an employment decision. This application for employment shall be considered active for a period of time not to exceed 6 months. Any applicant wishing to be considered for employment beyond this time period should inquire as to whether or not applications are being accepted at that time.

I hereby understand and acknowledge that, unless otherwise defined by applicable law, any employment relationship with this organization is of an "at will" nature, which means that the Employee may resign at any time and the Employer may discharge Employee at any time with or without cause. It is further understood that this "at will" employment relationship may not be changed by any written document or by conduct unless such change is specifically acknowledged in writing by an authorized executive of this organization.

In the event of employment, I understand that false or misleading information given in my application/interview may result in discharge. I understand, also, that I am required to abide by all rules and regulations of the employer.

Signature of Applicant _____ Date _____

FIGURE 9.2   **Job Application Questionnaire, Page 2**

Always mention the job *title,* as the employer may have advertised more than one. Also indicate how you learned of the job opening. Most employers find this information helpful in monitoring the productivity of their various advertising efforts, and they appreciate the courtesy. If you learned of the opening by word of mouth, however, do *not* mention the name of the person who told you about it, even if you have been given permission to do so. The individual may not be well regarded by the employer, and because you have no way of knowing this, you should not risk the possibility of an unfortunate association. In such a situation, use a sentence such as *"It has come to my attention that you have an opening for an electrician,* and I am applying for the job."

In the middle section, which can be anywhere from one to three paragraphs, provide a narrative summary of your experience, education, and other qualifications. Go into some depth, giving sufficient information to make the employer want to read your résumé, which you should refer to specifically. But avoid *excessive* detail. Dates, addresses, and other particulars belong in the résumé, not the letter. Be sure to mention, however, any noteworthy attributes—specialized licenses, security clearances, computer skills, foreign language fluency—that may set you apart from the competition. Do not pad the letter with vague claims that you cannot document. "I have five years of continuous experience as a part-time security guard" scores a lot more points than "I am friendly, cooperative, and dependable." Never mention weaknesses, and always strive for the most upbeat phrasing you can devise. "I'm currently unemployed," for example, creates a negative impression; the more positive "I am available immediately" turns this circumstance to your advantage.

The purpose, of course, is to make the employer recognize your value as a prospective employee. Using the "you" approach explained in Chapter 1, gear your letter accordingly. Without indulging in exaggeration or arrogant self-congratulation, explain why it would be in the employer's best interests to hire you. Sometimes a direct, straightforward statement such as this can be quite persuasive: "With my college education now completed, I am very eager to begin my career in banking and will bring a high level of enthusiasm and commitment to this position."

Your closing paragraph—no longer than two or three sentences—should briefly thank the employer for considering you and request an interview. Nobody has ever received a job offer on the strength of a letter alone. The letter leads to the résumé, the résumé (if you're lucky) secures an interview, and the interview (if you're *really* lucky) results in a job offer. By mentioning both the résumé and the interview in your letter, you indicate that you're a knowledgeable person familiar with conventions of the hiring process.

Understand, however, that even one mechanical error in your letter may be enough to knock you out of the running. You must make absolutely certain that there are no typos, spelling mistakes, faulty punctuation, or grammatical blunders—none whatsoever! Check and double-check to ensure that your letter (along with your résumé) is mechanically perfect.

Figure 9.3 is an effective application letter in response to the classified ad for an electrician on page 197. Figure 9.4 depicts the same letter as an e-mail transmittal submitted in response to an on-line job posting. The accompanying résumé, shown in Figure 9.5, enables you to see how the résumé and letter interrelate.

Résumé

As Figure 9.5 illustrates, a résumé is basically a detailed list or outline of a job applicant's work history and other qualifications. The following categories of information typically appear:

- Contact Information
- Career Objective
- Education
- Work Experience
- Military Service
- Computer Literacy
- Specialized Skills or Credentials
- Honors and Awards
- Community Activities

Of course, few résumés include *all* these categories. Not everyone has served in the military, for example, or received awards. Not everyone is active in the community or possesses special skills. But practically anyone can assemble an effective résumé. The trick is to carefully evaluate your own background, identify your principal strengths, and emphasize those attributes. A person with a college degree but little relevant experience, for example, would highlight the education component. Conversely, someone with a great deal of experience but relatively little formal schooling would emphasize the employment history. Both individuals, however, would follow these well-established guidelines:

1. The résumé, like the application letter, should be visually attractive. It should be printed on 8½ -by-11-inch white paper. Use capitalization, boldface, and white space skillfully to create an inviting yet

32 Garfield Avenue
Belford, CT 06100
April 2, 2007

Ms. Maria Castro
Director of Human Resources
The Senior Citizens' Homestead
666 Grand Boulevard
Belford, CT 06100

Dear Ms. Castro:

As an experienced electrician about to graduate from County Community College with an AOS degree in electrical engineering technology, I am applying for the electrician position advertised in the *Daily Herald*.

In college I have maintained a 3.60 grade point average while serving as vice president of the Technology Club and treasurer of the Minority Students' Union. In keeping with my ongoing commitment to community service, last year I joined a group of volunteer workers renovating the Belford Youth Club. Under the supervision of a licensed electrician, I helped rewire the building and acquired a great deal of practical experience during the course of this project. The combination of my academic training and the hands-on knowledge gained at the Youth Club equips me to become a valued member of your staff. Past and current employers, listed on the enclosed résumé, will attest to my strong work ethic. I can provide those individuals' names and phone numbers on request.

Thank you very much for considering my application. Please phone or e-mail me to arrange an interview at your convenience.

Sincerely,

James Carter

James Carter

FIGURE 9.3 **Application Letter**

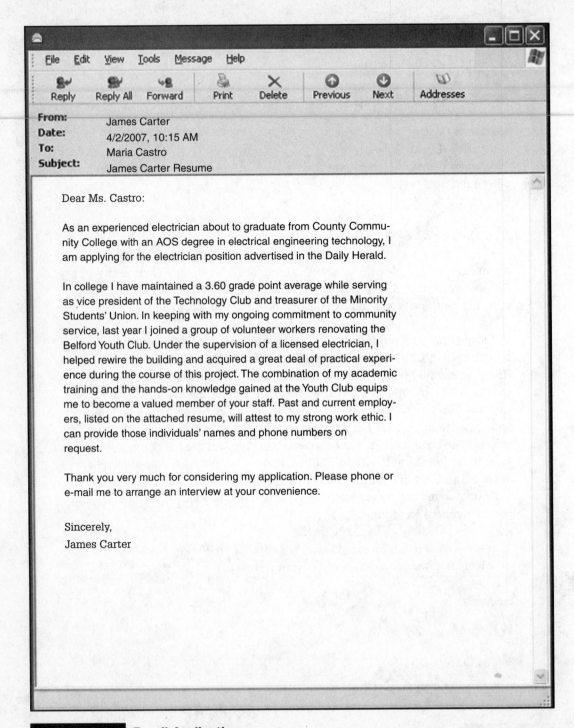

From: James Carter
Date: 4/2/2007, 10:15 AM
To: Maria Castro
Subject: James Carter Resume

Dear Ms. Castro:

As an experienced electrician about to graduate from County Community College with an AOS degree in electrical engineering technology, I am applying for the electrician position advertised in the Daily Herald.

In college I have maintained a 3.60 grade point average while serving as vice president of the Technology Club and treasurer of the Minority Students' Union. In keeping with my ongoing commitment to community service, last year I joined a group of volunteer workers renovating the Belford Youth Club. Under the supervision of a licensed electrician, I helped rewire the building and acquired a great deal of practical experience during the course of this project. The combination of my academic training and the hands-on knowledge gained at the Youth Club equips me to become a valued member of your staff. Past and current employers, listed on the attached resume, will attest to my strong work ethic. I can provide those individuals' names and phone numbers on request.

Thank you very much for considering my application. Please phone or e-mail me to arrange an interview at your convenience.

Sincerely,
James Carter

FIGURE 9.4   E-mail Application

James Carter

32 Garfield Ave., Belford, CT 06100
(203) 555-2557
jamcar@email.net

Career Objective

To secure a permanent, full-time position as an electrician.

Education

County Community College (2004–present)
1101 Belford Dr., Belford, CT

Will graduate in May 2007 with an AOS degree in electrical
engineering technology. Have maintained a 3.60 grade point average
while serving as vice president of the Technology Club and treasurer of
the Minority Students' Union.

Experience

Counter Clerk (2004–present)
Quik Stop Grocery, 255 Bergen St., Belford, CT

Part-time position to help meet college expenses.

Warehouse Worker (2001–2004)
S. Lewis & Sons, 13 North Rd., Belford, CT

Full-time job held after high school, before deciding to pursue college
education.

Community Activities

Assistant Little League baseball coach, church choir member, volunteer
for Belford Youth Club renovation project (helped rewire building).

FIGURE 9.5   **Résumé**

professional appearance. Unless you're applying on-line, you can lay out your résumé in any number of ways, but it must *look* good. Experiment with a variety of layouts until it does.

2. The various categories of information must be clearly labeled and distinct from one another so the employer can quickly review your background without having to labor over the page or screen. Indeed, most employers are unwilling to struggle with a confusing résumé and will simply move on to the next one.

3. All necessary details must appear—names, addresses, dates, and so on—and must be presented in a consistent manner throughout. For example, do not abbreviate words like *Avenue* and *Street* in one section and then spell them out elsewhere. Adopt one approach to abbreviation, capitalization, spacing, and other such matters.

4. Use reverse chronological order in categories such as Education and Work Experience. List the most recent information first and then work backward through time.

5. A printed résumé should be no longer than one page unless the applicant's background and qualifications truly warrant a second. This is not usually the case, except among applicants with ten or more years of work experience. If your résumé does have two pages, include your name at the top of the second page.

6. Some employers and Web sites provide on-line "fill in the blanks" résumé forms for electronic submission. The design of the form will govern the length of your on-line résumé. Otherwise, do not exceed three or four screens. Some employers, rather than providing on-line forms, request that you submit a scannable résumé on-line. This type of résumé is discussed in detail later in the chapter.

7. Like your letter, your résumé must be mechanically perfect, with absolutely no errors in spelling, punctuation, or grammar. Edit for careless blunders—typos, inconsistent spacing, and the like.

Here are some detailed pointers concerning the various categories of a résumé:

- ■ ***Contact Information:*** Such irrelevant personal details as birth date, religion, marital status, Social Security number, and so forth simply waste space. Include *only* your name, address, phone number, and e-mail address. Your contact information should appear at the top of the page or screen and need not be labeled. *Note:* Many e-mail addresses are somewhat silly (for example, bigsexydood©aol.com). If yours falls into this category, you should set up a "professional" e-mail account specifically for job-search purposes. Similarly, you should ensure that the message on your answering machine or cell phone also conveys an appropriate impression. And if you maintain a personal Web site, it should contain absolutely nothing that potential employers might find juvenile or irresponsible.

- **Career objective:** A brief but focused statement of your career plans can be useful. But if you wind up applying for a wide range of positions, you must revise it to suit each occasion. Whether to include this category depends on your individual circumstances, and whether you have room for it.

- **Education:** In reverse chronological order, provide the name and address of each school you've attended, and mention your program of study and any degrees, diplomas, or certificates received, along with dates of attendance. You may wish to list specific classes completed, but this consumes a lot of space and is not necessary. Do not list any schooling earlier than high school, and high school itself should be omitted unless you're attempting to "beef up" an otherwise skimpy résumé.

- **Work experience:** Besides the Education section, this is the most important category in the résumé. For each position you've held, provide your job title, dates of employment, the name and address of your employer, and—if they are not evident from the job title—the duties involved. Some résumés also include the names of immediate supervisors. As in the Education section, use reverse chronological order. If you have worked at many different jobs, some for short periods, you may list only your most important positions, omitting the others or lumping them together in a one-sentence summary like this: "At various times I have also held temporary and part-time positions as service station attendant, counter clerk, and maintenance worker."

- **Military service:** If applicable, list the branch and dates of your service, the highest rank you achieved, and any noteworthy travel or duty. Some applicants, especially those with no other significant employment history, list military activity under the Work Experience category.

- **Computer literacy:** This is a highly valued attribute—indeed, a necessary one—in today's technology-driven workplace. Mention specific word-processing and other software with which you're familiar (for example, Microsoft Word and Excel or Adobe Photoshop).

- **Specialized skills or credentials:** Include licenses, certifications, security clearances, foreign language competency, proficiency with certain machines—any "plus" that does not fit neatly elsewhere.

- **Honors and awards:** These can be academic or otherwise. In some cases—if you received a medal while in the military, for example, or made the college honor roll—it's best to include such distinctions under the appropriate categories. But if the Kiwanis Club awarded you its annual scholarship or you were cited for heroism by the mayor, these honors would probably be highlighted in a separate category.

- **Community activities:** Volunteer work or memberships in local clubs, organizations, or church groups are appropriate here. Most helpful are well-known activities such as Scouts, Little League, 4-H, PTA, and the like. Include full details: dates of service or membership, offices held, if any, and special projects or undertakings you initiated or coordinated. Obviously, community activities often bear some relationship to applicants' pastimes or hobbies. Employers are somewhat interested in this because they are seeking individuals who can not only perform the duties of the job but also "fit in" easily with co-workers. But don't claim familiarity with an organization or activity you actually know little about. You're likely to get caught because many interviewers like to open with some preliminary conversation about an applicant's interests outside the workplace.

- **References:** Employers no longer require applicants to list the names of references on their résumés, or even to include a "References available on request" line. Nevertheless, you'll probably be asked for references if you become a finalist for a position, so you should mention near the end of your application letter that you're ready to provide them. But never identify someone as a reference without the person's permission. Before beginning your job search, identify at least three individuals qualified to write recommendation letters for you, and ask them whether they'd be willing to do so. Select persons who are familiar with your work habits and who are likely to comment favorably. Teachers and former supervisors are usually the best choices for recommendations because their remarks tend to be taken the most seriously. You must be absolutely certain, however, that anyone writing on your behalf will have nothing but good things to say. Tentative, halfhearted praise is worse than none at all. If someone seems even slightly hesitant to serve as a reference, you should find somebody more agreeable. One way to determine whether someone is indeed willing to compose an enthusiastic endorsement is to request that a copy of the recommendation be sent to you as well as to the employer. Anyone reluctant to comply with such a request is probably not entirely supportive. In any case, securing copies of recommendation letters enables you to judge for yourself whether any of your references should be dropped from your list. Better to suffer the consequences of a lukewarm recommendation once than to be undermined repeatedly without your knowledge. Usually, however, anyone consenting to write a letter on your behalf (and provide you with a copy) will give an affirmative evaluation that will work to your advantage.

Traditional Résumé

A traditional résumé can be organized in accordance with any one of three basic styles: chronological, functional, or a combination of both.

A **chronological résumé** (sometimes called an archival résumé) is the most common and the easiest to prepare. Figures 9.5 and 9.6 typify this style. Schooling and work experience are presented in reverse chronological order, with the names and addresses of schools and employers indicated, along with the dates of attendance and employment. Descriptions of specific courses of study and job responsibilities are provided as part of the Education and Work Experience categories. This style is most appropriate for persons whose education and past experience are fairly consistent with their future career plans, or for those seeking to advance within their own workplace.

A **functional résumé,** on the other hand, highlights what the applicant has done, rather than where or when it has been done. The functional résumé is skills-based, summarizing in general terms the applicant's experience and potential for adapting to new challenges. Specific chronological details of the person's background are included but are not the main focus. Moreover, the list of competencies occupies considerable space on the page and may therefore crowd out other categories of information. In Figure 9.7, for example, the Service category has necessarily been omitted. This style is most appropriate for applicants wishing to emphasize their actual proficiencies rather than their work history.

Carole A. Greco

61 Stebbins Drive
Smallville, NY 13323
(315) 555-5555
cagrec@email.net

OBJECTIVE: A permanent position in financial services.

EDUCATION: Associate in Applied Science (Accounting), May 2006
County Community College, Elliston, NY

GPA 3.65, Phi Theta Kappa Honor Society, Phi Beta Lambda
Business Club, Ski Club.

EXPERIENCE: Intern (Fall 2005)
Sterling Insurance Company, Elliston, NY

Contacted and met with prospective clients, answered
client inquiries, performed general office duties.

Trust Administrative Assistant (Summers 2003–2005)
First City Bank, Elliston, NY

Researched financial investment data, organized trust
account information, screened and answered customer
inquiries, composed business correspondence.

Student Congress Treasurer (Fall 2004–Spring 2005)
County Community College, Elliston, NY

Maintained $300,000 budget funding 35 campus
organizations, approved and verified all disbursements,
administered Student Congress payroll.

SERVICE: Volunteer of the Year, 2005
American Red Cross, Elliston, NY

FIGURE 9.6   **Chronological Résumé**

Carole A. Greco

61 Stebbins Drive
Smallville, NY 13323
(315) 555-5555
cagrec@email.net

Objective

A permanent position in financial services.

Competencies

Financial
- Interpreted financial investment data
- Assisted with disbursement of trust accounts
- Administered $300,000 budget

Leadership and Management
- Participated in policy making
- Addressed client/customer concerns

Research and Organization
- Researched financial investment data
- Organized trust account data
- Coordinated funding for 35 organizations

Education

Associate in Applied Science (Accounting), May 2006, County Community College, Elliston, NY; GPA 3.65; Phi Theta Kappa Honor Society, Phi Beta Lambda Business Club, Ski Club

Experience

Intern (Fall 2005), Sterling Insurance Company, Elliston, NY

Trust Administrative Assistant (Summers 2003–2005), First City Bank, Elliston, NY

Student Congress Treasurer (Fall 2004–Spring 2005), County Community College, Elliston, NY

FIGURE 9.7   **Functional Résumé**

Carole A. Greco

61 Stebbins Drive
Smallville, NY 13323
(315) 555-5555
cagrec@email.net

OBJECTIVE

A permanent position in financial services.

COMPETENCIES

- Strong account management and financial analysis skills
- Effective leadership and management capabilities
- Well-developed research and organizational skills

EXPERIENCE

Intern (Fall 2005), Sterling Insurance Company, Elliston, NY: Contacted and met with prospective clients, answered client inquiries, performed general office duties.

Trust Administrative Assistant (Summers 2003–2005), First City Bank, Elliston, NY: Researched financial investment data, organized trust account information, screened and answered customer inquiries, composed business correspondence.

Student Congress Treasurer (Fall 2004–Spring 2005), County Community College, Elliston, NY: Maintained $300,000 budget funding 35 campus organizations, approved and verified all disbursements, administered Student Congress payroll.

EDUCATION

Associate in Applied Science (Accounting), May 2006, County Community College, Elliston, NY; GPA 3.65; Phi Theta Kappa Honor Society, Phi Beta Lambda Business Club, Ski Club

SERVICE

Volunteer of the Year (2005), American Red Cross, Elliston, NY

FIGURE 9.8   Combination Résumé

As the term suggests, the **combination résumé** is a blend of the chronological and functional approaches, featuring a relatively brief skills section at the outset followed by a chronological detailing of work experience. The combination approach is most appropriate for applicants whose experience is relatively diversified and whose skills span a range of functional areas. Figure 9.8 depicts a résumé prepared in the combination style.

Besides the variations in the ways the three styles of résumés present the candidate's credentials, there are also *layout* differences. In Figure 9.6 the category headings are in capitals and are flush with the left margin, in Figure 9.7 they are underlined and centered, and in Figure 9.8 they are capitalized and centered. These differences do not derive from the fact that the three résumés are in chronological, functional, and combination style, respectively. Rather, the variations simply reflect the open-ended nature of résumé design.

For many applicants this flexibility is liberating, allowing them to experiment and exercise creativity. But for others it can pose problems. Someone who is not visually oriented, for example, may find it difficult to choose among the many possible options that present themselves. For this reason some applicants prefer to use the predesigned résumé templates that accompany most word-processing programs. Figure 9.9 depicts one such template available in Microsoft Word. To use it, you'd simply highlight each section of text and replace it with yours, changing *"Max Benson"* to your own name, and so forth. Another template provided by Microsoft Word, called Resume Wizard, allows for a high degree of customization by offering choices of styles and headings. You can access Word's résumé templates by opening the File menu, clicking New, and then clicking the Other Documents tab.

Scannable Résumé

Rapid advances in computer technology have greatly changed every aspect of workplace communications. The hiring process is an obvious example. Many companies now advertise job openings on the Internet, inviting applicants to submit résumés electronically to be read on the screen rather than as hard copy. One problem with this development is that, depending on which software is used, a creatively formatted résumé may appear confusingly jumbled or downright illegible on the receiving end. Format enhancements such as bold print, italics, underlining, bullets, and the like can dress up a résumé on paper, but in the on-line environment they can create havoc. For this reason, many career counselors now urge applicants to greatly simplify the design of their résumés by adopting a no-frills, flush-left format. An on-line

[Click here and type address]   [Put Phone, Fax and E-mail here]

Max Benson

Objective   [Click **here** and type objective]

Experience   1990–1994   Arbor Shoe   Southridge, SC
National Sales Manager
- Increased sales from $50 million to $100 million.
- Doubled sales per representative from $5 million to $10 million.
- Suggested new products that increased earnings by 23%.

1985–1990   Ferguson and Bardell   Southridge, SC
District Sales Manager
- Increased regional sales from $25 million to $350 million.
- Managed 250 sales representatives in 10 Western states.
- Implemented training course for new recruits — speeding profitability.

1980–1984   Duffy Vineyards   Southridge, SC
Senior Sales Representative
- Expanded sales team from 50 to 100 representatives.
- Tripled division revenues for each sales associate.
- Expanded sales to include mass market accounts.

1975–1980   LitWare, Inc.   Southridge, SC
Sales Representative
- Expanded territorial sales by 400%.
- Received company s highest sales award four years in a row.
- Developed Excellence In Sales training course.

Education   1971–1975   Southridge State University   Southridge, SC
- B.A., Business Administration and Computer Science.
- Graduated Summa Cum Laude.

Interests   SR Board of Directors, running, gardening, carpentry, computers.

Tips   Select the text you would like to replace, and type your information.

FIGURE 9.9   **"Professional" Résumé Template**

résumé should always be sent as a Word document or RTF file, not as a compressed (zip) or PDF file, which might create problems for the recipient. To enable the employer to quickly locate your résumé, the file name should begin with your last name, like this: Smith_2008 apr.19.doc. Also, resist the urge to attach pictures, graphics, or URL links. Most employers will not bother to access these. Figure 9.10 depicts the same résumé as shown in Figure 9.6 but in a readily scannable format.

Streamlining for the computer's sake is probably a positive development. Simpler is generally better in workplace communications, and the trend toward a less complicated résumé layout serves to counterbalance the tendency to overbuild such documents. Indeed, most persons who have created scannable versions of their résumés eventually tone down their hard-copy originals as well. An incidental benefit of the simpler format is that more information can be included because limited space is used more effectively. Since scannable résumés are rapidly becoming the norm, many employers now use a strategy called the keyword search. Computerized scanning programs check all résumés received to identify those that include certain terms (that is, keywords) the employer considers particularly relevant. Of course, the computer can detect keywords wherever they may appear in a résumé, but many job-seekers are now creating a separate, keyword-loaded section—sometimes called the profile—in place of the job objective. Notice that the scannable résumé in Figure 9.10 includes this feature.

Since the mid-1990s innumerable Web sites have appeared that can be quite helpful if you're looking for employment. These enable you to post your résumé on-line in the hopes that prospective employers will seek you out. More realistically, you can inspect job announcements posted by the employers. Most of these sites enable you to focus efficiently, searching by job title, geographical location, company name, keyword(s), and other considerations. The sites often boast company profiles, on-line job fairs and newsletters, various forms of job search and career development advice, chat rooms and bulletin boards, links to other sites, and even on-line résumé tutorials. Here are ten such sites, all considered outstanding in a very crowded field:

- BestJobsUSA   www.bestjobsusa.com
- CareerBuilder   www.careerbuilder.com
- CareerPath.com   www.careerpath.com
- FlipDog   www.flipdog.monster.com
- HotJobs   www.hotjobs.yahoo.com
- Monster.com   www.monster.com
- NationJob.com   www.nationjob.com

CAROLE A. GRECO

61 Stebbins Drive
Smallville, NY 13323
(315) 555-5555
cagrec@email.net

PROFILE: Experienced financial services professional with accounting
degree and expertise in customer service, data retrieval, and budget, payroll,
and investment analysis and management. Administrative and research skills,
along with computer proficiency in Microsoft Word, Adobe Photoshop, and
PowerPoint.

EDUCATION: Associate in Applied Science (Accounting), May 2006, County
Community College, Elliston, NY: GPA 3.65; Phi Theta Kappa Honor Society,
Phi Beta Lambda Business Club, Ski Club

EXPERIENCE: Intern (Fall 2005), Sterling Insurance Company, Elliston, NY:
Contacted and met with prospective clients, answered client inquiries,
performed general office duties.

Trust Administrative Assistant (Summers 2003–2005), First City Bank,
Elliston, NY: Researched financial investment data, organized trust account
information, screened and answered customer inquiries, composed business
correspondence.

Student Congress Treasurer (Fall 2004–Spring 2005), County Community
College, Elliston, NY: Maintained $300,000 budget funding 35 campus
organizations, approved and verified all disbursements, administered Student
Congress payroll.

SERVICE: Volunteer of the Year (2005), American Red Cross, Elliston, NY.

FIGURE 9.10   **Scannable Résumé**

Tech Tips

For optimal results, you should create and save a résumé only as a Word document, not on-line. Save the document in hypertext markup language (HTML) so you can easily post your résumé to the Web. But you should adhere to several important rules:

- Create the résumé as plain text, using a conventional font in 12-point size throughout.
- Set 1.2" side margins.
- Position all text flush with the left margin.
- Enter your name and the category headings in uppercase letters.
- Insert only one space after periods and other end punctuation.
- Do not use the ampersand (&), bold print, centering, indentations, italics, line justification, the percent sign (%), ruling lines, the slash (/), bullets, or underlining.
- Limit each line to six inches on your computer screen, and advance down the screen by hitting the "Enter" key before reaching the end of the line, rather than allowing the lines to wrap around automatically.

Some employers will want your résumé in the body of the e-mail. If so, open the document you created it in, copy the text, and paste it into your e-mail window. Other employers may want you to attach your résumé. If so, from your e-mail screen, click Add Attachments (or a similar button, depending on your e-mail program), search through your computer directories until you find your file, highlight it and press Open (or Choose or Attach, depending on your program). The file should then attach. If you have posted your résumé to the Web, reference the URL in the body of your message so employers can click on it and go directly to your site. Whatever you do, follow the same three-part approach recommended for the traditional job application letter but without the inside addresses. For a subject line, use the job title or posting number.

- True Careers   www.truecareers.com
- WetFeet.com   www.wetfeet.com
- Worktree.com   www.worktree.com

Several Web sites are specifically geared to younger, relatively inexperienced applicants seeking entry-level positions. Here are a half-dozen of these "gateway" sites:

- College Grad Job Hunter   www.collegegrad.com
- Experience   www.experience.com

- InternshipPrograms.com   www.internshipprograms.com
- MonsterTrak   www.monstertrak.monster.com
- JobWeb   www.jobweb.com
- SnagAJob.com   www.snagajob.com

Interview

If your letter and résumé result in an interview, you can assume that you're in the running for the position; no personnel office deliberately wastes time interviewing applicants who are not. But now you must outperform the other finalists by excelling in the interview. For this to happen, you must have three assets going for you: preparation, composure, and common sense.

To prepare, find out everything you can about the position and the workplace. Read any existing literature about the employer (Web site, annual reports, promotional materials, product brochures, and so on). Consult some of the employment-related Web sites mentioned earlier in this chapter. If possible, talk to past and current employees or to persons in comparable jobs elsewhere. For generic information about the job title, consult the United States Department of Labor's *Occupational Outlook Handbook* (available in any good library or on-line at *www.bls.gov/oco*). By familiarizing yourself with the nature of the job and the work environment, you'll better equip yourself to converse intelligently with the interviewer. You'll *feel* more confident, a major prerequisite to successful interviewing.

If possible, locate the interview site beforehand and determine how much time you'll need to get there punctually. Be sure to get enough sleep the night before. Take a shower. Eat breakfast. Dismiss from your mind all problems or worries. All this may seem like obvious and rather old-fashioned advice, but it goes a long way toward ensuring that you'll be physically and mentally at ease and ready to interact smoothly. Of course, you should not be *too* relaxed; an employment interview is a fairly formal situation, and you should conduct yourself accordingly. Stand up straight, shake the interviewer's hand firmly, establish eye contact, and speak in a calm, clear voice. Sit down only when invited to or when the interviewer does. Do not smoke or chew gum, and—needless to say—*never* attend an employment interview with alcohol on your breath or while under the influence of any controlled substance. Also, turn off your pager and your cellular phone. No interviewer enjoys being interrupted by an applicant's incoming calls.

Whether you have applied by mail or on-line, be sure to have several copies of your résumé with you.

Anticipate key questions. As mentioned earlier, the interviewer might begin by asking you about your interests and hobbies, or perhaps by remarking about the weather or some other lightweight topic. From there, however, the conversation will become more focused. Expect discussion of your qualifications, your willingness to work certain hours or shifts, your long-range career plans, your desired salary, your own questions about the job, and so on. Here's a list of 20 typical questions often asked by interviewers:

1. Tell me about yourself. (A common variation is, If you had to describe yourself in just one word, what would it be?)
2. What do you do in your spare time?
3. Why did you choose your particular field of study?
4. What do you think you've learned in college?
5. How much do you know about computers?
6. Why aren't your grades higher?
7. Do you plan to further your education?
8. What are your long-range goals?
9. What kind of work do you like best? Least?
10. What was the best job you ever had? Why?
11. How do you explain the "gaps" on your résumé?
12. Can you provide three solid references?
13. Why do you think you're qualified for this position?
14. Why do you want to work for this particular company?
15. Are you willing to work shifts? Weekends? Overtime?
16. Are you willing to relocate?
17. If hired, when could you start work?
18. How much do you expect us to pay you?
19. Why should we hire you?
20. Do *you* have any questions?

Interviewers ask questions such as these partly because they want to hear your answers but also because they want to determine how poised you are, how clearly you express yourself, and how well you perform under pressure. Try to formulate some responses to such queries beforehand so you can reply readily, without having to grope for intelligent answers. Just as important, try to settle on several good questions of your own. Gear these to matters of importance, such as the employer's training and orientation procedures, the job description and conditions of employment, performance evaluation policies, likelihood of job stability, opportunities for advancement, and the like. You want the employer to know you're a serious candidate with a genuine interest in the job. But don't talk *too* much or attempt to control the interview. Answer questions fully—in three or four sentences—but know when to stop talking. Stay away from jokes or controversial topics. Avoid excessive slang. Don't try to impress the interviewer with "big words" or exaggerated claims. Maintain a natural but respectful manner. In short, just be yourself, but be your *best* self.

Many applicants are unsure about how to dress for an interview. The rule is actually quite simple: wear approximately what you would if you were reporting for work. If you are applying for a "dress-up" job, dress up. For a "jeans and sweatshirt" job, dress casually. Some employment counselors advise applicants to dress just a step above the position for which they are interviewing. In any case make sure your interview clothing fits properly, is neat and clean, and is not too outlandishly "stylish." Minimize jewelry. Small earrings are acceptable (two or three for a woman, one for a man), but nose and eyebrow rings, tongue studs, chains, or any other such adornments are better left at home, as are shower flip-flops, sweatpants, hats, and any clothing imprinted with crude or tasteless slogans. Just as the physical appearance of your letter and résumé will influence whether you're invited to an interview, your *own* appearance will influence whether you get hired. As mentioned at the beginning of this section, *common sense* is a major factor in interviewing well. You must "use your head" and "put your best foot forward." As threadbare as these well-known clichés may seem, they really are good advice.

Follow-Up

The follow-up to an interview is another exercise in common sense. Although it requires very little effort, many applicants neglect it. This is unfortunate, because a timely follow-up (within a day or two) can serve as a tie-breaker among several comparably qualified candidates. Every employer wants to hire someone willing to go a bit beyond what's required. Your follow-up is evidence that you are such a person, so it can enable you to get a step ahead of the other applicants.

In the form of a simple letter or e-mail, the follow-up expresses gratitude for the interview and assures the employer that you're still interested in the job. There's no need to compose anything elaborate; a brief note will do. For an example, see Figure 9.11.

32 Garfield Avenue
Belford, CT 06100
April 15, 2007

Ms. Maria Castro
Director of Human Resources
The Senior Citizens' Homestead
666 Grand Boulevard
Belford, CT 06100

Dear Ms. Castro:

Thank you for meeting with me to discuss the electrician position.

Having enjoyed our conversation and the tour of the Senior Citizens'
Homestead, I am still very interested in the job and am available to start
work immediately after my graduation from college next month. I can also
start sooner (on a part-time basis) if necessary.

Please contact me if you have any further questions about my background or
credentials, and thanks again for your time.

Sincerely,

James Carter

James Carter

FIGURE 9.11   Follow-up Letter

Evaluating an Application Letter, Résumé, and Follow-Up

A good application letter

___ follows a standard letter format (full block is best);

___ is organized into paragraphs:

☐ First paragraph asks for the job by name, and indicates how you learned of the opening

☐ Middle paragraphs briefly outline your credentials and refer the reader to your résumé

☐ Last paragraph closes on a polite note, mentioning that you would like an interview

___ does not exceed one page;

___ uses simple language, maintains appropriate tone, and contains no typos or mechanical errors in spelling, capitalization, punctuation, or grammar.

A good résumé

___ *looks* good, making effective use of white space, capitalization, boldface type, and other format features;

___ includes no irrelevant personal information;

___ includes separate, labeled sections for education, experience, and other major categories of professional qualifications;

___ maintains a consistent approach to abbreviation, spacing, and other elements;

___ does not exceed one page;

___ contains no typos or mechanical errors in spelling, capitalization, punctuation, or grammar.

A good follow-up letter

___ follows a standard letter format (full block is best);

___ is organized into paragraphs:

☐ First paragraph thanks the employer for the interview and mentions the job by name

☐ Middle paragraph restates your interest and availability

☐ Last paragraph politely invites further contact

___ does not exceed one page;

___ uses simple language, maintains appropriate tone, and contains no typos or mechanical errors in spelling, capitalization, punctuation, or grammar.

 **Exercises**

■ **EXERCISE 9.1**

Read the classified advertisements in a recent issue of your local newspaper and write a booklet report about what you find there. Include information not only about what kinds of jobs are listed but also about the qualifications required. Provide a breakdown of how many jobs require written responses as opposed to telephone or personal contact. Indicate whether there appears to be any correlation between the type of job and the likelihood that a written response will be requested.

■ **EXERCISE 9.2**

Using the URLs listed on page 215, explore the employment-related Web sites CareerBuilder, Monster.com, and WorkTree.com and write a memo report about what you discover. Compare and evaluate these sites. Which one is best for your purposes? Why? Which is the *least* useful to you? Why?

■ **EXERCISE 9.3**

Using the Internet along with print resources such as the Department of Labor's *Job Information Handbook,* research a particular job title, and write a booklet report discussing your findings. What are the principal responsibilities of the position? What qualifications are typically required? What is the salary range? Are there more openings for this job in certain geographical areas?

■ **EXERCISE 9.4**

Using the Internet along with print resources such as Standard and Poor's, research a particular employer and write a booklet report discussing your findings. What are the employer's main products or services? How long has the employer been in business? Where is the corporate headquarters? How large is the workforce? What kinds of skills or credentials are required to work for this company?

■ **EXERCISE 9.5**

Interview someone currently employed in a job related to your field of study, and write a memo report summarizing the conversation. Why did the person choose this kind of work? How long has the person been in the position? What kind of education and other qualifications does the individual possess? What was said about the best and worst features of the job? Does he or she find the work challenging, interesting, and rewarding?

■ EXERCISE 9.6

Find an actual classified advertisement for an opening in your field that specifically requests a written response. Compose a job application letter and a chronological résumé. Pretend you have been successful in getting an interview and have met with the personnel director. Compose a follow-up letter.

■ EXERCISE 9.7

Find an actual classified advertisement for an opening in some field unrelated to your own that specifically requests a written response. Compose a job application letter and a functional résumé. Pretend you have been successful in getting an interview and have met with the personnel director. Compose a follow-up letter.

■ EXERCISE 9.8

Find an actual classified advertisement for an opening in some field other than your own but related to it that specifically requests a written response. Compose a job application letter and a combination résumé. Pretend you have been successful in getting an interview and have met with the personnel director. Compose a follow-up letter.

■ EXERCISE 9.9

Design scannable versions of the chronological, functional, and combination résumés you created in response to Exercises 9.6–9.8.

■ EXERCISE 9.10

Three application letters accompanied by résumés follow. For a variety of reasons, all are badly flawed. Rewrite each to eliminate its particular weaknesses.

■ **EXERCISE 9.10** Continued

Carla Zogby
2400 Front St., Apt. 32
Kansas City, MO 64100

February 23, 2007

Diversified Services, Inc.
500 Tower Street
Kansas City, Missouri 64100

Dear Sirs:

I am writting this letter in reply to your recent add in the *Kansas City Star.*

As you can see from the enclosed resume, I have all the qualifications for which you are looking for.

Thank you for your time.

Your's Truely,

Carla Zogby

Carla Zogby

■ **EXERCISE 9.10**   **Continued**

NAME: Carla Zogby
ADDRESS: 2400 Front St., Apt. 32, Kansas City, MO 64100
TELEPHONE MUMBER: 816-555-4370
DATE OF BIRTH: October 1, 1983
RELIGION: Cathoilc
MARITAL STATUS: Single
HEIGHT: 5"3' WEIGHT: 110 lbs.

EXPERIENCE

9/2002–2/2003 Receptionist	St. Aedan's Church Answered phones, greeted visitors, handled weekly collection deposits, prepared and distributed weekly bulletin.
3/2002–8/2003 Store Trainer, Waitress	Friendly's Corporation Trained all new waitstaff, took food orders, cleared tables, washed dishes, helped cook.
11/2004–present Insurance Processor	City Bank Process disability and death claims, work with insurance companies to pay accounts.

EDUCATION

9/1998–6/2002	St. Aedan's High School • Honor Roll 3, 4 • Student Council 2
8/2006–present	Kansas City Technical College Secretarial Science

SKILLS
Personal computer systems, software proficiency with spreadsheets, word processing and database programs.

■ EXERCISE 9.10   Continued

Thomas Logan
105 Lincoln Ave.
Lincoln, Nebraska 68500
July 17, 2008

Conklin's Department Stores, Inc.
1400 West Carroll Street
Chicago, Illinois 60600

Gentlemen,

I am responding to an employment ad of yours that I found via the Internet for the Store Security postion. I am sure that you will find that I am highly qualified for this job.

As a military policeman in the United States Army from July 2002 until April 2008 I had over six years experience in law enforcement. My job responsibilities included public relations, emergency vehicle operations, weapons handling, equipment maintenance and personnel management. My training included interpersonal communication skills, radio communications procedures, weapons safety, police radar operations, unarmed self-defense and riot and crowd control operations. I enforced traffic regulations by monitoring high traffic areas, being visible to the public, and issuing citations as necessary. I performed law enforcement investigations as needed, as well as prepared, verified, and documented police reports to include sworn statements and gathering and processing evidence. I conducted foot and motorized patrols of assigned areas and applied crime prevention measures by maintaining control and discipline through ensuring that all laws and regulations were obeyed at all times. I also performed basic first aid as first responder when needed.

Earlier I served as a parachute rigger, rigging, assembling, and repairing several of the military parachutes used in Airborne operations. I rigged various vehcles, weapons, and supplies to be air-dropped as well as hold airborne status for the duration. I also trained in combat operations.

At present I have just enrolled in the Criminal Justice program at Lincoln (Nebraska) Community College, and I have also completed a Human Relations course at Texas Central College, a Combat Lifesaver course, a ten-week course at the United States Army Military Police School, as well as studies at the United States Army Airborne and Pararigger Schools and the United States Army Basic Training and Infantry Schools.

Additional Skills include knowledge of first aid, knowege of conversational Spanish, an accident-free driving record (nine years (civilian and military), and a United States Army Secret Security Clearance.

Sincrely,

Thomas Logan

■ **EXERCISE 9.10**   **Continued**

Résumé of

Thomas Logan, Jr.

105 Lincoln Avenue
Lincoln, Nebraska

Career Objective
Full-time position in law enforcement or security.

Education
Dickinson High School
Jersey City, NJ (Class of 2002)

Lincoln Community College
Lincoln, Nebraska (Currently enrolled)

Armed Forces
United States Army (2002–2008)

Interests
Fishing, Hunting, Snowmobiling

References
Professor John Dhayer
Sgt. Warren Landis
Mr. Thomas Logan, Sr.

July 17, 2009

Superior Steel, Inc.
c/o NYS Department of Labor
121 North Main Street
Herkimer, NY 13350

Dear Superior Stell;

I am applying for the machinist/production assembler position you have
posted with the Depratment of Labor. I have been a machinist at the Curtis
Arms Co. for two years with experience in the manufacture of low tolerance
parts from blueprints. I also have eight years experience as a self-employed
general contractor, and additional experience as a tree service worker. I am
now continuing my education at Proctor Technical College. I have completed
12 credits towArd an AOS degree and have maintained a 4.0 GPA. I am
looking forward to meeting with you for an interview as soon as possible.
Thank you for your consideration.

Sincerely;

Roland Perry

Roland Perry

Roland Perry
30 East Street
Proctor, NY 13500
(315)555-3806
e-mail: rolper30@aol.com

OBJECTIVE

To obtain a full-time position as a machinist with Superior Steel.

WORK HISTORY

Curtis Arms Company, Inc., Utica, NY

Machine operation/set-up on CNC, Pratt-Whitney bore reamers, NAPCO black oxide color line, neutral and hardening furnaces. (January 2007–present)

DUTIES
- machining gun parts to tolerances of +/– .005 inch
- metal fabricating from blue prints
- hardening parts to Rockwell hardness specifications
- maintaining quality standards

Larry's Tree Service, Kingston, NY

Ground crew member. (July 2006–January 2007)

DUTIES
- operated chain saws, chippers, stump machine
- controlled lowering lines and climbers lifeline
- operated and maintained trucks and machinery

■ **EXERCISE 9.10** **Continued**

-page 2-

Perry Construction, Inc., Poughkeepsie, NY

Self-employed general contractor. (August 1996–February 2006)

DUTIES

- carpentry, masonary , plumbing, electrical work
- contracts, book-keeping, customer service

EDUCATION

Proctor Technical College, Proctor, NY (August 2008-present)

COURSES COMPLETED

- Air Conditioning Technology 101–A
- Technical English 101–A
- Technical Math 101–A
- Public Speaking 101–A

COMMUNITY ACTIVITIES

Volunteer Fire Department
American Legion Post Secretary
Community Band (Tuba Player)

10

Oral Presentations: Preparation and Delivery

 **Learning Objective**

When you complete this chapter you'll be able to prepare and deliver successful oral presentations.

■ **Preparation**
Preliminaries
Rehearsal

■ **Delivery**
Introductions and Conclusions
Vocal Factors
Physical Factors
Eye Contact
Audiovisuals
Enthusiasm
Checklist: Evaluating a Public Speaker

Exercises

I f you're like most people, you dread the prospect of having to stand in front of an audience and make a speech. You feel unsure of yourself and fear you'll appear awkward or foolish. Nevertheless, you should make a real effort to overcome such misgivings. The ability to present your ideas clearly and forcefully to a group of listeners is a valuable skill that equips you for leadership in the workplace, where it is often necessary to address groups of supervisors, co-workers, clients, or customers. The skill is also quite useful in community contexts, such as club gatherings, town meetings, school board hearings, and other public forums. It's certainly helpful in the college setting, too, where oral reports are becoming a requirement in more and more courses.

A good speech is the result of three elements: preparation, composure, and common sense. If that sounds familiar, it should; in Chapter 9 the same was said of the employment interview. In many respects, the two endeavors are similar. Both are examples of oral communication, both are fairly formal speaking situations, and both place essentially the same demands on you. The main difference, of course, is that in a job interview you're usually speaking to one or two listeners, whereas an oral presentation generally involves addressing a group. After reading this chapter, you should be able to prepare and deliver successful oral presentations.

Preparation

A successful oral presentation nearly always is based on thorough preparation. This involves some preliminary activities followed by actual rehearsal of the speech.

Preliminaries

Preparing for an oral presentation is much like preparing to write. Just as if you were about to compose a memo, letter, or written report, you must first identify your purpose. Are you simply trying to inform your listeners, or are you attempting to entertain them? Are you perhaps seeking to persuade them of something or motivate them to action? In any case, you need a plan that enables you to achieve your goal.

It's crucial to assess your audience. What are your listeners' backgrounds and interests? How about their perspective on your topic? In short, what might influence their expectations or responses? Unless you gear your remarks to your audience, you probably won't connect satisfactorily with your listeners. For example, a mayoral candidate addressing a gathering of senior citizens would be foolish to focus a campaign speech on long-range outcomes the listeners may never live to see. Such a group would respond better to a presentation of the candidate's short-term goals, particularly those related to that audience's immediate concerns—crime prevention, perhaps, or health care. Just as you do in written communications, you must always bear in mind the nature of your audience when preparing your remarks.

It's also helpful to get a look in advance at the room where you will be speaking. This ensures that you'll be somewhat more at ease during the presentation, because you'll be on familiar turf. If you're planning to use audiovisual equipment, you should acquaint yourself with it as well. Nothing is more embarrassing than suddenly discovering that there's no convenient electrical outlet for your overhead projector, or that expected equipment is defective or unavailable. Guard against such setbacks by checking everything when you visit the site beforehand.

Of course you must be thoroughly familiar with your subject matter. Gather information about the topic and assemble an arsenal of facts, figures, and examples to support your statements. This requires some research and homework—an essential part of your preparation. You must know not only how to approach and organize the material but also how to *develop* it. Nobody wants to listen to a speaker who has nothing to say or who rambles on and on with no apparent direction or focus.

Therefore, the opening of your speech must include a clear statement of purpose, informing the audience about what to expect. From there you must follow a logical path, covering your material in a coherent, step-by-step fashion, dealing with one main idea at a time, in an orderly sequence. And, as in written communication, you should provide effective transitions to facilitate progress from point to point. For all this to happen, you must write out your entire speech ahead of time. Because it's best, however, to actually *deliver* the speech from notes or note cards, a finely polished, letter-perfect piece of writing is not absolutely necessary. But you do need to have a well-developed and well-organized draft from which you can select key points and supporting details for your notes or note cards. You must also ensure that your notes or cards are plainly legible so you can glance down and easily see them on the lectern as you deliver the speech. Prepare your notes or cards using a bold, felt-tipped pen, and write substantially larger than you normally do. It's very damaging to your presentation if you have to pause to decipher your own handwriting, or if you have to bend over or pick up your notes or cards to see them clearly. Figure 10.1 is a page from the draft of an oral presentation about various applications of radar technology. Figure 10.2 shows notes based on that same information, and Figure 10.3 depicts note cards.

As we have seen, radar has obvious military value and has been used to detect and track enemy planes, submarines, missiles, and so on. Permanent Ballistic Missile Early Warning Systems (BMEWS) are in place at various strategic locations around the globe: Clear, Alaska; Thule, Greenland; Fylingdale Moor, England; and elsewhere. An impressive recent development is Relocatable Over-the-Horizon Radar (ROTHR), which can bounce high-frequency signals in the 5–28 MHz range off the ionosphere to scan an area from 500 to 1,800 nautical miles away. But radar has many nonmilitary applications as well.

Radar permits astronomers to measure interplanetary distances precisely and to collect much data that otherwise might be unavailable, by obtaining radar echoes from the major bodies of the solar system . . . and deriving as much information as possible from them. Since radar can ascertain surface textures and details and can find objects as small as insects or as large as mountains, it's obviously very useful in making maps of distant, restricted, or otherwise inaccessible places—even planets.

Obviously, radar can be nearly as useful to civilian aviators as it is to the military, by detecting storms and other aircraft and by determining location and altitude. Indeed, one of the first applications of radar was in radio altimeters. And, of course, air traffic controllers use radar extensively to prevent "runway incursions" and other mishaps.

FIGURE 10.1   **Draft Page of an Oral Presentation**

Permanent Ballistic Missile Early
Warning Systems (BMEWS):
   Clear, Alaska
      Thule, Greenland
         Fylingdale Moor, England

Relocatable Over-the-Horizon Radar (ROTHR): bounces
high-frequency signals off ionosphere; can scan areas
500–1,800 nautical miles away.

Astronomers: measure interplanetary distances, collect
solar system data.

Cartographers: make maps—even of planets; can find
objs as small as insects or as large as mts.

Aviators: detect storms, other planes; determine location,
altitude; air traffic control, prevent "runway incursions."

FIGURE 10.2   **Oral Presentation Notes**

Permanent Ballistic Missile Early Warning
Systems (BMEWS):

Clear, Alaska

Thule, Greenland

Fylingdale Moor, England

Relocatable Over-the-Horizon Radar (ROTHR):
bounces high-frequency signals off ionosphere;
can scan areas 500–1,800 naut. miles away.

FIGURE 10.3 Note Cards

Rehearsal

Important as the preliminaries are, rehearsal is the most important part of your preparation. Many people skip this step, figuring they'll wing it when the time comes and rely their wits. Unless you're a very experienced speaker, however, this almost never works. Before attempting to deliver an oral presentation, you *must* practice it. You need not recruit a practice audience (although it certainly helps), but you must at least recite the speech aloud several times. This reveals which parts of the presentation seem the most difficult to deliver and establishes how *long* the speech really is. You don't want to run noticeably shorter or longer than the allotted time, because that would violate the audience's expectations. Remember that speeches tend to run shorter in actuality than in rehearsal; the pressures of live performance generally speed up the delivery. If aiming for a 5-minute presentation, you need 7 or 8 minutes in rehearsal. If you're expected to speak for half an hour, your rehearsal might take 40 to 45 minutes.

In addition to preparing your speech, you must prepare *yourself*. All the commonsense advice presented in Chapter 9 concerning the employment interview applies equally here. Get a good night's sleep. Shower. Eat, but do not consume any alcoholic beverages. Dismiss any troubling thoughts from your mind. Wear clothing appropriate for the occasion. All this preparation will contribute to your general sense of confidence and well-being, thereby helping you develop composure and deliver the presentation to the best of your ability.

Delivery

The key to successfully delivering your oral presentation in public is to relax. Admittedly, this is more easily said than done but not as difficult as it may seem. Most audiences are at least reasonably receptive, so you need not fear them. In the classroom setting, for example, all your listeners will soon be called on to present their own orals or will have done so already. This usually makes them sympathetic and supportive. It's simply not true that everyone in the room is scrutinizing your every word and gesture, hoping you'll perform poorly. (At any given moment, in fact, a certain percentage of the audience is probably not paying attention at all!) Nevertheless, there are several areas of concern you may wish to consider when delivering an oral presentation.

Introductions and Conclusions

Since first impressions are so important, a good oral presentation must begin with an effective introduction. Here are four useful strategies for opening your speech.

- ***Ask the audience a pertinent question.*** This is an effective introduction because it immediately establishes a connection between you and your listeners—especially if somebody responds. But even if no one does, you can provide the answer yourself, thereby leading smoothly into your discussion. In a presentation titled "Tourist Attractions in New York City," for example, you might open with the query, "Does anyone here know the name of the street the Empire State Building is on?"

- ***Describe a situation.*** There's something in human nature that makes us love a story, especially if it involves conflict. The enduring appeal of fairy tales, myths and legends, and even soap operas and sentimental country-western lyrics proves the point. You can capitalize on this aspect of your listeners' collective psychology by opening your presentation with a brief story that somehow relates to your subject. A speaker attempting to explore the dangers of tobacco, for example, might begin like this: "My friend Jane, a wonderful young woman with a bright future, had been smoking a pack a day since tenth grade. Finally, at age 25, she had decided to quit. But when she went to the doctor for her annual physical, she learned that it was already too late. Tragically, Jane died of lung cancer less than a year later."

- ***Present an interesting fact or statistic.*** This will help you grab the audience's attention by demonstrating that you're familiar with your topic. The annual edition of *World Almanac and Book of Facts* is an excellent source of statistical information on diverse topics, but there are many other resources. Any qualified librarian can direct you to government documents, corporate reports, computer databases, and other useful resources. Even though statistics can be deceptive, people like what they perceive as the hard reality of such data and therefore find numbers quite persuasive. A speech intended to demonstrate the need for stricter gun control legislation, for example, might open with the observation, "Every year, there are more than 10,000 handgun-related murders in the United States." Although many Internet sites are untrustworthy, the Internet is another good source of statistics if used judiciously. One useful Internet site is Statistical Resources on the Web at *www.lib.umich.edu/govdocs/stats.html*. Others are Infonation Advanced at *www.cyberschoolbus.un.org/* and the U.S. Department of Labor's Bureau of Labor Statistics at *www.bls.gov/home.htm*.

- ***Use a quotation.*** Get a "Big Name"—Shakespeare, Martin Luther King Jr., the Bible—to speak for you. Find an appropriate saying that will launch your own remarks with flair. Many useful books of quotations exist, but *Bartlett's Familiar Quotations* (available in virtually any good bookstore or library) is the best known, and for good reason. Bartlett includes nearly 100 quotes on the subject of money alone, for example. *Bartlett's* is available—along with *Simpson's Contemporary Quotations* and the *Columbia World of Quotations*—on the Web at *www.bartleby.com/*.

The conclusion to your talk is as important as the introduction. Always sum up when you reach the end of an oral presentation. Repeat your key points and show clearly how they support your conclusion. Like an airplane rolling smoothly to a stop on the runway rather than crashing to the ground after reaching its destination, you should not end abruptly. You can accomplish this by returning the audience to the starting point. When you reach the end of your speech, refer to the question, scenario, fact, statistic, or quotation with which you opened. This creates in your listeners the satisfying sense of having come full circle, returning them to familiar territory.

Another common concluding tactic is to ask whether members of your audience have any questions. If so, you can answer them, and then your work is done. If no questions are forthcoming, the audience has in effect ended the speech for you. Because this creates the sense of a letdown, however, you can instead have an accomplice or two in the audience ask questions to which you have prepared responses in advance. Although staged, this is a common practice among professional speakers. Whatever form of conclusion you choose, always close by thanking the audience for their time and attention.

Vocal Factors

Obviously, the *voice* is the principal instrument of any oral presentation. Therefore, pay attention to your vocal qualities. Speak at a normal rate of speed, neither too fast nor too slow, and at a normal volume, neither too loud nor too soft. Pronounce each word clearly so the audience can understand your entire speech without straining. When using a microphone, be sure it's approximately one foot away from your mouth—any farther, and it may not pick up your voice adequately; any closer, and your overly amplified *b*s and *p*s may create an annoyingly explosive sound. In addition, try to maintain the normal rhythms of everyday conversation. Nothing is more boring than listening to a speech delivered in an unvarying monotone. Conversely, it's irritating to be subjected to an overly theatrical delivery characterized by elaborate gestures or exaggerated vocal effects. The key is to be natural, as if you were speaking to one or two people rather than a whole group.

At the same time, however, an oral presentation is certainly a more formal speaking situation than a social conversation. Therefore, you should provide more examples and illustrations than you ordinarily might, along with more transitional phrases than usual. In addition, make a conscious effort to minimize verbal "ticks," those distracting little mannerisms that characterize everyday speech: *um, y'know, okay? right?*

and the like. Listening to a tape recording of your oral presentation enables you to assess the degree to which you need to work on your vocal mannerisms. Though you don't want to sound stiffly artificial, you should stay away from the more colorful vernacular. Avoid slang, expletives, and conspicuously substandard—"I ain't got no"—grammar. Achieving the right level of formality can be challenging, but practicing the presentation a few times helps.

Physical Factors

Although your voice is obviously important, your audience *sees* you as well as hears you. They respond to your body language as much as to your words. As you would in an employment interview, you must create a favorable physical impression. Get rid of any chewing gum or tobacco long before stepping up to the lectern. Stand up straight behind the lectern; don't slump or lean over it. Control your hand motions. Do not fold your arms, drum with your fingertips, click a ballpoint pen, or cling rigidly to the lectern with a stiff-armed, white-knuckled grip. Refrain from touching your face or hair, tugging at your clothes, or scratching your body. You can gesture occasionally to make a point, but only if such movements are spontaneous, as in casual conversation. In short, your hands should not distract the audience from what you're saying. Your feet, too, can create problems. Resist the tendency to tap your feet, shift from one leg to the other, or stray purposelessly from the lectern. Plant your feet firmly on the floor and stay put.

In the academic setting, your professors (much like many workplace supervisors) may impose certain regulations concerning proper attire for oral presentations. Baseball caps, for example, are sometimes prohibited, along with various other style and dress affectations such as those mentioned in the "Interview" section of Chapter 9. Whether in a college classroom or on the job, you should observe any such guidelines, even if you feel they're overly restrictive.

Eye Contact

As much as possible, *look* at your audience. This is probably the hardest part of public speaking, but it's imperative. Unless you maintain eye contact with audience members, you'll lose their attention. Keep your head up and your eyes directed forward. If you find it impossible to actually look at your listeners, fake it. Look instead at desk tops, chair legs, or the back wall. You must create at least the *illusion* of visual contact.

Holding your listeners' attention is one—although certainly not the only—reason you should absolutely avoid the dreadful error of simply reading to your audience from the text of your speech. Few practices are more boring, more amateurish, or more destructive of audience-speaker rapport. As mentioned in the section on preparation, you should deliver your presentation from notes or note cards rather than from a polished text to force yourself to adopt a more conversational manner. But keep your papers or cards out of sight, lying flat on the lectern. Do not distract the audience by nervously shuffling them.

Audiovisuals

To greatly enhance your oral presentation, consider using audiovisual aids in conjunction with the various visuals (tables, graphs, charts, pictures) discussed in Chapter 4. Audiovisual tools can be helpful to both you and your audience by illustrating key points throughout your talk. If the room where you are speaking is equipped with a chalkboard or dry-erase board, take advantage of it as appropriate. A flip chart—a giant, easel-mounted pad of paper that you write on with felt-tip markers—is another useful option. You may also choose to use large display posters prepared in advance, but you must remember to bring along tape or thumbtacks to secure them for viewing.

Whether using a chalkboard, flip chart, or poster to make your point, remember to position yourself *next to* it, not in front; you must not block the audience's view. Remember to face the audience rather than the display. Be sure your writing is plainly legible from a distance; write in large, bold strokes, using color for emphasis and incorporating the other design principles outlined in Chapter 5. Make sure your drawings and text are easy to see even from the back of the room. Follow this rule of thumb: The image must be at least one-sixth as large as the distance from which it will be seen. For example, a graph viewed from 30 feet should be 5 feet wide.

For lettering, use the following chart:

Distance	Size of Lettering
Up to 10 ft.	¾ in.
20 ft.	1 in.
30 ft.	1¼ in.
40 ft.	1½ in.
50 ft.	1¾ in.
60 ft.	2 in.

Although they require more preparation time, you may want to create slides or transparencies that can be projected onto a screen. They lend your presentation a great deal of credibility by making it much more professional and polished. One advantage is that you can control the size of the images on the screen, enlarging them as necessary to create displays that are easily visible even in a relatively big room.

Here are some basic guidelines to bear in mind when using slides or transparencies in conjunction with an oral presentation:

- Make certain beforehand that your slides are properly inserted in their tray. They must not be reversed, upside down, or out of sequence.

- Do not include too much information on a slide or transparency. Keep it simple. Use brief phrases instead of full sentences, and limit each screen to four or five main points. Similarly, do not use more than two type sizes, fonts, or styles on a given screen. Maintain consistency throughout a presentation, using capitalization, underlining, spacing, and other elements the same way on each screen. Figure 10.4 depicts a series of inconsistently formatted screens, and Figure 10.5 depicts the same screens consistently formatted.

- To draw the audience's attention to a detail on the screen, use a laser pointer rather than a yardstick or conventional pointer, which are effective only for pointing out details on chalkboards, posters, maps, and the like. If you don't have a laser pointer, highlight details by pointing to them on the transparency itself, but be sure to use a pen or freshly sharpened pencil rather than your finger, because the bulky shadow cast by your hand will block too much from view. Presentation software, of course, affords a variety of far more imaginative highlighting methods.

- When adding notations on a transparency during your presentation, be sure to write legibly, using a marker designed for that purpose. Again, software greatly simplifies this procedure.

- Avoid the glaring "empty white screen" effect; turn off your slide or transparency projector once you're done with it, or if you'll not be referring to it for more than a minute or two.

Depending on the length, scope, and topic of your speech, you may decide to supplement your remarks with videotape or sound recordings, provided they're of good quality. Relevant physical objects can also be displayed or passed around. If you were explaining how to tune a guitar, for example, you would certainly want to demonstrate the procedure on an actual instrument. Similarly, if you were explaining the workings of a particular tool or other device, ideally you would provide one (or more) for the audience to examine.

Of all the options available, however, the presentation software packages that have become so popular in recent years are perhaps the most helpful. Some well-known ones are Adobe Persuasion, Corel Presentations, and Lotus Freelance Graphics, but Microsoft PowerPoint is by far the preferred choice. These programs greatly facilitate the creation of tables, graphs, bulleted lists, and other images for use on transparencies and 35-mm slides. The software is at its best, though, when images are exhibited by a liquid crystal display (LCD) projector connected to a laptop or other computer controlled by the speaker. This technology provides a wide variety of type sizes, fonts, colors, clip art, backgrounds, three-dimensional effects, and other format features, as well as sound and animation. In addition, static images and streaming video can be imported from the Internet and other outside sources to create multimedia presentations. Although some training is required to fully exploit the technology's potential, anyone can easily learn the fundamentals. Figures 10.6 through 10.11 depict a series of PowerPoint slides outlining responses to several kinds of workplace emergencies.

Speakers using transparencies with traditional overhead projectors sometimes employ the "slow reveal" strategy, whereby information on a given transparency is projected a bit at a time rather than all at once, gradually adding on to or "building" the content. This can be done in two ways: either by manually superimposing transparencies over one another or by keeping the transparency partially covered with a piece of paper that is slid downward to uncover each section in turn. Thus the audience can concentrate on each point, rather than reading ahead and losing track of the speaker's comments. PowerPoint, of course, can achieve this and other effects electronically, either automatically or in response to mouse clicks or other manual commands from the speaker. This is just one of PowerPoint's many useful features, which include an array of techniques borrowed from Hollywood filmmakers. To move from one slide to the next, for example, PowerPoint is able to "wipe" the screen as if it were a windshield; one image is pushed from view while another moves in behind it. Similarly, the Dissolve option causes the slow fading out of one image and the gradual fading in of its successor, sometimes with a superimposition of images at the midpoint of

CULVERTS

- **Replace/repair**

- **Restore drainage capacity**

- **Return roadway to original elevation**

Drainage Ditches

- Remove Trees and Brush

- Restore Drainage Patterns

- Add Riprap to Control Flow

GATE SYSTEM

- *install locking gates*

- *provide pedestrian access alongside gates*

- *install signs at entry gate*

FIGURE 10.4 Inconsistent Format

CULVERTS

- **Replace/repair**

- **Restore drainage capacity**

- **Return roadway to original elevation**

DRAINAGE DITCHES

- **Remove trees and brush**

- **Restore drainage patterns**

- **Add riprap to control flow**

GATE SYSTEM

- **Install locking gates**

- **Provide pedestrian access alongside gates**

- **Install signs at entry gate**

FIGURE 10.5 **Consistent Format**

RESPONDING TO WORKPLACE EMERGENCIES

FIGURE 10.6   First PowerPoint Slide

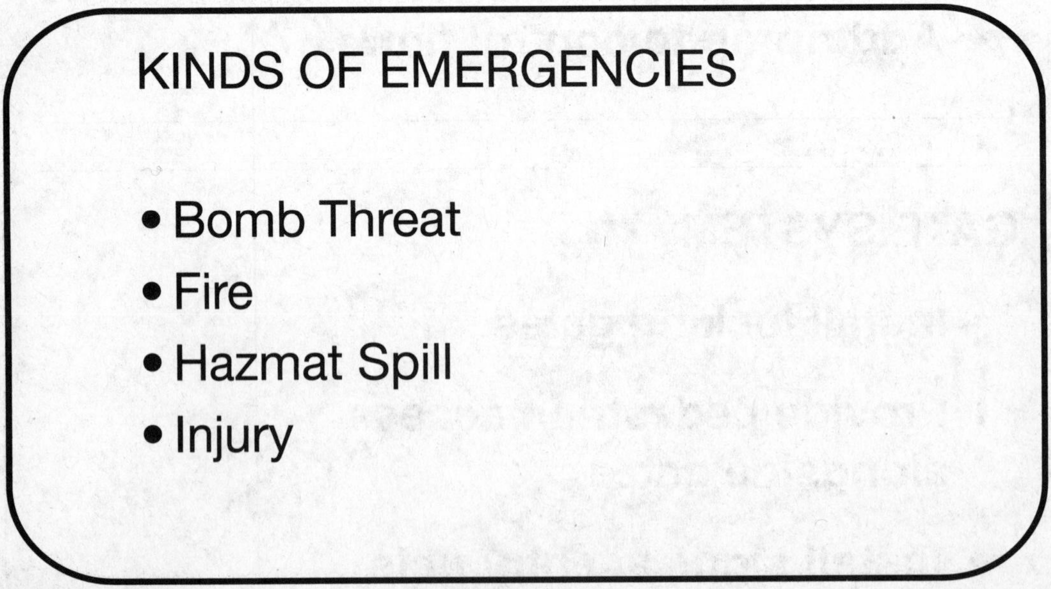

KINDS OF EMERGENCIES

- Bomb Threat
- Fire
- Hazmat Spill
- Injury

FIGURE 10.7   Second PowerPoint Slide

BOMB THREAT

- Get Info from Caller
- Call Fire or Police Department
- Call Security
- Alert Supervisor

FIGURE 10.8 Third PowerPoint Slide

FIRE

- Pull Nearest Alarm
- Use Stairs, NOT Elevators
- Leave Building
- Go to Designated Area

FIGURE 10.9 Fourth PowerPoint Slide

HAZMAT SPILL

- Alert Others in Area
- Get Away from Spill
- Call 911
- Call Security

FIGURE 10.10   **Fifth PowerPoint Slide**

INJURY

- Call 911
- Call Company Nurse
- Call Security
- Provide Aid and Comfort

FIGURE 10.11   **Sixth PowerPoint Slide**

Tech Tips

Here are some basic guidelines for creating an effective PowerPoint presentation:

- Don't get carried away with all the options at your disposal; exercise restraint. As with so many aspects of workplace communications, less is often more.
- Don't allow a patterned, textured, or incompatibly colored background to obscure your text. Use a dark background with light text for projection in a lighted room; use a light background with dark text for projection in a darkened room.
- Use relatively large print for greater legibility: 30- to 34-point for text, 44- to 50-point bold for headings.
- Use consistent formatting features on all slides.
- Avoid large segments of running text. Use lists and outlines instead.
- Include no more than five items of information and no more than 15 words per slide.
- Include no more than 25 slides in any given presentation.
- To guard against technical difficulties, have a backup plan that provides several options. Because not all computers have a CD drive, some will not be compatible with your flash, and some don't have Internet access, both e-mail your PPT presentation to yourself and bring an electronic version on CD and/or flash drive. And bring hard-copy handouts for distribution in case all else fails.

the transition. Among the program's most commonly used capabilities is the Fly In option, which makes a word or image appear to be airborne, "landing" on the screen like a lobbed dart, often accompanied by a sound effect.

A well-crafted PowerPoint component adds a high degree of professionalism to any oral presentation, revealing that the speaker is up-to-date and knowledgeable about current practices. As with any visual components of oral or written communications, however, you should use electronic options selectively and with restraint, not just for the sake of appearing tech-savvy but to genuinely enrich and enhance the content. A common mistake is to overload the presentation with special effects, creating a jumpy, hyperactive quality that deflects the audience's

☑ Checklist   Evaluating a Public Speaker

A good public speaker

___ opens with an interesting, attention-getting introduction;

___ follows a clear and logical pattern of organization;

___ provides enough detail to fully develop the subject;

___ closes with a smooth, satisfying conclusion;

___ speaks in a firm, clear, expressive voice;

___ makes frequent eye contact with the audience;

___ appears physically relaxed and composed, with no distracting mannerisms;

___ maintains an appropriate level of formality, neither too casual nor too solemn;

___ delivers in an alert, engaging manner;

___ satisfies but does not exceed the appropriate length for the presentation.

attention away from the content. An opposite but equally unproductive approach is to outline the entire speech on PowerPoint and then simply read aloud from these too-numerous slides while facing away from the audience. This can literally put listeners to sleep. Instead, you should use PowerPoint slides simply as background, greatly expanding on their content by presenting a fully developed speech delivered in accordance with the established principles of effective public performance. You want your audience to consider PowerPoint not as a substitute for the speech but as a tool for better delivering it. The purpose of any audio-visual aid is to reinforce and clarify, rather than overshadow, the speaker's remarks.

Remember, too, that electronic delivery systems can malfunction or present other unexpected difficulties. If you plan to use PowerPoint in an upcoming presentation, rehearsal (actually using the technology) is even more crucial than it would be otherwise. Even if everything appears to be ready, you should never approach a PowerPoint presentation without a backup plan. It's always a good idea to have a full set of printed copies of your slides to distribute to the audience in case of an equipment failure or other last-minute problem.

Enthusiasm

Try to deliver your oral presentations in a lively, upbeat, enthusiastic manner. This actually makes your job easier, since a positive attitude on your part will help to foster a more receptive attitude on the part of the audience. If your listeners sense that you'd rather be elsewhere, they will probably "tune out." When that occurs, you receive no encouraging feedback, and knowing you've lost your audience makes it even more difficult to continue. If you sense, however, that the audience is following along, this reinforcement in turn fuels your performance. That cannot happen, however, unless you project in an engaging way. From the start, *you* establish the tone. Therefore, it makes sense to adopt a positive attitude when giving an oral presentation, not only for the audience's sake but also to serve your own purposes.

The many factors that contribute to a good delivery may seem like a lot to keep track of. If you're like most speakers, however, you probably have real difficulty in only one or two areas. An especially useful strategy is to videotape your rehearsal to determine what you should work on to improve your delivery. As stated at the start of the chapter, a successful oral presentation is the result of preparation, composure, and common sense. If you take seriously the recommendations offered in this chapter and practice the strategies and techniques suggested, your performance as a public speaker will improve greatly.

Exercises

■ EXERCISE 10.1

Prepare and deliver a 5- to 10-minute oral presentation on one of the following autobiographical topics:

- A Childhood Memory
- My Brush with Danger
- An Angry Moment
- A Very Satisfying Accomplishment
- My Career Goals
- What I Expect My Life to Be Like in Ten Years

■ EXERCISE 10.2

Prepare and deliver a 5- to 10-minute oral presentation that summarizes a book, article, lecture, film, or television broadcast related to your field of study or employment (see Chapter 6).

■ EXERCISE 10.3

Prepare and deliver a 5- to 10-minute oral presentation that provides a specific mechanism description related to your field of study or employment (see Chapter 7). Present an actual example of such a mechanism, along with any audiovisual aids that may be helpful to your audience.

■ EXERCISE 10.4

Prepare and deliver a 5- to 10-minute oral presentation describing a process related to your field of study or employment (see Chapter 7). Present any audiovisual aids that may be helpful to your audience.

■ EXERCISE 10.5

Prepare and deliver a 5- to 10-minute oral presentation describing a procedure related to your field of study or employment (see Chapter 7). Present any audiovisual aids that may be helpful to your audience.

■ EXERCISE 10.6

Prepare and deliver a 5- to 10-minute oral presentation providing instructions related to your field of study or employment (see Chapter 8). Present any audiovisual aids that may be helpful to your audience.

■ EXERCISE 10.7

Prepare and deliver a 5- to 10-minute oral presentation based on Exercise 5.10. Present any audiovisual aids that may be helpful to your audience.

■ EXERCISE 10.8

Prepare and deliver a 5- to 10-minute oral presentation based on Exercise 7.18. Present any audiovisual aids that may be helpful to your audience.

■ EXERCISE 10.9

Prepare and deliver a 5- to 10-minute oral presentation based on Exercise 8.8. Present any audiovisual aids that may be helpful to your audience.

■ EXERCISE 10.10

Prepare and deliver a 5- to 10-minute oral presentation based on Exercise 9.4. Present any audiovisual aids that may be helpful to your audience.

11

Proposals

Learning Objective   When you complete this chapter you'll be able to use standard procedures to write successful solicited and unsolicited proposals.

- ▢ **Solicited Proposals**
- ▢ **Unsolicited Proposals**
- ▢ **Internal and External Proposals**
- ▢ **Formats of Proposals**
- ▢ **Objectives of Proposals**
    Checklist: Evaluating a Proposal

Exercises

L ike the various other kinds of workplace writing, proposals are a major example of business communication. Simply put, a proposal is a persuasive offer intended to secure authorization to perform a task or provide products or services that will benefit the reader. There are basically two kinds of proposals: solicited and unsolicited (that is, requested and unrequested). But there are sub-categories within those broad divisions, including internal and external proposals. This is not really as complicated as it seems, however, because the conventions governing proposal writing are well-established and quite logical. This chapter explores these issues and provides examples of solicited and unsolicited proposals.

Solicited Proposals

In this case the business, agency, or organization seeking proposals has already identified a situation or problem it wishes to address. Accordingly, it issues an RFP (request for proposal) that spells out the details of the project and provides instructions to outsiders for submitting bids. RFPs, many of which are quite lengthy and complex, commonly appear in trade publications, as government releases, and on the Internet. An individual or organization wishing to compete for a particular contract must craft a proposal that will convincingly demonstrate its superiority to the many others received.

In one sense, however, responding to an RFP is easier than writing an unsolicited proposal, because the problem or goal has already been established and there is no need to convince anyone of its existence or importance. In addition, the RFP usually provides explicit instructions regarding the format, design, and content of the proposal, so those requirements—which must be followed exactly—are already in place. Figures 11.1 and 11.2 show an RFP issued by a local government, soliciting bids for air-conditioning work on a city-owned building.

Unsolicited Proposals

In this case the proposal originates with the writer, who has perceived a problem or need that the writer's expertise might be able to remedy. Although an unsolicited proposal may face no direct competition, it's more challenging to compose because it must convince the reader of the potential benefits. In short, it must be more strategically persuasive than a solicited proposal, whose acceptance or rejection is often based largely

RFP Due Date: 12/23/2005
RFP Number: 2004–069

**CITY OF LEWISTON
REQUEST FOR PROPOSALS
CITY HALL BUILDING AIR QUALITY/HVAC SYSTEM STUDY**

INTRODUCTION:

The City of Lewiston is requesting proposals from qualified engineer consultant(s) to provide engineering services to complete an Air Quality/Heat/Ventilation/Air Conditioning System Study for the Lewiston City Building. The City Building is located on the corner of Park Street and Pine Street at 27 Pine Street. The facility is owned and operated by the City of Lewiston.

SCOPE OF SERVICES:

There are numerous problems with the existing City Building system including air quality, heat loss, air temperature control problems, etc. The City is soliciting the services of an engineering consultant(s) to inspect and evaluate the condition of the existing facility and to make recommendations for system modifications to the facility's HVAC system and building to enhance air quality, safety and energy efficiency. The study shall provide a phased approach, which will provide prioritized recommendations with cost estimates for various elements of the plan.

The engineering consultant(s) will work with representatives from the City's Building Division, Department of Public Services during the study. Significant input from several department representatives currently working in the City Building would be required throughout the study process.

The study will evaluate the following issues:

1. The current HVAC system is actually designed and built in three different phases. The third floor HVAC system was completed as part of the third floor renovation project completed in 2001. The third floor AC unit was replaced in 2001. The second floor system is part of the original heating system with the addition of AC wall units. The first floor heating system was built during the renovation project completed in 1990 and 1992 with cooling added in 1995. All these systems have problems. This study would look at all the systems and issues and recommend the best way to remediate the problems.

2. The ceiling on the third floor is a suspended ceiling with fiberglass insulation. Over the years the insulation has moved, been water damaged and lead paint has fallen from the fourth floor ceiling. It has lost most of its effectiveness in insulating the ceiling, resulting in tremendous heat loss. The heat loss has also created a condition, which allows for the formation of ice dams along the roof edge. This condition has created extensive water damage over the years to the interior walls and ceilings. The engineer will include as part of their recommendations how the City can best deal with the lead paint and how best to address the heat loss through the ceiling.

3. The current first floor heat and cooling system is now set up to either heat or cool. The conversion happens twice a year. During the spring and fall seasons, the temperature can vary, creating a situation where one day you need heat and the next you need to cool. Modifications to the existing system would allow conversion of the system at any time.

4. The Park Street and Pine Street entrances now have inadequate heating and cooling systems. This creates problems for the first floor because the double doors in the hallway need to be left open, which makes it difficult to maintain a comfortable environment. The engineer will recommend how best to improve this situation.

5. The second floor is now using wall mounted air conditioning units. The units are constantly being replaced, not very energy efficient, noisy and ineffective in cooling the workspace. The City expects a new central air conditioning system would enhance the working environment, reduce unit replacement and energy costs. The engineer will evaluate the feasibility and cost associated with doing this.

6. The third floor MIS offices and Pine street end of the building are using wall mounted air conditioning units and in some working spaces, they do not have any AC. The units are constantly being replaced, not very energy efficient, noisy and ineffective in cooling the workspace. The city expects a new central air conditioning system would enhance the working environment, reduce unit replacement and energy costs. The engineer will evaluate the feasibility and cost associated with doing this.

7. If at anytime during the study the engineering consultant(s) discovers an issue not listed above that may improve air quality, energy efficiency and other related issues, he/she shall submit a proposal to complete additional evaluations including cost estimate to the Director of Public Buildings. The City will review your proposal and respond yes or no as soon as possible.

Funding for this study will be provided from a City bond issue.

AVAILABLE INFORMATION:

The selected engineering consultant(s) will be provided a copy, if requested, of the original building construction plans and specifications for third floor and first floor renovation projects. The City does not have plans or specification for the construction of the original building. The City's Building Division, Department of Public Services shall provide all field support services needed to complete the study.

SCHEDULE:

Receive Proposals from Engineering Consultant(s)	December 23, 2004
Short List Engineering Consultant(s)	January 7, 2005
Recommendation of Selection Review Committee	January 18, 2005
Finance Committee Approval	January 24, 2005
Issue Notice to Award	January 25, 2005

FIGURE 11.1 **Request for Proposal** (Courtesy of the City of Lewiston)

Execute Contract   January 28, 2005
Stan Work   January 31, 2005
Study Completion Date   June 1,   2005

SELECTION:

The process for selection of a engineering consultant(s), as outlined in the tentative work schedule, will consist of interested engineering consultant(s) submitting proposals. The Selection Review Committee (SRC) will review the proposals, shortlist the engineering consultant(s) and may interview the shortlisted firms. The Selection Review Committee (SRC) will consist of the Director of Public Buildings, Director of Public Services, Director of Budget/Purchasing and the Building Maintenance Superintendent. The SRC will make a recommendation to the Finance Committee for award of the Contract.

The engineer consultant(s) shall address the proposed scope of services, including their approach, personnel who will do the work, in-house technical review and ability to meet the project schedule. Also, the engineering consultant(s) shall submit information helpful in evaluating the engineering consultant(s), such as experience, qualifications, references and the ability to work effectively with the involved parties.

The engineering consultant's proposal(s) shall discuss in sufficient detail the steps that the engineering consultant(s) will take to arrive at the desired results. The discussion shall be important for the selection process. The City of Lewiston reserves the right to solicit additional information from the engineering consultant(s) or their references and to refuse any or all proposals.

Each responding engineering consultant(s) will be ranked according to the City's evaluation of his/her proposal, qualifications based on experience and other information.

The SRC will use the following criteria in evaluating the proposals:

1. A successful record in completing similar projects to the one described in this RFP.

2. The quality and depth of the engineering consultant(s) team's applicable experience and expertise, especially with development of similar projects.

3. A list of relevant projects with the name, address and telephone number of a contact person to check references.

4. The ability of the engineering consultant(s) to complete the work as outlined in the schedule based on current and projected workload.

5. The firm's ability to maintain an appropriate relationship with the City, including working on the project with in-house personnel.

6. Resumes of the personnel who may be assigned to this project, including relevant experience

7. Other factors that would be helpful to the SRC in evaluating the engineering consultant(s) for this project.

8. Qualifications of sub-consultants similar to that described in item numbers one (1) through seven (7).

FEE STATEMENT:

Each proposal shall include a sealed fee statement under separate cover for the work to be performed. The fee statement shall include a cost for each of the tasks to complete the work outlined in the Scope of Services and additional tasks the consultant(s) feels are necessary to complete the work. The fee statement will not be opened until the engineering consultant(s) have been rated. The engineering consultant(s) may modify, combine or otherwise change the tasks in the Scope of Services as they see fit in order to meet the needs of the City. The engineering consultant(s) shall be paid on an hourly or per diem rate plus direct expenses with a "not to exceed" amount. The engineering consultant(s) shall break down the proposed labor cost for each task by hours for each person involved in that phase or task. To this shall be added any direct cost and the overhead cost for that phase or task.

The City reserves the right to negotiate with the engineering consultant(s) to determine the amount of work and fees to be included in the contract. The fee statement shall include a schedule of fees on a per diem or hourly basis for each of the key personnel and sub-contractors, as wall as a schedule of other basic costs, should additional services be necessary. The engineering consultant(s) should estimate the nature and cost of additional services deemed necessary to complete the project.

CONCLUSION:

Proposals will be received at the Office of the Director of Budget/Purchasing, City Building, 27 Pine St., Lewiston, Maine04240 until 4:30 P.M. on December 23, 2004. The consultant/airchitect(s) shall submit Five (5) copies of the proposals and one sealed fee statement (under separate cover). Proposals will not be opened until after the submittal deadline.

If you are interested in being considered for this work and wish to discuss the work in more detail or have questions, you may contact Mike Paradis P. E., Director Of Public Buildings (207) 784-5753 (ext. 203), or Norman Beauparlant, Director of Budget/Purchasing (207) 784-2951 (ext, 222).

The City of Lewiston prohibits discrimination and/or the exclusion of individuals from its municipal facilities, programs, activities and services based on the individual person's race, national origin, color, creed, religion, sex, age, disability, veteran status or inability to speak English. Individuals requiring auxiliary aids, modifications, interpreter or translation services in order to access the City's facilities or to participate in programs, activities or services should contact the City's Antidiscrimination Compliance Coordinator: Michael Paradis, Telephone: 784-5753, Ext. 203; TDD/TTY: 784-5999, FAX 777-4621. Such requests should provide, where possible, a minimum of 72 hours advance notice. All such auxiliary aids shall be free of charge. IN CASES WHERE THE COMPLIANCE COORDINATOR IS NOT AVAILABLE, ALL CONTACTS SHOULD BE DIRECTED TO THE CITY ADMINISTRATOR.

FIGURE 11.2 Request for Proposal (Courtesy of the City of Lewiston)

on cost and time projections as well as the writer's credentials and track record on similar projects, all of which is fairly objective information.

Internal and External Proposals

Like most other kinds of business writing, a proposal—solicited or not—may be either an in-house document or an external one.

Internal Proposals: These are often rather short because the writers and readers are already known to each other, and the context is mutually understood. Solicited in-house proposals are not usually written in response to a formal RFP, but rather to a direct assignment from a manager, supervisor, or other administrator. Unsolicited in-house proposals are motivated by an employee's own perception of need—for example, the belief that a particular policy or procedure should be adopted, modified, or abandoned.

External Proposals: As mentioned previously, solicited external proposals are nearly always in response to formal RFPs, but unsolicited external proposals—more difficult to create—obviously are not. External proposals are motivated primarily by the desire for financial reimbursement. In effect, they might almost be seen as a form of employment application.

Formats of Proposals

If in-house, short proposals usually take the form of a memo, e-mail, or memo report; if external, they are typically sent as a letter. Longer, more fully-developed proposals can include many sections and very much resemble long reports, and are sometimes written collaboratively (see Chapter 12). Actually, then, there are eight kinds of proposals, as Figure 11.3 illustrates.

Objectives of Proposals

Irrespective of whether a proposal is solicited or unsolicited, internal or external, short or long, it should accomplish several objectives, some of which may overlap:

- Clearly summarize the situation or problem that the proposal is addressing. If unsolicited, the proposal must convince the reader that there is in fact an important unmet need.

	SOLICITED	**UNSOLICITED**
INTERNAL short	short	short
INTERNAL long	long	long
EXTERNAL short	short	short
EXTERNAL long	long	long

FIGURE 11.3

Categories of Proposals

- Provide a detailed explanation of how the proposal will correct the situation or problem. This is sometimes called the "project description" and it typically contains several parts.
- Confirm the feasibility of the project and the anticipated benefits of completing it, as well as possible negative consequences of not doing so.
- Convincingly refute any probable objections.
- Establish the writer's credentials and qualifications for the project.
- Identify any necessary resources, equipment, or support.
- Provide a reliable timeline for completion of the project. A Gantt chart (see Chapter 4) is sometimes used for this.
- Provide an honest, itemized estimate of the costs. Deliberately understating the timeline or the budget is not only unethical (see Chapter 1) but also fraudulent. Doing so can incur legal liability.
- Close with a strong conclusion that will motivate the reader to accept the proposal. A convincing cost/benefit analysis is helpful here.

As mentioned in earlier chapters, workplace communications must always be sensitive to considerations of audience, purpose, and tone. But this is especially important in proposal writing because of its fundamentally persuasive nature. A proposal writer must be alert to the differing requirements of upward, lateral, downward, and outward communication. The phrasing should be reader-centered, using the "you" approach. And because by definition proposals seek to improve conditions by rectifying problems, it's important that they remain positive and upbeat in tone. The writer must refrain from assigning blame for existing difficulties and should instead focus on solutions. This is especially important when writing in-house, where a hostile climate can result if the writer neglects to consider people's needs and feelings, particularly if the proposal's recommendations might alter or otherwise affect the responsibilities of co-workers or departments.

Like any workplace document, a proposal is far more likely to succeed if well-written. Nothing tarnishes credibility more quickly than careless typos and basic errors in spelling, punctuation, or grammar. In addition, workplace writing should always be accurate, clear, and well-organized. And the wording should be simple, direct, and concise, using active verbs and everyday vocabulary, with no rambling, wordy expression. The crucial point to remember is that no amount of study from a textbook will enable you to compose your best writing on the first try. Any professional writer will tell you that the key is to revise, revise, and revise. And, finally, proofread—carefully.

In addition, a proposal should look inviting. As explained in Chapter 5, our ability to comprehend what we read is greatly influenced by its physical arrangement on the page or screen. We see a document—forming an involuntary subconscious opinion of it—before beginning to actually read. Obviously, a positive initial impression goes a long way toward fostering a more receptive attitude in a reader. Therefore, strive for a visually appealing page design by applying the principles outlined in Chapter 5.

Figures 11.4–11.25 present several sample proposals:

- A proposal from a student to her instructor, regarding a topic for her long report assignment
- A proposal from an employee to her supervisor, regarding improvements to the company's day care facilities
- A proposal from a landscaping company to a real estate agency, regarding improvements to the agency's grounds
- A proposal from a community group to a fund-granting agency, regarding improvements to a trail system in a local park

All of these are good examples of various formats, situations, and kinds of proposals.

Bayonne Technical College
Bayonne, New Jersey 07002

MEMORANDUM

DATE: 15 October 2008

TO: Professor Wade Rosenberg
          English Department

FROM: Tabitha Roetz
          Student, EN 110 (Section 034)

RE: Long Report Proposal

As you know, I am pursuing an A.O.S. degree in Rail Transportation Technology and am enrolled in your EN 110 (Workplace Communications) class to partially fulfill my English requirement. We have been assigned to submit a short proposal identifying our choice of topic for the long report due at the end of the semester, along with a brief outline of the report, a preliminary bibliography, and a timeline for completion. Here's my proposal.

Report Topic: Five Major Railway Museums in the United States

Outline: Introduction

                 1 - B & O Railroad Museum (Baltimore MD)

                 2 - California State Railroad Museum (Sacramento CA)

                 3 - Henry Ford Museum at Greenfield Village (Dearborn MI)

                 4 - Railroad Hall at Smithsonian Institution's Museum of
                     History & Technology (Washington DC)

                 5 - Steamtown National Historic Site (Scranton PA)

                 Conclusion

FIGURE 11.4   Solicited Internal Proposal, Page 1

Roetz, pg. 2

Preliminary Bibliography:	www.borail.org
	www.csrmf.org
	www.hfmgv.org
	www.americanhistory.si.edu
	www.nps.gov/stea
Timeline:	Oct. 20–Nov. 23: Research
	Nov. 24: Individual Conference
	Nov. 25–Dec. 10: Writing
	Dec. 11–13: Editing/Revising
	Dec. 14: Report Due

My report will focus on the history of each museum, along with its holdings and special features. Having personally visited each of these sites at least once during family vacations over the past several years, I am well acquainted with the topic and can illustrate the report with photos from my own collection. In addition, I have numerous books, brochures, flyers, and other promotional materials that I can use to supplement my bibliography.

Given my longtime interest in the subject, I'm confident I can do a good job with this topic, and I'm hoping you'll approve it. Please contact me if you need any further information. My student e-mail account is troetz.stu@btc.edu, and of course I can discuss this with you after class or during your office hours in Sisson Hall.

FIGURE 11.5   **Solicited Internal Proposal, Page 2**

RASCO INCORPORATED

Scudder Boulevard

Hyde Park, NY 12538

www.rascoinc@aol.com

MEMO

DATE: May 22, 2008

TO: Jim Sandiford
             Site Director

FROM: Maureen Noble
             Day Care Supervisor

SUBJECT: Day Care Proposal

As you know, Rasco Incorporated's free day care program has been a major factor in enabling the company to attract and retain a dependable, highly skilled workforce in a very competitive industry.

As you always say, however, "Good can always be better." Therefore, I have a proposal that would, if accepted, greatly improve our day care program.

The day care room itself leaves nothing to be desired. Bright, roomy, and fully equipped with everything needed, it's a model of what a day care facility should look like. And my two part-time workers, Patty and Michelle, are both excellent.

In the nice weather, however, there's not much for the children to do outdoors. We often bring them outside and let them run around or play soccer in the grassy area alongside the parking lot, but that's not fully appropriate for the really young ones, and there's always the danger factor to consider. What if somebody lost control of a car?

My proposal is to install a small playground surrounded by a sturdy chainlink fence and equipped with a picnic table and a manufactured play structure with swinging, sliding, and climbing accessories. One of us could still monitor the soccer players in the area behind the building while the others supervised the playground.

FIGURE 11.6   **Unsolicited Internal Proposal, Page 1**

Noble, pg. 2

The equipment could be installed in one day by our own maintenance personnel, although the fence would have to be erected by its supplier. The long-
established Valla's Fencing in nearby Poughkeepsie tells me they could do a
job this size (roughly 40 ft. by 50 ft.) in a couple of days.

Obviously, this would all cost some money, but I really think it would be a
wise investment. Here's a tentative budget, which I've estimated after re-
searching playground equipment on the Internet and at local stores, and after
pricing fence costs and installation charges at several local fencing companies
(including Valla's, whose quote was the lowest).

play set	$ 1000.
picnic table	100.
surface sand	150.
chainlink fence	3750.
Total	$ 5000.

Thanks very much for considering this proposal. I'll be happy to discuss it
with you in greater detail if you wish.

FIGURE 11.7 Unsolicited Internal Proposal, Page 2

GREEN THUMB
LANDSCAPING AND LAWNCARE

929 Lewis Road · Vanderpool, NY 13417
(315) 555–1234

May 12, 2008

Ms. Mary G. Chesebro
Chesebro Realty
21 West Main Street
Vanderpool, NY 13417

Dear Ms. Chesebro:

As you know, we have been maintaining the lawns at your business for several years, and everything looks very nice. But we have a suggestion about how we could make your grounds even more attractive.

During our weekly visits we've noticed that several of the trees surrounding the building might benefit from professional attention. Our proposal is as follows:

General Tree Work

Prune blue spruce located at left front of building according to following specifications:

- Remove all dead, diseased, and broken branches that are 1" in diameter and larger throughout crown to improve health and appearance and reduce risk of branch failure

- Reduce height approximately 8 to 10 feet to reduce risk of branch, stem, and/or root failure $275.

Prune Norway spruce located at left rear of building according to following specifications:

- Prune structurally to reduce risk of branch failure

- Subordinate co-dominant leader, remove dead and broken branches $165.

FIGURE 11.8   **Unsolicited External Proposal, Page 1**

Soil Management

Treat blue spruce, hemlock at right side of building, and hemlock behind parking area with slow-release fertilizer to help improve health following damage from site conditions, insects, and disease $ 265.

Total Amount: $ 705.

Here is the site plan:

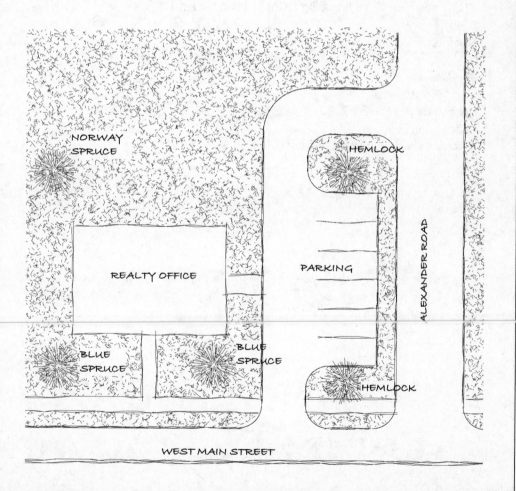

All Green Thumb Landscaping and Lawncare jobs are performed in a professional manner by highly trained workers provided with state-of-the-art tools and equipment. In addition, we clean up after every job, removing all wood, brush, and debris. We carry full liability insurance, and all our employees are covered by workers' compensation.

If you wish to discuss this proposal, please contact our office at your convenience. If you accept, we will send you a contract to sign and return.

Thank you very much for being a Green Thumb client!

Sincerely,

Elvir Vlasic

Elvir Vlasic
Office Manager
(e-mail: evlasic @greenthumb.com)

FIGURE 11.10 Unsolicited External Proposal, Page 3

ETHANTON STRIDERS
RUNNING CLUB

P.O. Box 4141 · Ethanton, VT 05201
www.etntnstriders@aol.com

March 16, 2009

Ms. Elizabeth Cortwright, Director
Ethanton Philanthropic Foundation
2600 Allen Boulevard
Ethanton, VT 05201

Dear Ms. Cortwright:

In response to the Ethanton Philanthropic Foundation's recent RFP focusing on local outdoor development projects, the Ethanton Striders Running Club is submitting the enclosed proposal which, as you will see, concerns the rehabilitation of the deteriorated footpath in the wooded area of Ethanton City Park.

For several years our club has been formulating plans to rehab this trail. The project will involve three phases. At this point we are requesting a matching grant of $20,000 from the Foundation to complete the first part of the project, which includes the following:

- Creation of a defining entrance vista and increased visibility; improving security of pavilion area by means of landscaping, tree & brush removal, and signage

- Installation of two locking gates—one near the pavilion and one below—to restrict vehicle access (except for service vehicles) while allowing easy entrance for pedestrians

- Improved drainage provisions above and near the pavilion

- Upgrade of existing pavilion parking area

- Resurfacing of roadway leading to the entrance

As a running club, we are obviously concerned with improving the trail for that activity. But the trail offers opportunities for many other outdoor activities as well: hiking, bicycling, bird-watching, cross-country skiing, snowshoeing, and the like. Unfortunately, the present conditions make the trail quite unsafe and inhibit full use. These conditions may eventually cause the trail to be closed to the public. The Striders are committed to preventing this, because we see the trail as an important community resource that must be preserved.

FIGURE 11.11 **Solicited External Proposal (Cover Letter, Page 1)**

Your RFP lists many specific guidelines that cannot be discussed here, but all are fully addressed in the body of the proposal.

Having secured the endorsement of the mayor's office and several other local organizations, we are confident that we can succeed with this project and are hoping that you will afford our proposal all due consideration. If you have any questions, please call me at 555-1234 or e-mail me at frdgrs71@aol.com.

Thanks very much for your time.

Sincerely,

Frank Rodgers

Frank Rodgers, President
Ethanton Striders Running Club

FIGURE 11.12 Solicited External Proposal (Cover Letter, Page 2)

CITY PARK
TRAIL RESTORATION
PROPOSAL

Submitted to

Ms. Elizabeth Cortwright, Director
Ethanton Philanthropic Foundation

by

Ethanton Striders
Running Club

March 16, 2009

FIGURE 11.13 Solicited External Proposal (Title Page)

CONTENTS

FIGURE 11.14 Solicited External Proposal (Table of Contents)

PROJECT SUMMARY

For several years the Ethanton Striders Running Club has been formulating plans to rehabilitate the deteriorating footpath in the wooded area of Ethanton City Park. The project will involve three phases. At this point we are requesting a matching grant of $20,000 from the Foundation to complete the first part of the project, which includes enhancement of the entrance to the woods, in part by installing gates and repaving the roadway. Funding for the second and third parts of the project will be sought from other nongovernmental sources.

PROJECT DESCRIPTION

Originally a carriage path, the present trail took shape as a Works Progress Administration (WPA) project during the Great Depression and enjoyed considerable popularity until fairly recently. Now, however, natural deterioration has taken its toll and the trail is endangered. Broken culverts and clogged drainage ditches have allowed water runoff to erode the trail, and in many places the road surface is badly damaged. In short, potentially unsafe conditions are inhibiting full use of the trail and may eventually cause it to be closed.

The Striders are committed to preventing this because we see the trail as an important community resource that must be protected. We envision a return to the trail's former diverse-use status. We want the trail to remain a resource for running and other outdoor sports, but we are hopeful that the proposed improvements will also afford a broad range of other nonmotorized leisure opportunities as well.

As mentioned previously, we envision a three-part plan:

Phase One

- Creating a defining entrance vista and increased visibility; improving security of pavilion area by landscaping, tree and brush removal, and signage

- Installing two locking gates—one near the pavilion and one below—to restrict vehicle access while allowing pedestrian access

- Improving drainage provisions above and near the pavilion

- Upgrading of existing pavilion parking area

- Resurfacing of roadway leading to the entrance

FIGURE 11.15 Solicited External Proposal, Page 1

Phase Two

- Replacing and backfilling 15 unsalvageable drainage culverts

- Cleaning out and repairing 7 additional salvageable culverts

- Boxing out and grading area around all 22 culverts

- Placing 2 inches of Type 3 binder to stabilize area around all 22 culverts in preparation for paving trail

- Cleaning out drainage ditches alongside trail.

Phase Three

- Installing riprap (filler stone) to inhibit water runoff

- Applying two layers of surfacing—a base and a covering of fine stone mixed with rolled petroleum slurry—all along the trail

- Paving entire two miles (10,560 linear feet) of trail, 8 feet across, with 1/2-inch of true and 1 inch of top macadam

RATIONALE

This project is currently the Striders' top priority for several reasons. A not-for-profit citizens' organization, we are dedicated to promoting physical fitness through running, and the trail plays a significant role in that endeavor. It comprises a major part of the annual Autumn Leaves 10k Roadrace course, and of the summer Thursday Training Runs course as well. The Autumn Leaves is a premier competitive running event and was recently featured in an article in *Runner's Times* magazine. Attracting participants from all over the Northeast, the Autumn Leaves pumps many thousands of dollars into the local economy the second weekend of every October. The family-oriented Thursday Training Runs are a long-established, ongoing series of weekly "fun runs" enjoyed by hundreds of local participants on 12 consecutive Thursday evenings during the months of May, June, and July.

But the importance of our project extends far beyond these two events, because the City Park trail is used year-round for a wide variety of nonvehicular recreational activities: hiking, bicycling, bird-watching, cross-country skiing, snow-shoeing, and the like. The Striders believe that the project will foster positive and

FIGURE 11.16 Solicited External Proposal, Page 2

significant changes in the community, ones that identify and enhance local strengths and that focus on identifiable outcomes that will make a difference. Our goals are quite clearly defined and—if achieved—will certainly impact most favorably on the quality of life here in Ethanton. Now that the area is undergoing something of a revitalization, we wish to contribute an additional dimension by championing a renewed commitment to one of our city's most valuable resources—the City Park Trail.

RFP CRITERIA

The Ethanton Philanthropic Foundation's RFP includes specific criteria by which each proposal will be judged. What follows is a point-by-point response to these parameters.

Describe the degree to which the project provides for enhanced public enjoyment of outdoor amenities in the greater Ethanton area.

Despite its deteriorated condition, the City Park Trail is used on a year-round basis. It is used primarily for running, hiking, and bicycling during the non-winter months of April through October. From November through March, the trail is used by cross-country skiers and snowshoers. The trail is central to the Thursday Training Runs series from May through July, to the annual Autumn Leaves 10k Roadrace every October, and to several other fund-raising running events. Our proposal will ensure that these activities will continue without fear of injuries caused by poor footing or surface conditions. In addition, the project will again provide the high school cross-country ski and running teams with a natural training site entirely within city limits. Until recently the school had used the trail in this way, but for the past three years school officials have considered the trail too unsafe. This has forced the ski team to travel to Little Davos Mountain (some 15 miles away) to practice, creating added expense.

Describe the degree to which the project furthers a specific goal of state, regional, or local planning bodies.

The Ethanton City Council has officially identified the City Park Trail problem as a high-priority issue. The Striders Board of Directors has been working closely with the Mayor's office about this, and we have received assurances of

FIGURE 11.17 **Solicited External Proposal, Page 3**

full cooperation. (See Appendix.) Indeed, at least some of the work involved will almost certainly be performed *pro bono* by Ethanton Parks Department personnel.

Specify the project's Index of Need (statistically driven rating assigned by Regional Grants Office).

The Regional Grants Office has assigned a preliminary rating of 78.

Describe the degree of citizen involvement in project conception and implementation.

The project is under the direction of the Ethanton Striders Running Club, a 200+ member not-for-profit citizens' organization whose mission is to promote health and fitness through running. Other citizens' groups from the greater Ethanton area have committed resources toward the completion of the project. Members of the Striders will provide project administration and supervision. In addition, a volunteer group consisting of employees of a large local business will provide equipment and operators for much of the tree removal, drainage ditch clearing, and drainage restoration. As mentioned previously, it is expected that additional assistance (engineering and oversight) will be provided by the City Parks Department.

Describe the degree to which the project relates to other Ethanton-area initiatives (natural, cultural, historical, or recreational).

City Park, located entirely within Ethanton city limits, is a large recreation area comprising a pavilion, a nine-hole municipal golf course, tennis courts, and playing fields. Until its deterioration, the trail through the wooded area was an integral part of this multi-use park. It is our intention to restore the trail to provide a safe environment for runners, hikers, bicyclists, cross-country skiers, and snowshoers, thereby promoting greater citizen enjoyment of the natural world. The trail in question connects to other park roads, which are currently shared-use roadways for nonmotorized and motorized access to park facilities.

Describe the degree to which volunteer labor, nontraditional labor, and other certified donations will be used to accomplish the project's goals.

FIGURE 11.18 Solicited External Proposal, Page 4

At least three area citizens' organizations, the Striders included, have committed resources to the completion of the trail restoration project. Two of the three will provide a considerable amount of volunteer labor and equipment. The third organization has committed up to $20,000 in financial support, pending approval of this proposal by the Ethanton Philanthropic Foundation. In addition, the Striders are able to call upon an extensive list of volunteers who have signed up to help during other club-sponsored initiatives. A community service group affiliated with a large local corporation will supply heavy equipment and operators for much of the work.

Describe the impact the proposal will have on the cultural, social, and recreational needs of the region.

As mentioned in several other parts of this proposal, the trail restoration project is specifically designed to serve the recreational needs of the region, by ensuring the continuation of the Thursday Training Runs, the Autumn Leaves Roadrace, and other community-oriented running events. In addition, successful completion of the project will greatly enhance the opportunities for recreational running, hiking, cross-country skiing, bicycling, and snowshoeing. And restoration of the trail will permit its use by the Ethanton High School cross-country ski and running teams. In addition, we expect that the refurbished trail will invite use by bird-watchers and other nature lovers, as part of the existing system of interlocking trails within the park.

TIMELINE

Obviously, any scheduling projections for a project of this scope must be tentative at best, because the project depends on several variables including funding and weather. The Striders are hoping to secure adequate financing through a variety of means (see Budget section of this proposal), but this may take longer than expected. In addition, the Vermont winters certainly preclude any progress during that season, leaving only the spring and fall seasons to complete work (we hope to keep the trail open for use during the summer). What follows, then, is a very optimistic timeline. We will make every effort to stay on schedule, but we realize that full completion of the project may take somewhat longer than planned.

FIGURE 11.19 Solicited External Proposal, Page 5

Phase One: Fall 2009
Phase Two: Spring 2010
Phase Three: Fall 2010

BUDGET

PHASE ONE

Expenses

architectural fees	$ 1,000
replacement of culvert at entrance	2,000
purchase and install main gate	6,500
erect main gate brick pillars	2,200
clear and pave two parking areas	5,000
clean out, repair, and reline 2 culverts	3,000
repave road from main gate to gate #2	9,500
clear trees and landscape east area	6,000
clean drainage trenches	3,500
purchase and install gate #2	800
purchase and install signage at both gates	500
	$ 40,000

Funding Sources

donated labor for landscaping	$ 4,000
donated labor and equipment for ditching	3,500
donated wrought iron for main gate	1,000
donated materials and installation of signage	500
partial contribution of architectural fees	700
cash contributions from Ethanton Striders	10,300
Ethanton Philanthropic Foundation Contribution	20,000
	$ 40,000

PHASE TWO

Expenses

replace and backfill 15 drainage culverts	$ 30,000
clean out, repair, and reline 7 drainage culverts	7,500

FIGURE 11.20 Solicited External Proposal, Page 6

box out and grade for blacktop at replaced culverts	5,500
place 2" of type 3 binder at replaced culverts	4,500
clean out 1 mile of drainage ditches	11,700
	$ 59,200

PHASE THREE

Expenses

pave 2 miles of road 8 feet wide, 1/2" true + 1" top	$ 42,500
	$ 42,500

Total Phase Two & Phase Three Expenses	$ 101,700

Funding Sources (Phase Two & Phase Three)

cash contributions from Ethanton Striders	$ 10,000
donated labor and equipment for ditching	11,700
monies from additional grant funding	80,000
	$ 101,700

ETHANTON STRIDERS BOARD OF DIRECTORS

President: Frank Rodgers (CEO, Rodgers Industries)
Vice President for Activities & Events: Joseph Carr (CPA, Donnelly & Co.)
Vice President for Administration & Finance: Rev. Thomas J. Moran (Clergy)
Secretary: Position currently vacant
Treasurer: Eugene Torpey (President, Glenwood, Inc.)
Member: Robert Catanzaro, Ph.D. (Professor, Ethanton Community College)
Member: Thomas Gibbons (Athletic Director, Ethanton High School)
Member: Dr. Cathleen McGovern (Physician, Meyers Medical Group)
Member: Charles McCabe (Owner, McCabe's Clothiers)
Member: Jane Scerbo (Owner, Ethanton Dry Cleaning)
Member: Robert F. Veale (Comptroller, Lincoln Co.)
Member: Grace Walsh (Principal, St. Aedan's Elementary School)

FIGURE 11.21 Solicited External Proposal, Page 7

CONCLUSION

A recognized, long-established, high-profile local organization with a large, active membership, the Ethanton Striders Running Club has been successful in eliciting project endorsements from the Mayor's office and several major local businesses. We have also secured pledges of assistance from such groups as the Ethanton Mountain Climbing Club, the Valley Bicycle Club, and the Phi Theta Delta service fraternity at Ethanton Community College. Given the range of expertise and the many professional affiliations represented on the club's Board of Directors, we are confident that we will be able to secure needed materials, services, and cash donations as the project moves forward. At present we are preparing a sizable grant application to be submitted to the Federal Recreational Trails Program, we are planning a new 5k race specifically to benefit the trail project, and we intend to conduct raffles and other fund-raising activities at the Thursday Training Runs and other area events. In short, we know we can succeed in this important endeavor, and we urge the Ethanton Philanthropic Foundation to assist us by approving our grant proposal.

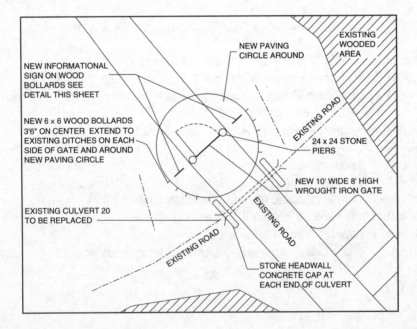

Figure 1 - Blowup of Gate Area

FIGURE 11.22 Solicited External Proposal, Page 8

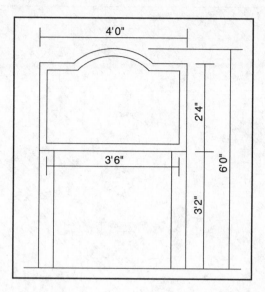

Figure 2 - Sign Detail

Figure 3 - Sketch View of Main Gate

FIGURE 11.23 Solicited External Proposal, Page 9

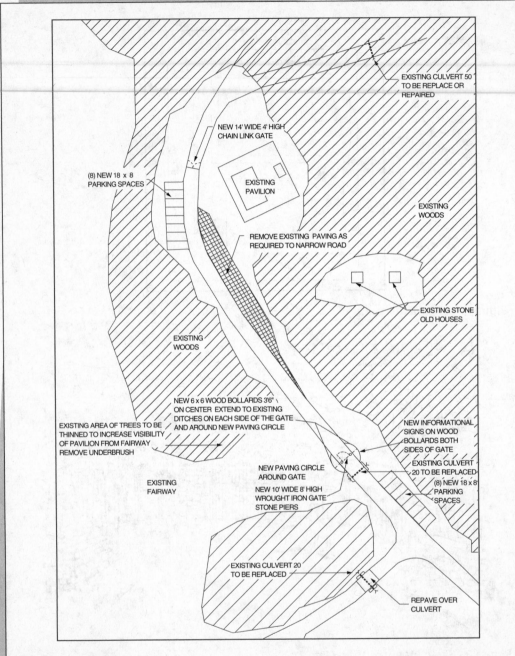

EXISTING CULVERT 50 TO BE REPLACE OR REPAIRED

NEW 14' WIDE 4' HIGH CHAIN LINK GATE

(8) NEW 18 x 8 PARKING SPACES

EXISTING PAVILION

EXISTING WOODS

REMOVE EXISTING PAVING AS REQUIRED TO NARROW ROAD

EXISTING STONE OLD HOUSES

EXISTING WOODS

NEW 6 x 6 WOOD BOLLARDS 3'6" ON CENTER EXTEND TO EXISTING DITCHES ON EACH SIDE OF THE GATE AND AROUND NEW PAVING CIRCLE

EXISTING AREA OF TREES TO BE THINNED TO INCREASE VISIBILITY OF PAVILION FROM FAIRWAY REMOVE UNDERBRUSH

NEW INFORMATIONAL SIGNS ON WOOD BOLLARDS BOTH SIDES OF GATE

EXISTING CULVERT 20 TO BE REPLACED

NEW PAVING CIRCLE AROUND GATE

(8) NEW 18 x 8 PARKING SPACES

EXISTING FAIRWAY

NEW 10' WIDE 8' HIGH WROUGHT IRON GATE STONE PIERS

EXISTING CULVERT 20 TO BE REPLACED

REPAVE OVER CULVERT

Figure 4 - Site Plan

FIGURE 11.24 Solicited External Proposal, Page 10

THE CITY
OF ETHANTON
Office of the Mayor

City Hall • Ethanton, Vermont 05201

January 5, 2009

Mr. Frank Rodgers, President
Ethanton Striders Running Club
P.O. Box 4141
Ethanton, VT 05201

Dear Frank,

Thanks very much for sharing with me the Ethanton Striders' wonderful plans to restore the trail in City Park. I'm sure you know of my great love for the park and my belief that it's one of the city's greatest assets.

For that reason, your trail restoration project greatly appeals to me, and I fully support your efforts.

I'm pleased that the Striders are willing to undertake this project, and I ask that you keep me informed of your progress. I look forward to the day when the entire community will be able to once again enjoy full use of the trail.

Thanks again! If I can assist in any way, please contact me.

Sincerely,

Hanna Julian

Mayor Hanna Julian

Figure 5 - Mayor's Endorsement

FIGURE 11.25 Solicited External Proposal, Page 11

✓ Checklist   Evaluating a Proposal

An effective proposal

__ is prepared in a format (e-mail, memo, memo report, letter, or booklet) appropriate to its nature;

__ clearly identifies the situation or problem and fully explains how the proposal addresses it;

__ confirms the feasibility of the proposal, refuting any probable objections and establishing the writer's credentials and qualifications for the project;

__ provides a reliable timeline for completion of the project; identifies any necessary resources, equipment, or support; and includes an itemized budget;

__ closes with a strong, persuasive conclusion that will motivate the reader to accept the proposal;

__ uses plain, simple language;

__ maintains an appropriate tone, neither too formal nor too conversational;

__ is well-designed and employs effective visuals—tables, graphs, charts, and the like;

__ contains no typos or mechanical errors in spelling, capitalization, punctuation, or grammar.

Exercises

■ EXERCISE 11.1

Write a proposal seeking approval from your college's student activities director to create a new campus club or organization.

■ EXERCISE 11.2

Write a proposal seeking approval from your college's athletic director to implement an improvement to the intramural sports program.

■ EXERCISE 11.3

Write a proposal seeking approval from the department head in your major field of study to take an elective course not among the program's recommended electives.

■ EXERCISE 11.4

Write a proposal seeking approval from your workplace supervisor to implement a change in a particular policy or procedure.

■ EXERCISE 11.5

Write a proposal seeking approval from one of your instructors to create a peer tutoring arrangement or study group designed to enhance students' performance in the course.

■ EXERCISE 11.6

Write a proposal seeking approval from your clergyperson to create a religion-based club or interest group.

■ EXERCISE 11.7

Write a proposal seeking approval from your local library director to present a public lecture at the library on a topic you're knowledgeable about.

■ EXERCISE 11.8

Write a proposal in response to an RFP found on the Internet or in a trade journal or magazine.

■ EXERCISE 11.9

Create a list identifying each of the proposals in Exercises 11.1–11.8 as solicited or unsolicited, and internal or external.

■ EXERCISE 11.10

Nearly all college-level workplace communications courses include an assignment requiring the completion of a long report. Using Figures 11.4–11.5 as a model, write a proposal seeking your instructor's approval of your chosen topic. If the topic has been assigned by the instructor, write a proposal seeking approval of your plan of approach.

12

Long Reports:
Format, Collaboration,
and Documentation

Learning Objective When you complete this chapter you'll be able to create well-designed long reports, whether working independently or with others, and to correctly document the sources of your information.

▪ Format
Transmittal Document
Title Page
Abstract
Table of Contents
List of Illustrations
Glossary
Text
Visuals
Pagination

▪ Collaboration

▪ Documentation
Bibliography
Parenthetical Citations
Checklist: Evaluating a Long Report

Exercises

n business, industry, and the professions, important decisions are made every day. Some concern routine matters, and others are more complicated, involving considerable risk and expense. Suppose, for example, that a hospital administration is debating whether to add a new wing to the main building. Or perhaps a police department wants to switch to a different kind of patrol car, or a successful but relatively new business venture must decide whether to expand now or wait a few years. Each situation requires in-depth study before a responsible decision can be reached. The potential advantages and drawbacks of each alternative have to be identified and examined, as well as the long-range effects. This is where the long report comes into play. This chapter discusses how to prepare such a report, explaining its formatting components, the dynamics of group-written reports, and some standard procedures for documenting sources.

Format

Obviously, both the subject matter and the formatting of long reports will vary from one workplace to another, and in the academic context, from one discipline to another and even from one instructor to another. Nevertheless, most long reports share the components described in the following paragraphs.

Transmittal Document

Prepared according to standard memo or business letter format (see Chapters 2 and 3) the transmittal document accompanies a long report, conveying it from whoever wrote it to whoever requested it. The transmittal document says, in effect, "Here's the report you wanted," and very briefly summarizes its content. The memo format is used for transmitting in-house reports, whereas the letter format is used for transmitting reports to outside readers. Often the transmittal document serves as a "cover sheet," although sometimes it's positioned immediately after the title page of the report. Figure 12.1 is a sample transmittal memo.

Title Page

In addition to the title itself, this page includes the name(s) of whoever prepared the report, the name(s) of whoever requested it, the names of the companies or organizations involved, and the date. In an academic context the title page includes the title, the name(s) of the student author(s)

PARAMOUNT CONSTRUCTION, INC.

MEMORANDUM

DATE: July 9, 2007

TO: Rosa Sheridan
             Director, Human Resources

FROM: William Congreve
             Administrative Assistant

SUBJECT: Drug-Testing Report

As you may recall, we recently decided that I should prepare a report on drug
testing in the American workplace, to help us explore the feasibility of introducing a program at Paramount. Here is the report. If you have any questions,
I would be happy to provide further details.

FIGURE 12.1   **Drug-Testing Report, Transmittal Memo**

DRUG TESTING
IN THE WORKPLACE

by

William Congreve
Administrative Assistant

Submitted to

Rosa Sheridan
Director of Human Resources

Paramount Construction, Inc.
Mission Viejo, California

July 9, 2007

FIGURE 12.2 Drug-Testing Report, Title Page

and the instructor who assigned the report, the course name (along with the course number and section number), the college, and the date. Figure 12.2 is a sample title page prepared for a workplace context.

Abstract

Sometimes called an executive summary, this is simply a brief synopsis—a greatly abbreviated version of the report (see Chapter 6). An effective abstract captures the essence of the report, including its major findings and recommendations. In the workplace the abstract assists those who may not have time to read the entire report but need to know what it says. Sometimes the abstract is positioned near the front of the report; at other times it appears at the end. For a 10- to 20-page report, the abstract should not be longer than one page and can be formatted as one long paragraph. Figure 12.3 offers an example of a concise abstract.

Table of Contents

As in a book, the table of contents for a long report clearly shows each numbered section of the report, along with its title and the page on which it appears. Many also show subdivisions within sections. When fine-tuning a report before submitting it, check to ensure that the section numbers, titles, and page numbers used in the table of contents are consistent with those in the report itself (see Figure 12.4).

List of Illustrations

This list resembles the table of contents, but rather than referring to text sections, it lists tables, graphs, charts, and all other visuals appearing in the report—each numbered and titled—and their page numbers. As with the table of contents, always check to ensure that your illustrations list accurately reflects the visual contents of the report and the corresponding labeling/captions (see Figure 12.5).

Glossary

A "mini-dictionary," the glossary defines all potentially unfamiliar words, expressions, or symbols in your report. Not all reports need a glossary; it depends on the topic and the intended audience. But if you are using specialized vocabulary or symbols that may not be well known, it's best to include a glossary page with terms alphabetized for easy reference and symbols listed in the order in which they appear in the text (see Figure 12.6).

ii

ABSTRACT

Paramount Construction is considering introducing a mandatory drug-testing program. Although intended to reduce the costs associated with workplace substance abuse, drug testing is quite controversial. Some experts argue that the extent of workplace drug abuse has been greatly exaggerated and that drug-testing programs—first introduced in large numbers in the 1980s—are a needless violation of employees' privacy. Most drug-testing programs rely on EMIT, a test that often yields inaccurate results, thus necessitating the use of confirmatory GC/MS testing to reduce the possibility of false positives. Drug testing appears to be least problematic when used to screen applicants for employment rather than administered to established employees. To avoid costly lawsuits and other setbacks, progressive companies observe several key features of successful drug-testing protocol: a clear policy statement, strict guidelines for specimen collection, use of NIDA-certified laboratories, confirmation of all positive test results, and employee assistance services. Paramount probably should introduce a drug-testing program, beginning by testing job applicants only, rather than the existing workforce, but we should first establish an EAP. In addition, we should seek assistance from an outside (NIDA) consultant.

FIGURE 12.3 Drug-Testing Report, Abstract

iii

TABLE OF CONTENTS

FIGURE 12.4   **Drug-Testing Report, Table of Contents**

iv

LIST OF ILLUSTRATIONS

FIGURE 12.5   **Drug-Testing Report, List of Illustrations**

v

GLOSSARY

ACLU	American Civil Liberties Union
CDC	Centers for Disease Control
EAP	Employee Assistance Program
EMIT	Enzyme Multiplied Immunoassay Technique
enzymes	Organic catalysts produced by living cells but capable of acting independently; complex colloidal substances that can induce chemical changes in other substances without undergoing change themselves
false negative	Test result that incorrectly indicates the absence of the substance(s) tested for
false positive	Test result that incorrectly indicates the presence of the substance(s) tested for
GC/MS	Gas Chromatography/Mass Spectrometry
immunoassay	Analysis of a substance to determine its constituents and the relative proportions of each
mass spectrum	Identifiable pattern of electromagnetic energy given off by a substance under specific test conditions
metabolites	Drug by-products that remain in the body after the effects of the drug have worn off
MRO	Medical Resource Officer, a licensed physician knowledgeable about substance abuse

FIGURE 12.6   **Drug-Testing Report, Glossary**

Text

One major difference between a long report and an academic term paper is that a report is divided into sections, usually numbered, and each with its own title. As mentioned previously, it's important that these divisions within the text be accurately reflected in the table of contents.

Every long report also includes an introduction and a conclusion. The introduction provides an overview of the report, identifying its purpose and scope, and explaining the procedures used and the context in which it was written. The conclusion summarizes the main points in the report and lists recommendations, if any.

Visuals

A major feature of many reports, visuals (see Chapter 4) sometimes appear in a separate section—an appendix—at the end of a report. A better approach, however, is to integrate them into the text, as this is more convenient for the reader. Either way, you should draw the reader's attention to pertinent visuals (stating, for example, "See Figure 5"), and every visual must be properly numbered and titled, with its source identified. The numbering/titling system must be the same system used in the list of illustrations.

Pagination

Number your report pages correctly. There are several pagination systems in use. Generally, page numbers (1, 2, 3, and so on) begin on the introduction page and continue until the last page of the report. Front-matter pages (abstract, table of contents, list of illustrations, glossary, and anything else that precedes the introduction) are numbered with lowercase Roman numerals (i, ii, iii, iv, and so on). There is no page number on the transmittal document or the title page, although the latter "counts" as a front-matter page, so the page immediately following the title page is numbered as ii. The best position for page numbers is in the upper-right corner, because that location enables the reader to find a particular page simply by thumbing through the report. Notice the page numbering throughout the sample report in this chapter (Figures 12.1–12.21).

■ Collaboration

A memo, letter, or short report nearly always is composed by one person working individually. This is sometimes true of long reports as well.

However, since the subject matter of long reports is often complex and multifaceted, they are often written collaboratively. Indeed, nearly all workplace writers are called on to collaborate at least occasionally. Teamwork is so common in the workplace because it provides certain obvious advantages. For example, a group that works well together can produce a long report *faster* than one person working alone. In addition, the team possesses a broader perspective and a greater range of knowledge and expertise than an individual. To slightly amend the old saying, two heads—or more—are better than one. In addition, with the increasing sophistication of *groupware* (word-processing and document design programs created specifically for collaborative use), teamworking has become easier and faster than ever.

Nevertheless, collaboration can pose problems if the members of a group have difficulty interacting smoothly. Real teamwork requires everyone involved to exercise tact, courtesy, and responsibility. The following factors are essential to successful collaboration:

1. Everyone on the team must fully understand the purpose, goals, and intended audience of the document.

2. There must be uniform awareness of the project's confidentiality level, especially if individual team members must consult outside sources for data, background information, or other material.

3. Team members must agree to set aside individual preferences in favor of the group's collective judgment.

4. A team leader must be in charge of the project—someone whom the other members are willing to recognize as the coordinator. Ideally, the leader is elected from within the group (although sometimes the leader is appointed by someone at a higher level of authority). The leader must be not only knowledgeable and competent but also a "people person" with excellent interpersonal skills. The leader has many responsibilities:

   - Schedules, announces, and conducts meetings
   - Helps establish procedural guidelines, especially regarding progress assessment
   - Monitors team members' involvement, providing encouragement and assistance
   - Promotes consensus and mediates disagreements
   - Maintains an accurate master file copy of the evolving document

In short, the leader operates in a managerial capacity (much like a professor in a college class), ensuring a successful outcome by keeping everyone on task and holding the whole effort together.

5. The team must assign clearly defined roles to the other members, designating responsibilities according to everyone's talents and strengths. For example, the group's most competent researcher takes charge of information retrieval. Someone trained in drafting or computer-assisted design agrees to format the report and create visuals. The member with the best keyboarding skills (or clerical support) actually produces the document. The best writer is the overall editor, making final judgments on matters of organization, style, mechanics, and the like. If an oral presentation is required, the group's most confident public speaker assumes that responsibility. A given individual might assume more than one role, but everyone must feel satisfied that the work has been fairly distributed.

6. Once the project has begun, the team meets regularly to assess its progress, prevent duplication of effort, and resolve any problems that arise. All disagreements or differences of opinion are reconciled in a productive manner. In any group undertaking, a certain amount of conflict is inevitable and indeed necessary to achieve consensus. This interplay, however, should be a source of creative energy, not antagonism. Issues must be dealt with on an objectively intellectual level, not in a personal or emotional manner. To this end, the group should adopt a code of interaction designed to minimize conflict and maximize the benefits of collaboration. Here are some guidelines:

- Make a real effort to be calm, patient, reasonable, and flexible—in short, *helpful*.
- Voice all reservations, misgivings, and resentments rather than letting them smolder.
- Direct criticism at the issue, not the person ("There's another way of looking at this" rather than "You're only looking at this one way"), and try not to *interpret* criticism personally.
- Make an effort to really *listen* to others' remarks and not interrupt.
- Paraphrase others' statements to be sure of their meaning ("What you're saying, then, is . . .").
- Identify strengths in other people's work before mentioning weaknesses ("This first section is very well written, but I have a suggestion for revising the second section").

- Avoid vague, unhelpful criticism by addressing specifics ("In paragraph 3, it's unclear whether Dept. A or Dept. B will be in charge" rather than "Paragraph 3 is unclear"). This is especially important when providing *written* feedback.
- Try not to concentrate on picky, inconsequential fine points. Although glaring errors in spelling, grammar, and the like should certainly be corrected, the focus should be on the "big picture."
- Accentuate the positive rather than the negative ("Now that we've agreed on the visuals, we can move on" instead of "We can't seem to agree on anything but the visuals").
- Suggest rather than command ("Maybe we should try it this way" instead of "Do it this way!") and offer rather than demand ("If you'd like, I'll . . ." instead of "I'm going to . . .").
- Be aware of your "body language," which can send negative signals that impede progress by creating resistance on the part of your teammates.
- In cases of major conflict the leader must mediate to prevent the group from bogging down. One solution is to table the problematic issue and move on, addressing it at a later meeting after everyone has been able to consider it in greater depth. If there's a severe clash between two group members, it's usually best for the leader to meet privately with them to reach compromise.

7. All members of the group must complete their fair share of the work in a conscientious fashion and observe all deadlines. Nothing is more disruptive to a team's progress than an irresponsible member who fails to complete work punctually or "vanishes" for long periods of time. To maintain contact between regularly scheduled meetings of the group, members should exchange phone numbers and/or e-mail addresses. If all team members are sufficiently tech savvy, they can maintain contact through synchronous electronic discussion in real time using a virtual conference room or multiuser domain (MUD) accessible via the Internet. But exchanges in such settings should be brief and to-the-point, as lengthy comments take too long to write and read, thus inhibiting the free and spontaneous flow of ideas so necessary to productive collaboration. Another option is to use file transfer protocol (FTP) to create a common Web site to which group members can post drafts for review by their teammates. In any case electronic communication should be seen simply as a way to keep in touch between meetings and should not become a substitute for frequent face-to-face interaction.

Regardless of how the team goes about its work, however, it's extremely helpful to the eventual editor if all sections of the document have been prepared according to uniform procedures. Therefore, unless the workplace has adopted an organization-wide style manual that governs such matters, the team should formulate its own guidelines. The editor then does not have to waste valuable time imposing conformity on various members' work but can concentrate instead on more important matters such as organization and content. To be useful, however, the guidelines should not be too extensive. Their purpose is simply to ensure that all members are preparing their drafts in a consistent way. Here are 10 areas to consider:

- Margins: Usually, 1-inch or 1½-inch margins are used.
- Fonts: Simple fonts are the most legible; the standard Microsoft Word font for documents is Times New Roman.
- Type size: 12-point type is the norm, although headings can be larger.
- Spacing: Double-spacing is best for drafts (to facilitate editing), but final versions of documents are often single spaced.
- CAPITALS, **bold face**, *italics*, and <u>underlining</u>: There must be agreement on when and how to use these options.
- Abbreviations, acronyms, and numbers: Again, the team must agree on their use.
- Page numbers: Position numbers in the upper-right corners of all draft pages.
- Placement and labeling of visuals: For recommendations, see Chapter 4.
- Headings: Depending on the nature of the document, headings can take many forms, including single words, phrases, statements, questions, and commands. As with all other format features, however, there should be uniformity in all sections.
- Documentation: If documentation is required, the same system should be used throughout.

Theoretically, a group can handle the writing of a report or other document in one of three ways:

- The whole team writes the report collectively, and then the editor revises the draft and submits it to the group for final approval or additional revisions.

- One person writes the entire report, and then the group—led by the editor—revises it collectively.
- Each team member writes one part of the report individually, and then the editor revises each part and submits the complete draft to the whole group for final approval or additional revisions.

Of these alternatives, the first is the most truly collaborative but is also extremely difficult and time consuming, requiring uncommon harmony within the group. The second method is preferable but places too great a burden on one writer. The third approach is the most common and is certainly the best, provided the editor seeks clarification from individuals whenever necessary during the editing process. For this reason, the third approach is the one that underlies most of what's been said here. Note, however, that in all three approaches the whole group gets to see and comment on the report in its final form. Because everyone's name will be on it, no one should be surprised when the finished product is released. Collaboration is, after all, a team effort with the goal of producing a polished document approved by all members of the team.

Documentation

Documentation is simply a technical term for the procedure whereby writers identify the sources of their information. In the workplace and in popular periodicals, this is often accomplished by inserting the pertinent information directly into the text, as in this example:

> As journalist James Fallows says in his article "Microsoft Reboots" in the December 2006 issue of the *Atlantic Monthly*, "the debut of a new operating system usually leads to a surge in PC sales, as people who have been waiting to upgrade buy machines with the new software installed" (168).

This straightforward approach eliminates the need for a bibliography (list of sources) at the end of the piece. Documentation in academic writing, however, nearly always includes both a bibliography and parenthetical citations identifying the origin of each quotation, statistic, paraphrase, or visual within the text.

Documentation is necessary to avoid *plagiarism*—the use of someone else's work without proper acknowledgment. As the Modern Language Association (MLA) handbook explains, the term derives from the Latin *plagiarius*, meaning "kidnapper." Accordingly, it's a serious offense:

"a form of cheating . . . theft. Passing off another person's ideas, information, or expressions as your own" (66). In several highly publicized recent cases, plagiarism has resulted in the firing of journalists at the *New York Times*, the *New Republic*, and other publications. Similarly, the president of a prestigious northeastern college was forced to resign a few years ago after delivering a speech (later posted on the college's Web site) that included material borrowed from Internet sources but not documented as such. Not surprisingly, then, "students exposed as plagiarists suffer severe penalties, ranging from failure in the assignment or in the course to expulsion from school" (67).

Here are the MLA's useful guidelines for recognizing and avoiding plagiarism:

You have plagiarized if:

- You took notes that did not distinguish summary and paraphrase from quotation, and then you presented wording from the notes as if it were all your own.
- While browsing the Web, you copied text and pasted it into your paper without quotation marks or without citing the source.
- You presented facts without saying where you found them.
- You repeated or paraphrased someone's wording without acknowledgment.
- You took someone's unique or particularly apt phrase without acknowledgment.
- You paraphrased someone's argument or presented someone's line of thought without acknowledgment.
- You bought or otherwise acquired a research paper and handed in part or all of it as your own.

You can avoid plagiarism by:

- Making a list of the writers and viewpoints you discovered in your research and using this list to double-check the presentation of material in your paper.
- Keeping the following three categories distinct in your notes: your ideas, your summaries of others' material, and exact wording you copy.
- Identifying the sources of all material you borrow—exact wording, paraphrases, ideas, arguments, and facts.
- Checking with your instructor when you are uncertain about your use of sources.

Bibliography

There are several standard ways to format a list of citations. The MLA format, which titles the list "Works Cited," and the American Psychological Association (APA) format, which titles the list "References," are the most commonly taught in college courses, although a great many others do exist: American Chemical Society (ACS), American Institute of Physics (AIP), American Mathematical Society (AMS), and the Council of Biology Editors (CBE), to name just a few. Here is a typical bibliography entry formatted according to the MLA and APA guidelines:

MLA Baron, Naomi S. *Alphabet to Email: How Written English Evolved and Where It's Heading.* London: Routledge, 2000.

APA Baron, N. S. (2000). *Alphabet to email: How written English evolved and where it's heading.* London: Routledge.

Notice the differences between the two formats. Perhaps the most obvious is the placement of the date of publication. But variations also exist with respect to capitalization, punctuation, and abbreviation. In both systems, however, double-spacing is used throughout, and book titles—like the titles of newspapers, magazines, journals, and other periodicals—are italicized. (MLA style is a bit more flexible in this regard, allowing titles to be either italicized or underlined.) In both formats, entries appear in alphabetical order by authors' last names or, in the case of an anonymous work, by the first significant word of the title.

There are many other kinds of sources besides a single-author book, however, and each requires a slightly different handling. Some of the most common citations are as follows:

Book by Two Authors

MLA Willis, Tracey R., and Gemma C. Siringo. *Academic Advisement for the 21st Century.* 2nd ed. Washington: NEA, 2006.

APA Willis, T. R., & Siringo, G. C. (2006). *Academic advisement for the 21st century* (2nd ed.). Washington, DC: National Education Association.

Book by Three Authors

MLA Whitman, William C., William M. Johnson, and John A. Tomczyk. *Refrigeration & Air Conditioning Technology.* 5th ed. Clifton Park: Thomson Delmar, 2005.

APA Whitman, W. C., Johnson, W. M., & Tomczyk, J. A. (2005). *Refrigeration & air conditioning technology* (5th ed.). Clifton Park, NY: Thomson Delmar.

Book by a Corporate Author

MLA   American Welding Society. *Welding Inspection Handbook.* 3rd ed. Miami: AWS, 2000.

APA   American Welding Society. (2000). *Welding inspection handbook* (3rd ed.). Miami, FL: Author.

Edited Book of Articles

MLA   Stangor, Charles, ed. *Stereotypes and Prejudice: Essential Readings.* Philadelphia: Psychology Press, 2000.

APA   Stangor, C. (ed.). (2000). *Stereotypes and prejudice: Essential readings.* Philadelphia: Psychology Press.

Article in an Edited Book

MLA   Allport, Gordon. "The Nature of Prejudice." *Stereotypes and Prejudice: Essential Readings.* Ed. Charles Stangor. Philadelphia: Psychology Press, 2000. 20–48.

APA   Allport, G. (2000). The nature of prejudice. In C. Stangor (Ed.), *Stereotypes and prejudice: Essential readings* (pp. 20–48). Philadelphia: Psychology Press.

Article in a Newspaper

MLA   Clark, Nicola. "One Word for Airplane Makers: Plastics." *New York Times* 16 June 2007: C3.

APA   Clark, N. (2007, June 16). One word for airplane makers: plastics. *The New York Times*, p. C3.

Anonymous Article in a Newspaper

MLA   "Nuclear Power Sets off a Debate in the Senate." *Wall Street Journal* 15 June 2007: A2.

APA   Nuclear power sets off a debate in the Senate (2007, June 15). *The Wall Street Journal*, p. A2.

Article in a Weekly or Biweekly Magazine

MLA   Hobson, Katherine. "Injury-Free Workouts." *U.S. News & World Report* 25 June 2007: 62–70.

APA   Hobson, K. (2007, June 25). Injury-free workouts. *U.S. News & World Report, 142,* 62–70.

Article in a Monthly or Bimonthly Magazine

MLA   Sovoboda, Elizabeth. "The Fuel Cell." *Popular Science* July 2007: 76–82, 99.

APA   Sovoboda, E. (2007, June). The fuel cell. *Popular Science, 271,* 76–82, 99.

Anonymous Article in a Magazine

MLA   "Beyond the Prius." *The Economist* 16 June 2007: 72.

APA   Beyond the Prius. (2007, June 16). *The Economist, 383,* 72.

Article in a Trade Journal or Academic Journal

MLA   Fahey, Richard. "Clean Drinking Water for All." *Civil Engineering* 77.4 (2007): 45–54.

APA   Fahey, R. (2007). Clean drinking water for all. *Civil Engineering, 77*(4), 45–54.

Entry in an Encyclopedia or Other Reference Work

MLA   Gran, Richard J. "Magnetic Levitation Train." *World Book Encyclopedia.* 2000 ed.

APA   Gran, R. J. (2000). Magnetic levitation train. In *The World Book Encyclopedia* (Vol. 13, pp. 55–56). Chicago: World Book, Inc.

Entry in a Portable Electronic Encyclopedia or Other Reference Work

MLA   Engelhardt, A. G., and M. Kristiansen. "Ohm's Law." *Grolier Multimedia Encyclopedia for Windows.* CD-ROM. Danbury: Grolier, 2002.

APA   Engelhardt, A. G., & Kristiansen, M. (2002). Ohm's law. *Grolier Multimedia Encyclopedia for Windows* [CD-ROM]. Danbury, CT: Grolier.

Personal Interview

MLA   Britton, William. Personal interview. 10 Nov. 2008.

APA   In APA style, all personal communications (conversations, interviews, and the like) are excluded from the list of references. Such sources are documented only within the text, like this:

Financial officer William Britton (personal communication, November 10, 2008) stated that the "total cost of the project may be well over a million dollars."

Online Sources

Internet Site

MLA   American Federation of Labor - Congress of Industrial Organizations. *AFL-CIO: America's Union Movement.* 2007. 21 June 2007. <http://www.aflcio.org/>.

APA   American Federation of Labor - Congress of Industrial Organizations. (2007). *America's union movement.* Retrieved June 21, 2007, from http://www.aflcio.org

Link Within an Internet Site

MLA   American Federation of Labor - Congress of Industrial Organizations. "Workers' Rights." *AFL-CIO: America's Union Movement.* 2007. 21 June 2007. <http://www.aflcio.org/issues/jobseconomy/workersrights/>.

APA   American Federation of Labor - Congress of Industrial Organizations. (2007). Workers' rights. *AFL-CIO: America's union movement.* Retrieved June 21, 2007, from http://www.aflcio.org/issues/iobseconomy/workersrights

Article in a Newspaper

MLA   Labaton, Stephen. "Microsoft to Alter Windows Vista." *New York Times on the Web.* 20 June 2007. 22 June 2007. <http://www.nytimes.com/>. Path: NYT Archive since 1981.

APA   Labaton, S. (2007, June 20). Microsoft to alter Windows Vista. *New York Times.* Retrieved June 22, 2007, from http://www.nytimes.com

Article in a Magazine

MLA   Krisher, Tom. "Chrysler to Boost Fuel Efficiency." *TIME* 21 June 2007. <http://www.time.com/>. Path: Business & Tech.

APA   Krisher, T. (2007, June 21). Chrysler to boost fuel efficiency. *TIME.* Retrieved June 21, 2007, from http:www.time.com

Article in a Database

MLA   Oh, William. "Preventing Damage to Motor Bearings." *HPAC Engineering* 79.4 (2007): 46–49. *Academic Search Premier.* Mohawk Valley Community College Library, Utica, NY. 10 May 2007. <http://www.ebscohost.com/>.

APA Oh, W. (2007). Preventing damage to motor bearings. *HPAC Engineering, 79.4*, 46–49. Retrieved May 10, 2007, from Academic Search Premier database.

E-Mail Message

MLA Russo, Linda. E-mail to the author. 15 Jan. 2009.

APA In APA style, personal communications (e-mail, conversations, interviews, and the like) are excluded from the list of references. Such sources are documented only within the text, like this:

Human Resources director Linda Russo (e-mail, January 15, 2009) agrees that Thursday's meeting "did not fully accomplish its objectives."

The examples just given follow the basic formats recommended by the MLA and the APA for documenting on-line sources. As you can see, both styles provide essentially the same information used to identify print sources: the author's name (if known), the title of the work, and—by way of publication data—the date the material was accessed and the URL or Web address at which it appeared. But electronic sources are of many different kinds, not all of which easily lend themselves to these formats. For a more complete explanation of how electronic (and print) sources are handled, you should consult the two organizations' handbooks, readily available in most libraries:

Gibaldi, Joseph, ed. *MLA Handbook for Writers of Research Papers.* 6th ed. New York: MLA, 2003.

American Psychological Association. (2001). *Publication Manual of the American Psychological Association* (5th ed.). Washington, DC: Author.

As the *MLA Handbook* says, "Recommendations on citing electronic works . . . will doubtless change as technology, scholarly uses of electronic materials, and electronic publication practices evolve" (208). Meanwhile, help is available on the Internet itself. Numerous Web sites exist to assist you in preparing correct bibliography entries in various styles including MLA and APA. Typically these sites employ a "fill in the blanks" approach. You provide the information, and the computer does the rest, creating a bibliography entry based on the publication data you've given. Of course you must be careful to enter the data correctly for the program to work. Here are three such sites:

www.citationmachine.org
www.easybib.com
www.noodles.com

Even more conveniently, the 2007 edition of Microsoft Word includes a documentation feature that works much the same way. To access it, simpy go to the Reference tab on the tool bar, and click on Manage Sources.

Parenthetical Citations

Every time you use a source within the body of a report, whether quoting directly or paraphrasing in your own words, you must identify the source by inserting parentheses. The contents and positioning of these parentheses vary somewhat depending on whether you're using MLA or APA style. Here are examples of how to cite quotations:

MLA   "E-mail has emerged as a medium that allows communication in situations where neither speech nor writing can easily substitute" (Baron 259).

APA   "E-mail has emerged as a medium that allows communication in situations where neither speech nor writing can easily substitute" (Baron, 2000, p. 259).

If you mention the author's name in your own text, neither MLA nor APA requires that the name appear in the parentheses, although the APA system then requires *two* parenthetical insertions:

MLA   As Baron observes, "E-mail has emerged as a medium that allows communication in situations where neither speech nor writing can easily substitute" (259).

APA   As Baron (2000) observes, "E-mail has emerged as a medium that allows communication in situations where neither speech nor writing can easily substitute" (p. 259).

When you're paraphrasing, the differences between the two styles are as follows:

MLA   E-mail is sometimes more practical than speech or writing (Baron 259).

APA   E-mail is sometimes more practical than speech or writing (Baron, 2000).

MLA   As Baron observes, e-mail is sometimes more practical than speech or writing (259).

APA   As Baron (2000) observes, e-mail is sometimes more practical than speech or writing.

To credit a quote from an unsigned source (such as the "Anonymous Article" example shown on p. 313) do it as follows:

MLA   "Even if the Prius is pushed aside by other forms of hybrid, it has done wonders for Toyota's reputation" ("Beyond" 72).

APA   "Even if the Prius is pushed aside by other forms of hybrid, it has done wonders for Toyota's reputation" ("Beyond the Prius," 2007, p. 72).

To credit a paraphrase from an unsigned source, follow these examples:

MLA   Whatever its future, the Prius has greatly enhanced Toyota's status as an industry leader ("Beyond" 72).

APA   Whatever its future, the Prius has greatly enhanced Toyota's status as an industry leader ("Beyond the Prius," 2007).

MLA   "The combination of a frugal 1.5-litre petrol engine with an electric motor provides the performance of a 2.0-litre petrol engine with lower fuel consumption than a diesel" ("Beyond" 72).

APA   "The combination of a frugal 1.5-litre petrol engine with an electric motor provides the performance of a 2.0-litre petrol engine with lower fuel consumption than a diesel" ("Beyond," 2007, p. 72).

The purpose of parenthetical citations is to enable readers to find your sources on the Works Cited or References page, in case they wish to consult those sources in their entirety. As the *MLA Handbook* explains, "Documentation . . . tends to discourage the circulation of error, by inviting readers to determine for themselves whether a reference to another text presents a reasonable account of what that text says" (67).

Obviously, proper documentation is an important part of any report or other paper that has drawn on sources beyond the writer's own prior knowledge. On the following pages is a correctly prepared report, "Drug Testing in the Workplace," with documentation prepared according to MLA guidelines. As mentioned earlier, actual reports written in the workplace may employ other styles of documentation. But the *format* of this report is fairly typical of the kind used in the workplace and in most college courses focusing on workplace communications. Once you've mastered this format, you can adapt it to a wide range of situations, whatever documentation system you may be using.

Tech Tips

The MLA Handbook says it quite well:

> Assessing Internet resources is a particular challenge. Whereas the print publications that researchers depend on are generally issued by reputable publishers, like university presses, that accept responsibility for the quality and reliability of the works they distribute, relatively few electronic publications currently have comparable authority. (42)

Consequently, you must exercise great selectivity when gathering information on-line. Here are some questions to ask when evaluating electronic sources:

■ Who has posted or sponsored the site? An individual? An organization? A special interest or advocacy group? What are their credentials or qualifications? The final suffix in the URL indicates a site's origins:

.com	Commercial enterprise
.org	Nonprofit organization
.edu	College, university, or other educational institution
.gov	Government agency
.mil	Military group
.net	Network

Sometimes it's helpful to enter the individual's or group's name in a search engine to see what related sites emerge. This often reveals affiliations and biases that have an impact on credibility.

■ Does the site itself provide links to related sites? Does it credit its own sources?

■ Is the information presented in a reasonably objective fashion, or does the site seem to favor or promote a particular viewpoint or perspective?

■ Does the site provide an e-mail address or other contact information that you can use to seek more information?

■ What is the date of the posting? Is the information current?

■ How well written is the site? How well designed? In short, does it seem to be the work of professionals or amateurs?

✓ Checklist   **Evaluating a Long Report**

An effective long report

____ is accompanied by a transmittal document (memo or letter);

____ includes certain components:

☐ Title page that includes the title of the report, name(s) of author(s), name of company or organization, name(s) of person(s) receiving the report, and the date

☐ Abstract that briefly summarizes the report

☐ Table of contents, with sections numbered and titled and page numbers provided

☐ List of illustrations, each numbered and titled, with page numbers provided

☐ Glossary, if necessary

____ is organized into sections numbered and titled in conformity with the table of contents, covering the subject fully in an orderly way;

____ is clear, accurate, and sufficiently detailed to satisfy the needs of the intended audience;

____ uses plain, simple language;

____ maintains an appropriate tone, neither too formal nor too conversational;

____ employs effective visuals—tables, graphs, charts, and the like— each numbered and titled in conformity with the list of illustrations;

____ includes full documentation (bibliography and parenthetical citations) prepared according to MLA or APA format;

____ contains no typos or mechanical errors in spelling, capitalization, punctuation, or grammar.

I - INTRODUCTION

Since the founding of the company in 1952, Paramount Construction has always sought to achieve maximum productivity while providing safe, secure, and conducive work conditions for our employees. In keeping with these goals, management has determined that it may now be time for Paramount to take a more active role in the war against drugs by adopting measures to ensure a substance-free workplace. One such measure that has been suggested is the creation of a mandatory drug-testing policy for all new and established employees, and this idea is currently under consideration.

As Figure 1 illustrates, our industry incurs more fatal occupational injuries than any other. And, as shown in Figure 2, the numbers have been steadily rising since the 1990s, with laborers suffering the highest incidence, as shown in Figure 3. Many of these fatalities resulted from falls, as shown in Figure 3 and Figure 4. When we consider that seven million persons are estimated to be drug dependent or abusers (see Figure 5), it's certainly possible that at least some of these fatalities can be attributed to drug-related impairment.

Drug testing first became popular after President Reagan's Executive Order 12564 in 1986 mandated the testing of federal employees in jobs entailing safety risks. The Drug Free Workplace Act, passed by Congress in 1988, along with the rapid evolution of reliable testing technology, further accelerated the spread of testing (Knudsen 623). But drug testing has always been somewhat controversial, and we need to carefully consider all aspects of the subject before reaching a determination about whether we should adopt the practice here. This report, compiled after an in-depth review of recent professional literature on the subject, is intended as a first step in that process.

II - KINDS OF TESTING

Although there are no truly definitive figures on the percentage of employers that require drug testing, most estimates are at least 50%, with larger companies (which can better afford testing programs) contributing disproportionately to that number (Hawkins 42). Among companies that test, several approaches are used: pre-employment, routine, reasonable suspicion/post-accident, return to work, and random. (Brunet 6–7)

Pre-Employment: Required of successful job applicants about to be hired, as a condition of employment. Indeed, some employers don't even bother to

FIGURE 12.7 **Drug-Testing Report, Page 1**

2

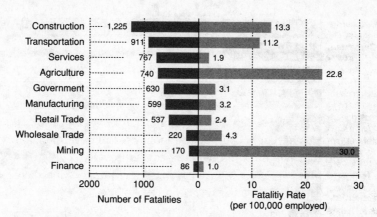

Note: Data exclude fatalities resulting from September 11, 2001 terrorist attacks.

Note: Data exclude fatalities resulting from September 11, 2001, terrorist attacks.
Figure 1. Fatal Occupational Injuries by Industry (*Source:* United States Centers for Disease Control and Prevention. "Construction Fatalities.")

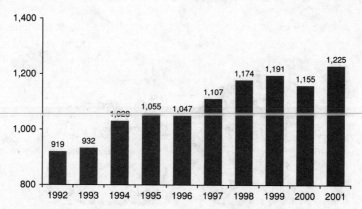

Figure 2. Fatal Occupational Injuries in Private Construction (*Source:* CDC. "Construction Fatalities.")

FIGURE 12.8 **Drug-Testing Report, Page 2**

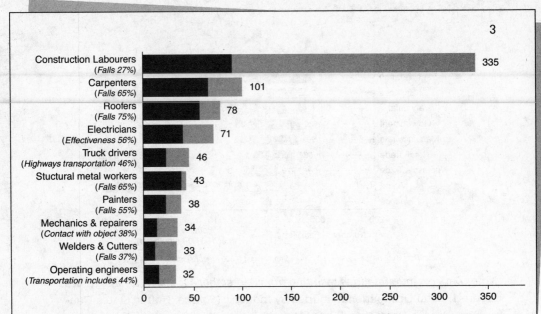

* *Selected occupations had a minimum of 40 fatalities and 45,000 employed workers in 2001. Note: Data exclude fatalities resulting from September 11 terrorist attacks.*

Figure 3. Construction Occupations with Most Fatalities (*Source:* CDC. "Construction Fatalities.")

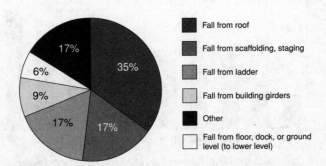

Figure 4. Falls by Detailed Event (*Source:* CDC. "Construction Fatalities.")

FIGURE 12.9 Drug-Testing Report, Page 3

4

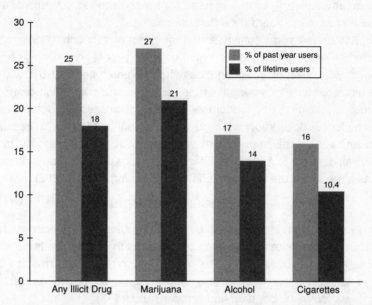

Figure 5. Persons Using Drugs During Past Year (2006) *(Source: CDC Policy.)*

confirm a positive pre-employment test result, even though most guidelines strongly recommend such confirmation of all positive results (Hawkins 44). Sometimes a follow-up test is required after the new worker's probationary period or when the worker is being transferred or promoted. Pre-employment testing is the most common kind. (White 1895)

Routine: Required of all employees at regular intervals, sometimes as part of an annual physical exam or performance review and sometimes more often.

Reasonable Suspicion/Post-Accident: Required of all employees whose supervisors have observed behaviors that seem to indicate substance abuse. Similarly, required of employees who have been involved in a workplace accident, on the assumption that controlled substances may have been a cause.

Return to Work: Required of all returning employees who have been off the job because of a prior violation and have completed a treatment program. This assumes, of course, that the company offers such a program as part of its EAP.

FIGURE 12.10 **Drug-Testing Report, Page 4**

5

Many companies do not, opting instead for immediate termination of anyone who fails a drug test, even if it's a first offense.

Random: Required of some employees without prior notification. "Computer-based, random-name generated software keeps the process completely objective. Consequently, some employees might be tested several times in a row, or they may not be tested for a long period of time—it's the nature of random testing. It is for this reason, however, that random testing both decreases and deters drug usage—employees don't know when they'll be tested." (Swartley 25) Because of its haphazard nature, this approach is the most effective. But it's also the most controversial, drawing fire from civil libertarians, labor unions, and workers themselves. As a result, it's the least common kind of testing. (White 1895)

III - METHODS OF TESTING

Simply put, drug testing is done by analyzing biological specimens for drugs or drug metabolites in the body of the test subject. Typically, an initial immunoassay test such as an EMIT is used, followed by a confirmatory GC/MS test if the first test is positive. Several different kinds of specimens can be analyzed: sweat, saliva, blood, hair, and urine. (Brunet 4–5)

Sweat: A sweat specimen can be obtained by having the test subject wear an adhesive patch that in effect soaks up the person's perspiration, which can then be tested for drug residue. This test is almost impossible to falsify, but its critics contend that the patch is susceptible to outside contamination that can produce false positives as well as false negatives. In any case, it's not widely used. (Hawkins 45)

Saliva: A saliva specimen can be obtained by placing in the subject's mouth a small, specially designed sponge that soaks up oral fluids, which can then be tested for drugs or drug residue. Like the sweat test, this procedure is fairly reliable and quite noninvasive, but it has not yet gained wide acceptance.

Blood: A blood specimen can be obtained through the usual clinical procedure and is quite reliable, but has the disadvantage of being highly invasive. In addition, it requires "stringent medical conditions, because of the risk of blood-borne infectious diseases" (White 1893). For these reasons, it is not widely used.

Hair: A hair specimen can be easily obtained by simply cutting some off the subject's head, starting near the scalp. Analysis of such a 1.5-inch specimen will provide an accurate 90-day drug history. Thousands of employers are

FIGURE 12.11 **Drug-Testing Report, Page 5**

6

using this kind of test, but it's controversial because results can be skewed by certain shampoos, airborne contaminants, and the like. In addition, NIDA research has revealed that certain drug molecules bind more readily to darker hair, thus putting some racial and ethnic groups at a disadvantage. As one Substance Abuse and Mental Health Services Administration official put it, "If two employees use cocaine, the blond may barely test negative, and the other will get caught." (Hawkins 46)

Urine: A urine specimen is readily obtainable, and an uncontaminated sample is generally reliable. But the urine test is the easiest to falsify, because the subject is usually afforded privacy while producing the sample. Obviously, then, this allows for various ways to alter, dilute, or even substitute for the sample. Nevertheless, the urine test remains by far the most popular method of testing. Despite its relative unreliability, urine is "preferred over blood samples because it requires a less invasive procedure, contains the metabolite . . . and is available in greater quantities." (Brunet 4)

IV - ARGUMENTS IN FAVOR

At first glance, the question of whether to test for drugs in the workplace seems quite uncomplicated. Obviously, a drug-free workplace is preferable to one in which employees' performance—and safety—may be compromised by substance abuse. And statistics seem to bear this out. According to several sources, drug abusers are one-third as productive as nonabusers, three times more likely to be late, almost four times more likely to be in a workplace accident, and five times more likely to file a workers' compensation claim. Indeed, 47% of all such claims are drug-related, with drug-related problems costing businesses an estimated $75 billion to $100 billion annually (Swartley 24, 28). As Figure 6 shows, our own industry (along with mining) is the hardest hit by workers' compensation costs.

"By deterring employees from using illegal drugs . . . organizations can reduce theft, absenteeism, accidents, and productivity losses. Furthermore, workplace drug testing fits within widely held American values and offers an opportunity for employers to be 'good citizens' while demonstrating symbolic support for the state's War on Drugs." (Knudsen 623) Not surprisingly, drug testing has gained increased acceptance over the years, with most people expressing support for testing, especially of employees in safety-sensitive positions. (Brunet 27)

FIGURE 12.12 **Drug-Testing Report, Page 6**

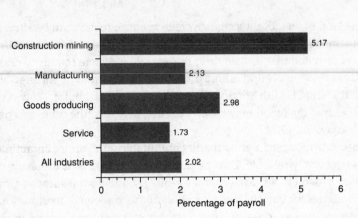

Figure 6. Workers' Compensation Costs, by Industry (*Source:* CDC. "Employer Spending.")

V - ARGUMENTS AGAINST

Although drug testing certainly enjoys great intuitive appeal, there exist a number of arguments against the practice. Most fundamentally, it's been said that drug testing creates an adversarial climate in the workplace, leading to distrust and lowered morale. Along those lines, ethicists and civil libertarians—particularly the ACLU—have been quick to remind us that drug testing is an invasion of privacy and can even be seen as an infringement on Fourth Amendment rights. See Table 1. They have also pointed out that the oft-cited statistics about drug users' productivity deficits, tardiness, absenteeism, and accident involvement derive from the so-called Firestone Study of 1972, which has never been documented and can be fairly categorized as an example of "junk science." Indeed, it would appear that no such study ever actually existed. (Zimmer 7; White 1896)

Opponents argue that employers have been influenced not only by faulty data, but also by sensationalized media accounts and pressure from government agencies and the powerful—because it is highly profitable—testing industry itself. In addition, even the National Academy of Science has admitted that "when post-accident drug screening reveals . . . marijuana, it does not mean that marijuana . . . played a causal role" (Zimmer 9), because tests do not measure impairment; rather, by detecting metabolites they reveal past use, which

FIGURE 12.13   **Drug-Testing Report, Page 7**

8

Table 1: Ethical Acceptability of Specific Drug Tests
(Source: Brunet. 41)

Type of Drug Test	Policy Justification	Ethical Determination
Preemployment	Symbolic	Unacceptable: Benefits of testing do not outweigh the harms, especially the infringement of personal privacy
	Deterrence	Unacceptable: Same rationale as above
	Public and Worker Safety	Not addressed in ethics literature
Existing Workforce		
Universal	Productivity	Unacceptable: Economic interests of employers are secondary to the autonomy interests of workers
	Treatment	Unacceptable: Protecting individual's autonomy is a stronger moral duty than beneficence
	Public and Worker Safety	Not addressed in ethics literature
Random	Deterrence	Unacceptable: "With no showing of a significant problem there is too little evidence that there will be any deterrent effect or any progress made to combat drug use" (DeCew 1994, 22)
	Public and Worker Safety	Acceptable: Preventing harm to third parties overrides individual privacy considerations
For Cause	Treatment	Acceptable: Beneficence is an acceptable rationale if person is in danger
	Public and Worker Safety	Acceptable: If the safety of others is in jeopardy and a problem is evident, then the privacy concerns of the individual are trumped by the need to prevent harm

FIGURE 12.14 **Drug-Testing Report, Page 8**

9

may have occurred up to three weeks prior to the incident (see Table 2). As one researcher puts it, "Drug testing is not necessarily a measure of performance impairment, but instead may reveal illegal behavior" (Knudsen 623). We have known for some time that workplace accidents are caused by a number of other factors besides impairment. (See Table 3.)

Table 2: Approximate Duration of Detectability of Selected Drugs in Urine (Source: Rothstein, 294)

Drugs	Approximate Duration of Detectability
Amphetamines	2 days
Barbiturates	1–7 days
Benzodiazepines	3 days
Cocaine metabolites	2–3 days
Methadone	3 days
Codeine	2 days
PCP	8 days
Cannabinoids	
Single use	3 days
Moderate smoker (4 times/week)	5 days
Heavy Smoker(daily)	10 days
Chronic heavy smoker	21 days

And the actual tests themselves have been criticized as unreliable. "The accuracy of some on-site urine tests can be as low as 52 percent" (Hawkins 41). Indeed, a CDC study of 13 testing facilities found error rates approaching 100%, which led to the creation of strict accreditation criteria that labs must now meet for NIDA certification (Brunet 33). As with anything, however, employers can choose among a wide range of testing instruments, and the cost varies accordingly. Unfortunately, "the least expensive drug tests, favored by employers, are also the most error-prone" (Hawkins 41). But even if an employer chooses a NIDA-certified lab, there is still the problem of employees attempting to beat the test. There are a variety of products sold on the open market for this purpose, and countless Internet Web sites dispense related advice and information.

FIGURE 12.15 Drug-Testing Report, Page 9

10

Table 3: Percentage of Job Injuries Associated With Each Variable
(Source: Macdonald, pg. 711)

Variable		Injuries [% (N)]	Total N	Injuries Associated with Variable
Trouble sleeping	No	5.7(12)	210	77.8
	Yes	15.4(42)	273	
Noise and dirt	No	6.2(20)	324	62.3
	Yes	22.0(33)	150	
Danger	No	6.8(26)	380	50.9
	Yes	28.1(27)	96	
Shift work	No	8.2(31)	365	41.5
	Yes	21.8(22)	101	
Worry	No	9.0(35)	387	34.0
	Yes	19.8(18)	91	
Boredom	No	9.1(37)	408	28.8
	Yes	21.7(15)	69	
Conflict	No	9.1(42)	419	28.3
	Yes	25.0(15)	60	
Illicit drug use	No	9.8(43)	440	20.4
	Yes	25.6(11)	43	

"The more usual methods of attempting to avoid detection are through use of diuretics and laxatives, adulteration, and substitution." (White 1898)

VI - CHARACTERISTICS OF AN EFFECTIVE PROGRAM

Employers agree that for any drug-testing program to succeed, every effort must be made to safeguard against error (and attendant liability) and to minimize any potentially negative impact on employee morale. To this end, most progressive companies design their programs according to the NIDA guidelines. Some key features are as follows:

Clear policy statement: Using input from human resources, employee relations, union and legal department representatives, and employees themselves, a clear, comprehensive policy statement must be written. The statement

FIGURE 12.16 Drug-Testing Report, Page 10

11

should spell out the company's standards of employee conduct, details of how and under what circumstances testing will occur, and what steps will be taken in response to a positive test result.

Strict guidelines for specimen collection: A company may choose to collect specimens in-house (usually at the company's health or medical facility) or off site, at a hospital or clinic or at a facility specializing in such procedures. In any case, it is absolutely crucial that collection be conducted according to the strictest NIDA standards. "Because the first few links in the chain of custody are forged here . . . many experts feel that choosing your collection site merits greater attention than choosing your lab." (Brookler 130)

NIDA-certified laboratory: To become NIDA-certified, a lab must meet the most stringent standards of accuracy and protocol, especially regarding the chain of custody governing the handling of specimens. In short, NIDA-certified laboratories are the most reliable and certainly the most credible in court.

Confirmation of positive results: Positive test results should be confirmed by means of a GC/MS follow-up test. "Without the GC/MS confirmation, you aren't legally defensible" (Brookler 129). In the event of a positive confirmation, the case must then be referred to the company's MRO, who searches for alternative medical explanations for the positive test result before providing final confirmation. The MRO may refer the case back to management only after the employee has been given the opportunity to meet with the MRO. At most companies, the MRO is a contract employee. When enlisting an MRO it's important to ensure that the person is certified by the AAMRO, the American Association of Medical Review Officers. (Kerns and Stopperan 232)

Employee assistance program: Because substance abuse is recognized as a disease, many employers now provide employee assistance programs. Rather than being terminated, employees who test positive may instead be referred for counseling. In such instances, the rehabilitation option is usually presented as a condition of continued employment. This approach, which stresses rehabilitation rather than punishment, is consistent with nationwide trends. Currently, for example, there are nearly 2000 "drug courts" throughout the country (See Figure 7). "Using the coercive power of the court system coupled with the support of family, friends, counselors, and treatment providers, drug courts bring a unique mix of sanctions and incentives to help people achieve abstinence from drug use." (United States Office of National Drug Control Policy)

FIGURE 12.17 Drug-Testing Report, Page 11

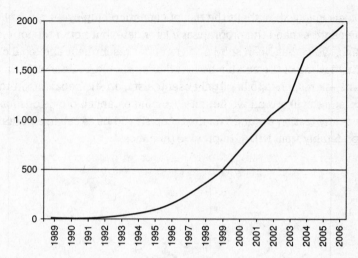

12

Figure 7: Increase in Drug Courts (1989—2006) (*Source:* United States Office of National Drug Control Policy.)

VII - CONCLUSION

Certainly, the whole subject of drug testing in the workplace is rather complicated, but several things do seem clear:

Substance abuse costs employers, both directly and indirectly. Substance abuse in employees leads to reduced productivity, additional costs of hiring and training workers, and administrative costs of absenteeism and worker's compensation claims. It can also result in loss of customers and sales, and damage your organization's reputation. . . . The right drug and alcohol testing program protects employees, customers, and your bottom line. It can increase employee productivity and retention, decrease absenteeism, and save you money. (Current 34)

Paramount Construction probably should introduce a testing program, but the way to begin would be to require testing of job *applicants* only—at least at first. This would enable us to become gradually acquainted with the procedures

FIGURE 12.18   **Drug-Testing Report, Page 12**

13

and problems involved, without the risk of alienating employees already on board. We might expand the program at a later date, but not in the form of random testing, which has been shown to engender resentment and legal challenges. Any testing of the established workforce should be done only on a for-cause basis—in response to habitual absenteeism, erratic behavior, on-the-job accidents, and the like. And we definitely should establish provisions for an EAP before any testing occurs. The next step should be to call in an outside consultant, preferably from NIDA, to provide guidance.

FIGURE 12.19   **Drug-Testing Report, Page 13**

14

WORKS CITED

Brookler, Rob. "Industry Standards in Workplace Drug Testing." *Personnel Journal* April 1992: 128–132.

Brunet, James R. *Drug Testing in Law Enforcement Agencies: Social Control in the Public Sector*. New York: LFB Scholarly Publishing, 2005.

Current, Bill. "New Solutions for Ensuring a Drug-Free Workplace." *Occupational Health & Safety* 71.4 (2002): 34–35.

DeCew, Judith Wagner. *In Pursuit of Privacy: Law, Ethics, and the Rise of Technology*. Ithaca: Cornell UP, 1997.

Hawkins, Dana. "Drug Tests Are Unreliable." *Drug Testing*. Ed. Cindy Mur. Farmington Hills, MI: Greenhaven, 2006. 41–46.

Kerns, Dennis L., and William I. Stopperan. "Keys to a Successful Program." *Occupational Health & Safety* 69.10 (2000): 230–233.

Knudsen, Hannah K., Paul M. Roman, and J. Aaron Johnson. "Organizational Compatibility and Workplace Drug Testing: Modeling the Adoption of Innovative Social Control Practices." *Sociological Forum* 18.4 (December 2003): 621–640.

Macdonald, Scott. "The Rote of Drugs in Workplace Injuries: Is Drug Testing Appropriate?" *Journal of Drug Issues* 25 (1995): 703–722.

Minchin, R. Edward, Jr., Charles R. Glagola, Kelu Guo, and Jennifer L. Languell. "Case for Drug Testing of Construction Workers." *Journal of Management in Engineering* 22.1 (2006): 43–50.

Rothstein, Mark A. "Drug Testing in the Workplace: The Challenge to Employment Relations and Employment Law." *Ethical Theory and Business*. Eds. Tom L. Beauchamp and Norman E. Bowie. Upper Saddle River, NJ: Prentice Hall, 1997: 292–309.

Swartley, Judith A. "Workplace Drug Testing Is Cost Effective." *Drug Testing*. Ed. Cindy Mur. Farmington Hills, MI: Greenhaven, 2006. 23–28.

United States Centers for Disease Control. "Construction Fatalities 2001: Census of Fatal Occupational Injuries." *eLCOSH: Electronic Library of Construction Occupational Safety and Health*. 15 June 2007. <www.cdc.gov/elcosh/docs/d0100/d000041/d000041.html>

FIGURE 12.20 **Drug-Testing Report, Page 14**

15

United States Centers for Disease Control. "Employer Spending on Workers' Compensation, by Industry, 2000." *eLCOSH: Electronic Library of Construction Occupational Safety and Health.* 15 June 2007. <www.cdc.gov/elcosh/docs/d0500/d000534/d000534.html>

United States Office of National Drug Control Policy. "The President's National Drug Control Strategy, February 2007." 15 June 2007. <www.whitehouse-drugpolicy.gov/publications/policy/ndcs07.html>

White, Tony. "Drug Testing at Work: Issues and Perspectives." *Substance Use & Abuse* 38.11–13 (2003): 1891–1902.

Zimmer, Lynn. *Drug Testing: A Bad Investment.* New York: ACLU, 1999.

FIGURE 12.21   **Drug-Testing Report, Page 15**

Exercises

■ EXERCISE 12.1

Rewrite the transmittal memo (Figure 12.1) and the title page (Figure 12.2), as if the report were your own work submitted as an assignment in your workplace communications course.

■ EXERCISE 12.2

Create a Table of Contents for a report on one of these aspects of your college:

- Degree or certificate program in your field of study
- Student Services provisions
- Athletic program
- Affirmative Action guidelines
- Physical Plant

■ EXERCISE 12.3

Rewrite the "Works Cited" in Figures 12.20 and 12.21, using APA format.

■ EXERCISE 12.4

Guided by the table of contents on the following page, team up with two or three other students to write a collaborative report entitled "Radar: History, Principles, Applications."

■ EXERCISE 12.5

Practically all workplace communications courses include a long report assignment at some point during the semester, usually near the end. Specific features of the project, however, vary greatly from instructor to instructor. Write a long report designed to satisfy your instructor's course requirements.

TABLE OF CONTENTS

Appendix

A Guide to Avoiding Plagiarism

Plagiarism is using someone else's work—words, ideas, or illustrations, that are published or unpublished—without giving the creator of that work sufficient credit. A serious breach of scholarly ethics, plagiarism can have severe consequences. Students risk a failing grade or disciplinary action ranging from suspension to expulsion. A record of such action can adversely affect professional opportunities in the future as well as graduate school admission.

DOCUMENTATION: THE KEY TO AVOIDING UNINTENTIONAL PLAGIARISM

It can be difficult to tell when you have unintentionally plagiarized something. The legal doctrine of **fair use** allows writers to use a limited amount of another's work in their own papers and books. However, to make sure that they are not plagiarizing that work, writers need to take care to credit the source accurately and clearly for every use. **Documentation** is the method writers employ to give credit to the creators of material they use. It involves providing essential information about the source of the material, which enables readers to find the material for themselves. It requires two elements: (1) a list of sources used in the paper and (2) citations in the text to items in that list. To use documentation and avoid unintentionally plagiarizing from a source, you need to know how to:

- Identify sources and information that need to be documented.
- Document sources in a Works Cited list.
- Use material gathered from sources: in summary, paraphrase, and quotation.
- Create in-text references.
- Use correct grammar and punctuation to blend quotations into a paper.

IDENTIFYING SOURCES AND INFORMATION THAT NEED TO BE DOCUMENTED

Whenever you use information from **outside sources,** you need to identify the source of that material. Major outside sources include books, newspapers, magazines, government sources, radio and television programs, material from electronic databases, correspondence, films, plays, interviews, speeches, and information from Web sites. Virtually all the information you find in outside sources requires documentation. The one major exception to this guideline is that you do not have to document common knowledge. **Common knowledge** is widely known information about current events, famous people, geographical facts, or familiar history. However, when in doubt, the safest strategy is to provide documentation.

DOCUMENTING SOURCES IN A WORKS CITED LIST

You need to choose the documentation style that is dominant in your field or required by your instructor. Take care to use only one documentation style in any one paper and to follow its documentation formats consistently. The most widely used style manuals are *MLA Handbook for Writers of Research Papers*, published by the **Modern Language Association (MLA)**, which is popular in the fields of English language and literature; the *Publication Manual of the American Psychological Association* (APA), which is favored in the social sciences; and *The Chicago Manual of Style*, published by the **University of Chicago Press (CMS)**, which is preferred in other humanities and sometimes business. Other, more specialized style manuals are used in various fields.

Certain information is included in all citation formats in all styles:

- Author or other creative individual or entity
- Source of the work
- Relevant identifying numbers or letters

- Title of the work
- Publisher or distributor
- Relevant dates

Constructing a Works Cited List in MLA Style

As an accompaniment to your English text, this guide explores MLA style. MLA lists are alphabetized by authors' last names. When no author is given, an item can be alphabetized by title, by editor, or by the name of the sponsoring organization. MLA style spells out names in full, inverts only the first author's name, and separates elements with a period. In the MLA Works Cited list below, note the use of punctuation such as commas, colons, and angle brackets to separate and introduce material within elements.

Books

Bidart, Frank. Introduction. Collected Poems. By Robert Lowell. Ed. Frank
    Bidart and David Gewanter. New York: Farrar, Strauss and Giroux, 2003.
    vii-xvi.

Chernow, Ron. Alexander Hamilton. New York: Penguin, 2004.

Conant, Jennet. 109 East Palace: Robert Oppenheimer and the Secret City of
    Los Alamos. New York: Simon, 2005.

---. Tuxedo Park: A Wall Street Tycoon and the Secret Palace of Science That
    Changed the Course of World War II. New York: Simon, 2002.

Maupassant, Guy de. "The Necklace." Trans. Marjorie Laurie. An Introduction to Fiction. Ed. X. J. Kennedy and Dana Gioia. 7th ed. New York: Longman, 1999. 160–66.

Periodicals

"Living on Borrowed Time." Economist 25 Feb.–3 Mar. 2006: 34–37.

"Restoring the Right to Vote." Editorial. New York Times 10 Jan. 2006, late ed., sec. A: 24.

Spinello, Richard A. "The End of Privacy." America 4 Jan. 1997: 9-13.

Williams, N. R., M. Davey, and K. Klock-Powell. "Rising from the Ashes: Stories of Recovery, Adaptation, and Resiliency in Burn Survivors." Social Work Health Care 36.4 (2003): 53–77.

Zobenica, Jon. "You Might As Well Live." Rev. of A Long Way Down by Nick Hornby. *Atlantic*. July–Aug. 2005: 148.

Electronic Sources

Glanz, William. "Colleges Offer Students Music Downloads." Washington Times. 25 Aug. 2004. 17 Oct. 2004 <http://washingtontimes.com/business/20040824-103654-1570r.htm>.

Human Rights Watch. Libya: A Threat to Society? Arbitrary Detention of Women and Girls for "Social Rehabilitation." Feb. 2006. Index No. E1802. Human Rights Watch. 4 Mar. 2006 <http://hrw.org/reports/2006/libya0206/1.htm#_Toc127869341>.

McNichol, Elizabeth C., and Iris J. Lav. "State Revenues and Services Remain below Pre-Recession Levels." Center on Budget Policy Priorites. 6 Dec. 2005. 10 Mar. 2006 <http://www.cbpp.org/12-6-05sfp2.html>.

Reporters Without Borders. "Worldwide Press Freedom Index 2005." Reporters Without Borders. 2005. 28 Feb. 2006 <http://www.rsf.org/article.php3?id_article=15331>.

USING MATERIAL GATHERED FROM SOURCES: SUMMARY, PARAPHRASE, QUOTATION

You can integrate material into your paper in three ways—by summarizing, paraphrasing, and quoting. A quotation, paraphrase, or summary must be used in a manner that accurately conveys the meaning of the source.

A **summary** is a brief restatement in your own words of the source's main ideas. Summary is used to convey the general meaning of the ideas in a source, without giving specific details or examples that may appear in the original. A summary is always much shorter than the work it treats. Take care to give the essential information as clearly and succinctly as possible in your own language.

Rules to Remember

1. Write the summary using your own words.
2. Indicate clearly where the summary begins and ends.
3. Use attribution and parenthetical reference to tell the reader where the material came from.

4. Make sure your summary is an accurate restatement of the source's main ideas.
5. Check that the summary is clearly separated from your own contribution.

A **paraphrase** is a restatement, in your own words and using your own sentence structure, of specific ideas or information from a source. The chief purpose of a paraphrase is *to maintain your own writing style* throughout your paper. A paraphrase can be about as long as the original passage.

Rules to Remember

1. Use your own words and sentence structure. Do not duplicate the source's words or phrases.
2. Use quotation marks within your paraphrase to indicate words and phrases you do quote.
3. Make sure your readers know where the paraphrase begins and ends.
4. Check that your paraphrase is an accurate and objective restatement of the source's specific ideas.
5. Immediately follow your paraphrase with a parenthetical reference indicating the source.

A **quotation** reproduces an actual part of a source, word for word, to support a statement or idea, to provide an example, to advance an argument, or to add interest or color to a discussion. The length of a quotation can range from a word or a phrase to several paragraphs. In general, quote the least amount possible that gets your point across to the reader.

Rules to Remember

1. Copy the words from your source to your paper exactly as they appear in the original. Do not alter the spelling, capitalization, or punctuation of the original. If a quotation contains an obvious error, you may insert [sic], which is Latin for "so" or "thus," to show that the error is in the original.
2. Enclose short quotations (four or fewer lines of text) in quotation marks, and set off longer quotations as block quotations.
3. Immediately follow each quotation with a parenthetical reference that gives the specific source information required.

CREATING IN-TEXT REFERENCES

In-text references need to supply enough information to enable a reader to find the correct source listing in the Works Cited list. To cite a source properly in the text of your report, you generally need to provide some or all of the following information for each use of the source:

- Name of the person or organization that authored the source.
- Title of the source (if there is more than one source by the same author or if no author is given).
- Page, paragraph, or line number, if the source has one.

These items can appear as an attribution in the text ("According to Smith. . .") or in a parenthetical reference placed directly after the summary, paraphrase, or quotation. The examples that follow are in MLA style.

Using an Introductory Attribution and a Parenthetical Reference

The author, the publication, or a generalized reference can introduce source material. Remaining identifiers (title, page number) can go in the parenthetical reference at the end, as in the first sentence of the example below. If a source, such as a Web site, does not have page numbers, it may be possible to put all the necesssary information into the in-text attribution, as in the second sentence of the example below.

> Recently *The Economist* noted that since 2004, "state tax revenues have come roaring back across the country" ("Living" 34). However, McNichol and Lav, writing for the Center on Budget and Policy Priorities, claim that recent gains are not sufficient to make up for the losses suffered.

Identifying Material by an Author of More Than One Work Used in Your Paper

The attribution and the parenthetical reference combined must provide the title of the work, the author, and the page number of the citation.

> Describing the testing of the first atom bomb, Jennet Conant says, "The test had originally been scheduled for 4:00 A.M. on July 16, when most of the surrounding population would be sound asleep and there would be the least number of witnesses" (*109 East Palace* 304–05).

Identifying Material That the Source Is Quoting

To use material that has been quoted in your cited source, add *qtd. in,* for "quoted in." Here, only one source by Conant is given in the Works Cited list.

> The weather was worrisome, but procrastination was even more problematic. General Groves was concerned that "every hour of delay would increase the possibility of someone's attempting to sabotage the tests" (qtd. in Conant, 109 East Palace 305).

USING CORRECT GRAMMAR AND PUNCTUATION TO BLEND QUOTATIONS INTO A PAPER

Quotations must blend seamlessly into the writer's original sentence, with the proper punctuation, so that the resulting sentence is neither ungrammatical nor awkward.

Using a Full-Sentence Quotation of Fewer Than Four Lines

A quotation of one or more complete sentences can be enclosed in double quotation marks and introduced with a verb, usually in the present tense and followed by a comma. Omit a period at the close of a quoted sentence, but keep any question mark or exclamation mark. Insert the parenthetical reference, then a period.

> One commentator asks, "What accounts for the government's ineptitude in safeguarding our privacy rights?" (Spinello 9).

> "What accounts," Spinello asks, "for the government's ineptitude in safeguarding our privacy rights?" (9).

Introducing a Quotation with a Full Sentence

Use a colon after a full sentence that introduces a quotation.

> Spinello asks an important question: "What accounts for the government's ineptitude in safeguarding our privacy rights?" (9).

Introducing a Quotation with "That"

A single complete sentence can be introduced with a *that* construction.

> Chernow suggests that "the creation of New York's first bank was a formative moment in the city's rise as a world financial center" (199–200).

Quoting Part of a Sentence

Make sure that quoted material blends grammatically into the new sentence.

> McNichol and Lav assert that during that period, state governments were helped by "an array of fiscal gimmicks."

Using a Quotation That Contains Another Quotation

Replace the internal double quotation marks with single quotation marks.

> Lowell was "famous as a 'confessional' writer, but he scorned the term," according to Bidart (vii).

Adding Information to a Quotation

Any addition for clarity or any change for grammatical reasons should be placed in square brackets.

> In *109 East Palace*, Conant notes the timing of the first atom bomb test: Conant says, "The test had originally been scheduled for 4:00 A.M. on July 16, [1945,] when most of the surrounding population would be sound asleep" (304–05).

Omitting Information from Source Sentences

Indicate an omission with ellipsis marks (three spaced dots).

> In *109 East Palace*, Conant says, "The test had originally been scheduled for 4:00 A.M. on July 16, when . . . there would be the least number of witnesses" (304–05).

Using a Quotation of More Than Four Lines

Begin a long quotation on a new line and set off the quotation by indenting it one inch from the left margin and double spacing it throughout. Do not enclose it in quotation marks. Put the parenthetical reference *after* the period at the end of the quotation.

> One international organization recently documented the repression of women's rights in Libya:

The government of Libya is arbitrarily detaining women and girls in "social rehabilitation" facilities, . . . locking them up indefinitely without due process. Portrayed as "protective" homes for wayward women and girls, . . . these facilities are de facto prisons . . . [where] the government routinely violates women's and girls' human rights, including those to due process, liberty, freedom of movement, personal dignity, and privacy. (Human 132-133)

IS IT PLAGIARISM? TEST YOURSELF ON IN-TEXT REFERENCES

Read the Original Source excerpt. Can you spot the plagiarism in the examples that follow it?

Original Source

To begin with, language is a system of communication. I make this rather obvious point because to some people nowadays it isn't obvious: they see language as above all a means of "self-expression." Of course, language is one way that we express our personal feelings and thoughts—but so, if it comes to that, are dancing, cooking and making music. Language does much more: it enables us to convey to others what we think, feel and want. Language-as-communication is the prime means of organizing the cooperative activities that enable us to accomplish as groups things we could not possibly do as individuals. Some other species also engage in co-operative activities, but these are either quite simple (as among baboons and wolves) or exceedingly stereotyped (as among bees, ants and termites). Not surprisingly, the communicative systems used by these animals are also simple or stereotypes. Language, our uniquely flexible and intricate system of communication, makes possible our equally flexible and intricate ways of coping with the world around us: in a very real sense, it is what makes us human. (Claiborne 8)

Works Cited entry:

Claiborne, Robert. _Our Marvelous Native Tongue: The Life and Times of the English Language_. New York: New York Times, 1983.

PLAGIARISM EXAMPLE 1

One commentator makes a distinction between language used as **a means of self-expression** and **language-as-communication**. It is the latter that distinguishes human interaction from that of other species and allows humans to work cooperatively on complex tasks (8).

> **_What's wrong?_** The source's name is not given, and there are no quotation marks around words taken directly from the source (in **boldface** in the example).

PLAGIARISM EXAMPLE 2

Claiborne notes that language "is the prime means of organizing the cooperative activities." Without language, we would, consequently, not have civilization.

What's wrong? The page number of the source is missing. A parenthetical reference should immediately follow the material being quoted, paraphrased, or summarized. You may omit a parenthetical reference only if the information that you have included in your attribution is sufficient to identify the source in your Works Cited list and no page number is needed.

PLAGIARISM EXAMPLE 3

Other animals also **engage in cooperative activities**. However, these actions are not very complex. Rather they are either the very **simple** activities of, for example, **baboons and wolves** or the **stereotyped** activities of animals such as **bees, ants and termites** (Claiborne 8).

What's wrong? A paraphrase should capture a specific idea from a source but must not duplicate the writer's phrases and words (in **boldface** in the example). In the example, the wording and sentence structure follow the source too closely.

EVALUATING SOURCES

It's very important to evaluate critically every source you consult, especially sources on the Internet, where it can be difficult to separate reliable sources from questionable ones. Ask these questions to help evaluate your sources:

- Is the material relevant to your topic?
- Is the source well respected?
- Is the material accurate?
- Is the information current?
- Is the material from a primary source or a secondary source?

AVOIDING PLAGIARISM: NOTE-TAKING TIPS

The most effective way to avoid unintentional plagiarism is to follow a systematic method of note taking and writing.

- **Keep copies of your documentation information.** For all sources that you use, keep photocopies of the title and copyright pages and the pages with quotations you need. Highlight the relevant citation information in color. Keep these materials until you've completed your paper.

- **Quotation or paraphrase?** Assume that all the material in your notes is direct quotation unless you indicated otherwise. Double-check any paraphrase for quoted phrases, and insert the necessary quotation marks.

- **Create the Works Cited or References list *first*.** Before you start writing your paper, your list is a **working bibliography,** a list of possible sources to which you add source entries as you discover them. As you finalize your list, you can delete the items you decided not to use in your paper.

LINDA STERN
PUBLISHING SCHOOL OF CONTINUING AND PROFESSIONAL STUDIES
NEW YORK UNIVERSITY

Index